Analyzing the Global
Political Economy

Analyzing the Global Political Economy

Andrew Walter and Gautam Sen

FOREWORD BY
Benjamin J. Cohen

PRINCETON UNIVERSITY PRESS PRINCETON AND OXFORD

Library of Congress Cataloging-in-Publication Data

Walter, Andrew, 1961–
Analyzing the global political economy / Andrew Walter and Gautam Sen ;
foreword by Benjamin J. Cohen.
p.   cm.
Includes bibliographical references and index.
ISBN 978-0-691-13958-6 (cl.)
ISBN 978-0-691-13959-3 (pb.)
1. Economic policy. 2. International economic relations. I. Sen, Gautam. II. Title.
HD87.W255 2009
337—dc22   2008026665

British Library Cataloging-in-Publication Data is available

This book has been composed in Minion

Printed on acid-free paper. ∞

press.princeton.edu

Printed in the United States of America

10   9   8   7   6   5   4   3   2   1

Contents

Figures and Tables

Figures

Tables

Foreword
Benjamin J. Cohen

What is the nature and scope of the scholarly discipline of international political economy? Most people would agree that IPE, at its most fundamental, is about the complex interrelationship of economics and politics in international affairs. In the words of Robert Gilpin, one of the field's pioneers, IPE is about "the reciprocal and dynamic interaction in international relations of the pursuit of wealth and the pursuit of power." By pursuit of wealth, Gilpin had in mind the realm of economics: the role of markets and material incentives, which are among the central concerns of mainstream economists. By pursuit of power, he had in mind the realm of politics: the role of the state and management of conflict, which are among the principal concerns of political scientists. IPE was to marry the two disciplines, integrating market studies and political analysis in a single field of inquiry.

Remarkably, the field has not existed for very long—at least not as a recognized academic specialty. Sharp observers had long understood, of course, that connections existed between economics and politics in the real world. As a practical matter, political economy has always been part of global relations. But as a distinct scholarly domain, surprisingly enough, IPE was born just a few decades ago. Prior to the 1970s, in the English-speaking world, economics and political science were treated as entirely different disciplines, each with its own view of international affairs. Relatively few efforts were made to bridge the gap between the two. Exceptions could be found, often quite creative, but mostly among Marxists or others outside the "respectable" mainstream of Western scholarship. A broad-based movement to integrate market studies and political analysis is really of very recent origin. IPE is a true "interdiscipline." Its achievement has been to build new bridges between older established disciplines, providing fresh perspectives for our study of the world economy.

Early on, the role of economics in IPE was allowed to wither a bit as the field came to be dominated by scholars from political science or other cognate disciplines. People like myself, who came to IPE from a background in economics, were far outnumbered as the interdiscipline gravitated toward departments of political science or international studies or to self-standing programs of their own. Even as the sophistication and accomplishments of the field grew, its grasp of the latest developments in economic theory weakened. Students of IPE were all too frequently underprepared to handle contemporary economic concepts or methodology.

More recently, the pendulum has begun to swing back. Growing numbers of specialists have turned once again to economics, with its emphasis on hard scientific method—what elsewhere I have referred to as "creeping economism" in IPE. More and more, the field finds inspiration in the twin principles of positivism and empiricism, which hold that knowledge is best accumulated through an appeal to objective observation and systematic testing. This is particularly true in the United States and increasingly the case elsewhere as well. Yet the development is barely evident in our textbooks. Most of the basic texts available to our students still reflect the field's early roots in political science and international studies.

Enter Andrew Walter and Gautam Sen. *Analyzing the Global Political Economy* offers a valuable corrective, bringing the economics in IPE back to the front and center of the stage. Economic theory is not prioritized, but neither is it discounted. In a balanced treatment, Walter and Sen demonstrate just how much insight can be gained from a serious, critical engagement with the economics discipline. Students could not hope for a better introduction to scholarship in the field as it is actually practiced today.

Preface

Why yet another textbook in international political economy (IPE), you might ask? Since this is a reasonable question, we should explain at the outset why we think this book is distinctive and worthwhile for those beginning serious studies in this field. IPE emerged as an academic discipline in the 1970s, and is thus one of the younger fields in the social sciences. It is marked by controversy and by basic differences of approach in theory, in method, and in the identification of its central questions. At the time we began our own studies in what was then a very new subject, the use of economic theory and concepts was seen as misplaced or dangerous. Since then, however, IPE's center of gravity has shifted, and much recent research in the field has an economic orientation. We hope that students who come to the study of IPE with little or no background in economics will find this book useful, but we also hope that students of economics interested in questions of political economy will find that the book increases their awareness of the advantages and disadvantages of economic approaches to political economy and to the comparative strengths of political science.

In teaching IPE to upper undergraduates and master's students at the London School of Economics and Political Science (LSE) for some years, we have found no single text that provides a relatively concise overview of IPE theory and approaches. Outside of the United States, and in the LSE in particular, Susan Strange still casts a long shadow. As one of the founders of the subject and of IPE studies at the LSE, her iconoclasm and forthrightness inspired a generation of students, some of whom went on to teach and research in the subject. Her antagonism toward economics as a social science is well known. She dismissed most economics as detached from the real world, as the modern-day equivalent of the debate between medieval scholars over the number of angels that could fit on a pinhead. Whether or not this position was justified, her attitude helped to carve out space for IPE in its early days as a separate field of study. It also earned her admirers within economics, as well as antagonism and outright dismissal. Later in her career, Strange was also critical of scholars of political science, especially in the United States, whom she perceived as too prone to the allures of economics with its pretensions to value-free social science.

The rapprochement between IPE, comparative politics, and economics that began in the 1980s has accelerated to the point where much contemporary IPE takes its primary inspiration from economic theory rather than from international relations or political science generally. This book reflects this state of affairs, but it also assesses what we have learned from economics and identifies the problems raised by this rapprochement. It is our view that IPE should draw on the theory, techniques, and findings of a range of academic disciplines, including international relations, political science, economics, sociology, history, and human biology, without making any one discipline paramount. However, as the term itself implies, political economy primarily concerns the investigation of interactions between political and economic factors in social life. The primary argument in this book is for an active but critical engagement between IPE and economics. Basic economic literacy is essential for modern students of IPE, as is clear from a perusal of the major journals. Economic theory has been a source of both inspiration and innovation in research in our subject, particularly via its advocacy of rationalist social science. However, students also need to be aware that other disciplines make important contributions, especially political science and international relations. An exclusive focus on economic theory limits the possibility of importing concepts and techniques from other fields.

Our main objective, therefore, is to provide a balanced and up-to-date assessment of the relationship between IPE and economics for upper undergraduate and master's students in IPE, avoiding the opposing pitfalls of economics phobia and economics envy. This book is not "economics for dummies," nor is it a paean to economic science. Our goal is to provide an introduction to international political economy that captures the evolving debates in the field. We hope to convince those students of IPE who remain wary of economics that a critical engagement with economic theory and concepts is essential both to understanding contemporary IPE and to doing good research in this field.

Our empirical focus is on the core issues of international trade, money and finance, and production. It would have been possible to include chapters on immigration, the environment, crime, and other subjects. But since our primary intention is to demonstrate the benefits of a critical engagement of IPE with economics, we decided that our empirical scope should be limited to the essential issues. We have thus traded some empirical breadth for greater depth and focus, while keeping the book to a readable length. This means that we do not provide historical accounts of the development of the systems of international trade, money, finance, and production (except where overviews are absolutely necessary). In the recommended further reading at the end of each chapter we list sources that offer further historical detail.

Two other points about the structure of the book should be made at this stage. First, although trade, money and finance, and international production can be dealt with separately, they are interrelated in practice. Yet we treat them separately, on the grounds that they are largely distinct theoretical topics (in the concluding chapter we discuss some of the issues raised by the empirical connections between these aspects of the global political economy). Second, we believe that although monetary and financial issues are also in principle separable, they are so closely intertwined that it is best to deal with them together. As a result, chapters 4 and 5 on monetary and financial issues are somewhat longer than those on trade and production. We hope that this asymmetry is outweighed by the advantages of a joint treatment.

At the end of each chapter we provide suggestions for further reading on key topics. We also provide web-links to useful sources of data and other helpful information, and we refer students to key sources so that they can follow up particular topics. In some cases we provide relevant web links in footnotes. Instead of a glossary of terms, we provide definitions of important terms in the text. (A growing number of websites offer such definitions, and they are more easily updated than printed texts. Some of these sites we list at the end of chapter 8.)

The preparation of this book took much longer than it would have in an ideal world, and many people have provided valuable assistance along the way. Richard Baggaley was steadfastly positive and encouraging through thick and thin, and we are very grateful to him and his colleagues at Princeton University Press. Heath Renfroe shepherded the book efficiently through the publication process, and Richard Isomaki provided numerous excellent suggestions for improving the text. A number of anonymous reviewers provided critical, constructive comments on the text and many specific suggestions of which we have taken full advantage. We thank Steven Kennedy for his encouragement and his interest in this project. We are grateful to many former and current students at Oxford and at the LSE, who kept us on our toes and who acted as an ideal readership. Finally, this book is dedicated to our respective families, who provided constant support, steady encouragement, and much happiness.

Andrew Walter and Gautam Sen
London, January 2008

Abbreviations

BCBS	Basle Committee for Banking Supervision
BIT	bilateral investment treaty
BoP	balance of payments
DSM	dispute settlement mechanism
DTT	double taxation treaty
EEC	European Economic Community
EMS	European Monetary System
EPZ	export-processing zone
EU	European Union
FDI	foreign direct investment
GATS	General Agreement on Trade in Services
GATT	General Agreement on Tariffs and Trade
H-O-S	Heckscher-Ohlin-Samuelson
HST	hegemonic stability theory
ICSID	International Centre for the Settlement of Investment Disputes
IFI	international financial institution
ILO	International Labor Organization
IMF	International Monetary Fund
IPE	international political economy
IR	international relations
ISI	import substitution industrialization
IT	information technology
ITO	International Trade Organization
LLR	lender of last resort
MAI	multilateral agreement on investment

MF   Mundell-Fleming
MNC   multinational corporation
NGO   nongovernmental organization
OECD   Organization for Economic Cooperation and
            Development
OFC   offshore financial center
OLI   ownership, location, internalization
NAFTA   North American Free Trade Agreement
PR   proportional representation
PTA   preferential trade agreement
R&D   research and development
RE   rational expectations
RIA   regional investment agreement
RTAA   Reciprocal Trade Agreements Act
TED   turtle excluder device
TRIMS   Trade Related Investment Measures
TRIPS   Trade-Related Aspects of Intellectual Property Rights
UNCTAD   United Nations Conference on Trade and Development
URA   Uruguay Round Agreement
WTO   World Trade Organization

Analyzing the Global
Political Economy

1 | International Political Economy

What is international political economy (IPE)? A simple answer is that IPE is concerned with the way in which political and economic factors interact at the global level. More specifically, political economists usually undertake two related kinds of investigations. The first concerns how politics constrains economic choices, whether policy choices by governments or choices by actors or social groups. The second concerns how economic forces motivate and constrain political choices, such as individuals' voting behavior, unions' or firms' political lobbying, or governments' internal or external policies.

An example of the first kind of investigation is provided by the European Union's policies protecting domestic agriculture and restricting trade in agricultural products. The EU's resistance to the liberalization of such trade, as demanded by agricultural exporting countries, may stem from the political organization of farm lobbies, the sympathy of urban consumers for the plight of national farmers (which may in turn stem from a concern to protect a national identity or way of life), a desire to promote "food security," or perhaps other factors. The political economist's task is to investigate which of these factors matter in explaining the EU's stance in negotiations over trade in agriculture.

An example of the second kind of investigation is provided by the claim that growing financial integration between countries has constrained the political choices of left-of-center governments more than those of right-of-center governments. Global financial integration makes possible the movement of capital to environments investors find most congenial. Has the threat of capital flight encouraged such left-of-center politicians as Brazil's President Lula (Luiz Inácio da Silva) and Britain's Gordon Brown to adopt "conservative" economic policies to reassure panicky investors? Manifestations of this phenomenon might include political pledges to pursue fiscal balance, to limit or reduce taxes on capital, and to place responsibility for monetary policy in the hands of politically independent and conservative central bankers. Do financial markets systematically punish left-wing financial policies? Is the asserted shift in policy by leftist political figures a myth? If it is real, is it due to some factor other than capital mobility? These have been popular questions for political economists in recent years (see chapter 5).

As we shall see, asking how politics and economics interact makes good sense. Economic outcomes have political implications because they affect opinions and power. For example, where individuals or groups fall in the hierarchy of wealth influences their political preferences. Similarly, decisions about economic policies are almost invariably politicized because different choices have different effects on the distribution of wealth. Political power is therefore a means by which individuals or groups can alter the production and distribution of wealth, and wealth is a means of achieving political influence. Although the pursuit of wealth is not the only motivating factor in human behavior, it is an important one, and often the means by which other goals can be achieved. In short, economic and political factors interact to determine who gets what in society.

In light of the preceding comments, one would be forgiven for assuming that the academic subjects of economics and political science were nearly indistinguishable. Although they indeed were aligned for many decades, new boundaries between the emerging academic disciplines of economics and political science in the early twentieth century led to distinct research questions, methods, and empirical focus. Furthermore, as we explain later, cross-disciplinary dialogue was muted because IPE grew out of international relations and because its founding scholars saw it as a response to irredeemable flaws in the discipline of economics.

We argue that IPE should move on—and indeed for the most part it has—from this early position of hostility to international economics. Most observers accept that contemporary students of political economy need more understanding of economic concepts than was initially thought necessary. As the purposes of studying political economy evolve, so too does appropriate methodology. Today, when so many IPE scholars plunder economics for testable theories of political economy, some ask whether the pendulum has swung too far in that direction. We cannot answer this question without a clear sense of both the benefits and the costs of close engagement between economics, political science, and international relations. Hence our argument for an IPE that engages fully but critically with economic theory and method.

ECONOMICS AND POLITICAL ECONOMY

Although most scholars in our subject could agree with the general definition of political economy offered at the beginning of this chapter, students coming to the subject for the first time may be confused by the plethora of approaches to the field, which include, among others, formal political economy within the neoclassical economic tradition,[1] Marxist or neo-Marxist historical sociology,[2] mainstream political sciences,[3] and offshoots of international relations.[4] These different orientations have soft boundaries, and authors often straddle one or more of them. The intellectual antecedents of modern approaches go back to the mercantilist thinkers of early modern Europe and to strands of Enlightenment thought.[5]

[1] James E. Alt and K. Alec Chrystal, *Political Economics* (Berkeley and Los Angeles: University of California Press, 1983); Gary S. Becker, "A Theory of Competition among Pressure Groups for Political Influence," *Quarterly Journal of Economics* 98:3, 1983, 371–400; James M. Buchanan, "The Constitution of Economic Policy," *American Economic Review* 77:3, 1987, 243–50; Allen Drazen, *Political Economy in Macroeconomics* (Princeton, N.J.: Princeton University Press, 2002); Bruno S. Frey, *International Political Economics* (Oxford: Blackwell, 1984).

[2] Fred H. Block, *The Origins of the International Economic Disorder* (Berkeley and Los Angeles: University of California Press, 1977); Robert W. Cox, *Power, Production, and World Order: Social Forces in the Making of History* (New York: Columbia University Press, 1987).

[3] Geoffrey Garrett, *Partisan Politics in the Global Economy* (Cambridge: Cambridge University Press, 1998); Robert O. Keohane and Helen V. Milner, eds., *Internationalization and Domestic Politics* (Cambridge: Cambridge University Press, 1996).

[4] Robert Gilpin, *War and Change in World Politics* (Cambridge: Cambridge University Press, 1981); Stephen D. Krasner, "State Power and the Structure of International Trade," *World Politics* 28:3, 1976, 317–47; Susan Strange, *States and Markets* (London: Pinter, 1988).

[5] Peter Groenewegen, "'Political Economy' and 'Economics,'" in John Eatwell, Murray Milgate, and Peter Newman, eds., *The New Palgrave: The World of Economics* (London: Macmillan, 1991), 556–62.

In our view, political economy is not any particular approach or tradition but an attitude to social science that does not privilege any single category of variable, whether political or economic. In this way, it harks back to a pre-twentieth-century tradition of political economy, in which thinkers as different as Adam Smith and Karl Marx understood that governments made economic policy in a political context and that economic outcomes had political and social implications.

As political economy developed over the course of the nineteenth century and as the modern subject of economics took shape, economics and political economy diverged. By the mid-twentieth century, most economists asked questions quite different from those political economists were asking. A central concern of economists has been to develop theoretical arguments about the relative optimality of different public policies. For example, economists often claim that one of the crowning achievements of their subject is the theory of comparative advantage, which holds that free trade policies generally maximize national and global (economic) welfare. Although many political economists have disputed this claim, the scholarly territory of optimal economic policy is not one where political economy has, so to speak, a comparative advantage.

Political economists more often ask what factors explain actual policy outcomes. Even when there is a consensus on the best policies (such as on the optimality of free trade), actual policies vary across countries and often diverge from economists' prescriptions. Why do most countries ignore economists and raise barriers to trade, and why do levels of protection vary across countries and sectors? These are classic questions of political economy. Indeed, the gap between standard economic prescription and the reality of trade policy is so large that most textbooks on international economics include sections on the political economy of trade policy (although new developments in the theory of strategic trade policy have opened new debates about the theoretical superiority of free trade). In a range of areas, policies that are bad from the perspective of economic welfare can make good politics, opening up space for explorations in political economy.

Moreover, as Kirshner has pointed out, in most areas economics generally has *not* reached a consensus on the relative optimality of particular policies.[6] Once again, this means that explanations of actual economic policy outcomes must turn to other factors, especially political variables. For example, there is little consensus in economics regarding the net benefits of financial openness, especially for developing countries, but in practice countries have widely varying patterns of financial openness. The position is similar with respect to policies in areas such as exchange rates, labor markets, welfare, education and training, corporate governance, and accounting regulation, to name but a few. Even in areas where there is a broad consensus among economists, such as the optimality of politically independent central banks, the empirical evidence in favor of the policy can be quite weak.[7] Hence, it seems that in a range of areas, factors other than empirically validated economic theory explain actual choices among policies.

One important strand of political economy explains such choices using the language and methods of neoclassical economics. This strand is often called *positive political economy* in reference to its relative lack of concern with normative questions and its use of deductive theories and rigorous empirical methods to explain outcomes.[8] With respect to one of the issues we have mentioned—the question of why many developed countries protect domestic agriculture—positive political economy answers that the beneficiaries of such policies (farmers) are better organized and more politically influential than the consumers of food.[9] Other economists have analyzed how different kinds of political institutions can affect choices on economic policy.[10]

---

[6] Jonathan Kirshner, "The Study of Money," *World Politics* 52:3, 2000, 407–36; Jonathan Kirshner, ed., *Monetary Orders: Ambiguous Economics, Ubiquitous Politics* (Ithaca, N.Y.: Cornell University Press, 2003).

[7] Ilene Grabel, "Ideology, Power, and the Rise of Independent Monetary Institutions in Emerging Economies," in Kirshner, *Monetary Orders*, 25–54.

[8] James E. Alt and Kenneth A. Shepsle, eds., *Perspectives on Positive Political Economy* (Cambridge: Cambridge University Press, 1990).

[9] Becker's "Theory of Competition among Pressure Groups" provides the classic statement of this approach. It is notable that a number of prominent Nobel prize-winners in economics, including Becker, have been centrally concerned with questions of political economy. See James E. Alt, Margaret Levi, and Elenor Ostrom, *Competition and Cooperation. Conversations with Nobelists about Economics and Political Science* (New York: Russell Sage Foundation, 1999).

[10] James M. Buchanan and Gordon Tullock, *The Calculus of Consent: Logical Foundations of Constitutional Democracy* (Ann Arbor: University of Michigan Press, 1962); Mancur Olson, *Power and Prosperity: Outgrowing Communist and Capitalist Dictatorships* (New York: Basic Books, 2000).

Building on this tradition of positive political economy within economics, a number of political scientists, mainly in the United States, have also employed economic theory to explain broad patterns in policy outcomes.[11] They share the economist's goal of achieving progress (i.e., factual knowledge) in the explanation and understanding of social outcomes. In so doing, they often accept the methodological principle that political variables, like economic ones, can be measured, compared, and (often) quantified. The method of positive political economy is straightforward: competing hypotheses are derived from theories built on simplifying assumptions, and these hypotheses are tested empirically. More often than not, the theories themselves are drawn from neoclassical economics and adopt its standard assumption of rational actors.[12]

Another broad strand of political economy is critical of positive political economy and suspicious of its proximity to the theory and methodology of economics. Often this critique begins from an explicitly normative standpoint, arguing that political economy must be concerned with equity, justice, and questions of what constitutes the "good life."[13] In this view, political economy needs not only to bring political variables into explanatory theories, but return to the original unity of the social sciences and humanities, including ethics and philosophy. That is, political economy should be "critical" and politically engaged. For these authors, focusing simply on explanation risks entrenching the status quo and ignoring the *cui bono* (who benefits?) question.[14] This

---

[11] E.g.: James E. Alt et al., "The Political Economy of International Trade: Enduring Puzzles and an Agenda for Enquiry," *Comparative Political Studies* 29:6, 1996, 689–717; Jeffry A. Frieden, "Invested Interests: The Politics of National Economic Policies in a World of Global Finance," *International Organization* 45:4, 1991, 425–51; Michael J. Hiscox, *International Trade and Political Conflict: Commerce, Coalitions, and Mobility* (Princeton, N.J.: Princeton University Press, 2002); Ronald W. Rogowski, *Commerce and Coalitions: How Trade Affects Domestic Political Alignments* (Princeton, N.J.: Princeton University Press, 1989).

[12] Actors are said to be rational when they choose actions that maximize the likelihood of their achieving certain goals. In doing so, they are assumed to use available information efficiently to identify causal relationships between possible actions and the achievement of their desired objectives.

[13] Within economics itself, Amartya Sen also rejects the standard "value neutral" approach in welfare economics as wholly unsuitable for welfare analysis. He argues that positive economics privileges economic goods over other human values, such as freedom (including, but not limited to, political freedom). See Amartya Sen, *On Ethics and Economics* (Oxford: Blackwell, 1987).

[14] Cox, *Power, Production, and World Order*; Strange, *States and Markets*.

school usually defines political economy as the investigation of power and wealth, the central subject matters of politics and economics respectively. The study of power is especially important to this approach and distinguishes it from mainstream economics, which, according to Galbraith, is largely blind to the social phenomenon of power.[15] The "Who benefits?" question should be addressed both to economic outcomes and to economic theories themselves, which can be seen as part of social power structures. Marx held that capitalism and classical economic theory, preoccupied with exchange relations and other surface phenomena rather than the reality of class struggle, privileged the interests of the bourgeoisie.

In our view, these positive and normative perspectives on political economy are not incompatible. Indeed, both are necessary. A well-grounded desire to change the world can only proceed from a proper understanding of it. Furthermore, explanation is often a precursor to a deeper understanding of social relations, including relations of power and domination. After all, even Marx was interested in explaining both the emergence and the working of capitalism as a means to understanding why it was unjust. Similarly, if one wished to argue, for example, that existing global economic institutions operate against the interests of poorer countries, one would first have to demonstrate that they have causal effects in the expected direction. Any amelioration of the plight of the poorest countries would also require a systematic understanding of the factors that result in poverty and low levels of economic development. Hence, positive explanation and normative critique are compatible approaches within the social sciences. This provides another reason why political economy should engage actively though critically with economics.

THE EVOLUTION OF IPE AS A SUBJECT IN THE SOCIAL SCIENCES: EARLY APPROACHES

All the founders of IPE shared the view that economics, and international economics in particular, had failed to explain the shape and evo-

---

[15] J. Kenneth Galbraith, *The New Industrial State* (Boston: Houghton Mifflin, 3rd ed., 1978), 48–61.

lution of the international economic system. This was because it ignored power, especially the distribution of power between states in the international political system.[16] In retrospect, this critique was hardly surprising given that these founding scholars came from the academic discipline of international relations (IR). Their disciplinary origin naturally led to a focus on big questions about the shape and dynamics of the international system. These scholars also argued that IR, in particular the realist tradition, had ignored economic issues, which, they claimed, were of growing salience in international affairs. With the breakdown of the Bretton Woods pegged exchange rate system, the 1973–74 oil shock and associated global recession, and the "new" protectionism, international economic conflict appeared to be growing. Important questions for these early IPE scholars included why the world economy has oscillated between phases of relative economic openness and closure, and why international economic relations had become more institutionalized over the past century.

Most of these scholars sought answers to such questions in the structure of the international political system rather than in domestic politics or in economic theory. Indeed, the main theories in early IPE were drawn from scholarly orientations familiar to IR researchers, such as realism, liberalism, and Marxism.[17] Economic issues became increasingly important in part because of the emergence of superpower détente, which apparently reduced the threat of major war and nuclear catastrophe. Another source of interest in economics was the growing contradiction between international economic interdependence on the one hand and national political sovereignty on the other, with the demand for national stabilization that the latter produced.[18] For realists,

[16] Robert Gilpin, *US Power and the Multinational Corporation* (New York: Basic Books, 1975); Robert O. Keohane and Joseph S. Nye, eds., *Transnational Relations and World Politics* (Cambridge: Harvard University Press, 1971) and *Power and Interdependence: World Politics in Transition* (Boston: Little, Brown, 1977); Stephen D. Krasner, *Defending the National Interest: Raw Materials Investments and US Foreign Policy* (Princeton, N.J.: Princeton University Press, 1978) and "State Power"; Susan Strange, "International Economics and International Relations: A Case of Mutual Neglect," *International Affairs* 46:2, 1971, 304–15.

[17] See Gilpin, *US Power*, and his *The Political Economy of International Relations* (Princeton, N.J.: Princeton University Press, 1987).

[18] Richard N. Cooper, *The Economics of Interdependence: Economic Policy in the Atlantic Community* (New York: Published for the Council on Foreign Relations by McGraw-Hill, 1968).

it was natural to argue that the decentralization of political power in the states-system militated against coordination of policy in response to economic interdependence.[19] For liberals, realists ignored how economic interdependence could transform state interests and promote international peace.[20]

Approaching IPE from the perspective of IR fostered the "states versus markets" dichotomy that characterized the dominant IPE approaches exemplified by Gilpin and Strange.[21] These authors criticized economics for privileging the interaction of actors in economic markets and for conceptualizing politics as a mere "constraint" on the pursuit of optimal policies (as, they argued, Cooper had done). From the perspective of IR, it seemed obvious that a strictly economic approach ignored the preeminence of the state as a political actor in the international system, with its demand for national security and sovereignty in its policies. However, in its obsession with war and security, IR was guilty of ignoring the central importance of economic factors in international affairs. For Gilpin and Strange, IPE should investigate the interaction between states (as the source of political authority in the international system) and markets (as the main source of wealth).

Rather than draw on contemporary economic theory for inspiration, these scholars returned to classical sources of political economy. For Strange most explicitly, a key motivation for doing IPE was a deep-rooted opposition to economics and the direction it had taken toward formal theory and depoliticization. Her stance had considerable appeal in the 1970s, when economic instability and the apparent breakdown of the Keynesian policy paradigm made the achievements of economics subject to greater skepticism. And yet economics still produced a certain defensiveness in the other social sciences, partly driven by the "imperialistic" ambitions of some economists (notably the Chicago school, led by figures such as Gary Becker). For some scholars, opposition to economics derived from an aversion to formal theory; others were con-

[19] Kenneth N. Waltz, The Theory of International Politics (Reading, Mass.: Addison-Wesley, 1979).

[20] Richard N. Rosecrance, The Rise of the Trading State: Commerce and Conflict in the Modern World (New York: Basic Books, 1986).

[21] Strange, States and Markets; Gilpin, Political Economy of International Relations.

cerned that rapprochement with economics would lead to a coloniza-
tion of their fields by economists.[22]

These twin concerns led early IPE scholars to emphasize the conceptual tools already available in political science and international relations. In his *Political Economy of International Relations,* Gilpin discussed modern economic theories of trade and monetary and financial
relations, but economics was not an important source of his conceptual
framework or of his method. Gilpin categorized IPE into three broad
paradigms describing the relationship between states and markets: liberalism, mercantilism, and Marxism. It was difficult to know whether
these paradigms constituted testable theories, though both Gilpin and
Krasner preferred a hybrid realism-mercantilism, which emphasized
the central role of states in the global political economy and the en-
demic nature of conflict and protectionism. Others, such as Keohane
and Nye, criticized this view as excessively static and pessimistic, arguing from within the liberal tradition that greater economic interdependence could have pacifying effects on international relations.

These broad paradigms, while elucidating competing positions on
the likelihood of international economic conflict or cooperation, were
of limited help in explaining the details of real-world outcomes. Although their main explanatory purpose consisted in elaborating system-level outcomes, their generality made it difficult to define decisive
tests. For example, realism emphasized the likelihood of economic conflict and protectionism, but it did not rule out interstate cooperation
driven by mutual self-interest.[23] In Gilpin's formulation, the deeply normative foundations of the three paradigms implied that these were
worldviews more than rival explanations. But if one could see the world
only through the warped lenses of one of the three major paradigms,
then IPE as an academic subject could look forward to little theoretical
and empirical progress.

In the late 1970s, one theory appeared that offered hope to those in
search of testable hypotheses. It arose from the observation that states
and other social institutions provide foundational conditions for the
emergence and operation of domestic markets, but such conditions are

---

[22] We thank an anonymous reviewer for this clarification.
[23] Krasner, "State Power."

lacking at the international level. What, then, could explain the rise of a global economy?

Gilpin first argued that the "liberal" international economies of the late nineteenth century and the period after 1945 were the respective products of the Pax Britannica and Pax Americana.[24] Gilpin also spoke of a "leadership vacuum" in the 1930s that resulted in the Great Depression and eventually World War II. Not long afterward, Charles Kindleberger's *The World in Depression* made very similar claims, arguing that leadership provided by powerful states was an international public good that could provide stability to the world economy.[25] What was soon termed *hegemonic stability theory* (HST) had broadly pessimistic implications.[26] Krasner, for example, argued that rival large states would not favor an open international trading system; only a sufficiently "hegemonic" state could force others to accept openness, which would primarily benefit itself as the leading economic power. Thus, international economic closure would likely follow from the continued relative decline of the United States, as it had Britain's decline half a century earlier.[27] In this context, the analogy between the economic disorder of the 1970s and that of the interwar period struck many, especially Americans, as apt.

[24] Robert Gilpin, "The Politics of Transnational Economic Relations," *International Organization* 25:3, 1971, 398–419.

[25] Charles P. Kindleberger, *The World in Depression, 1929–1939* (London: Allen and Unwin, 1973).

[26] Robert O. Keohane, "The Theory of Hegemonic Stability and Changes in International Economic Regimes, 1967–77," in Ole R. Holsti, Randolph M. Siverson, and Alexander L. George, eds., *Change in the International System* (Boulder, Colo.: Westview Press, 1980), 131–62. As David Lake ("Leadership, Hegemony, and the International Economy: Naked Emperor or Tattered Monarch with Potential?" *International Studies Quarterly* 37:4, 1993, 459–89) later pointed out, this formulation underplayed the differences between Kindleberger's finance-oriented leadership theory and Krasner's trade-oriented hegemony theory (Krasner, "State Power"). The former emphasized the need for leadership to provide international public goods that would *stabilize* a potentially unstable world economy. Krasner's account focused rather on hegemonic coercion to promote international economic *openness*. As Snidal showed, following Schelling, there was no strong theoretical reason for Kindleberger's claim. A small group of countries (a "k-group") might also have incentives for providing international public goods such as stabilizing supplies of short- and longer-term international liquidity. See Duncan Snidal, "The Limits of Hegemonic Stability Theory," *International Organization* 39:4, 1985, 579–614; Thomas Schelling, *The Strategy of Conflict* (Cambridge: Harvard University Press, 1960).

[27] Krasner, "State Power."

On balance, tests of HST have cast doubt on it.[28] The theory did not explain why an economically dominant United States avoided international leadership in the 1930s, only to embrace it during and after World War II. The answer, presumably, lay in domestic politics and in the realm of ideas, both of which HST largely ignored. As time wore on, predictions of the dire consequences of US decline also became less compelling because international trade was not becoming more restricted. Possible explanations were that US decline was exaggerated or that there was a "lag" before hegemonic decline led to economic closure.[29] However, these responses only underlined the ambiguity of the concept of hegemony itself.

The failure of HST to provide IPE with a foundational theory led many scholars to look elsewhere. Showing a new willingness to look to economics for inspiration, neoliberals drew on game theory and institutionalist economics to argue that cooperation (and the provision of public goods) could occur even on pessimistic realist assumptions of states' self-interest.[30] If self-interested actors expected to engage in repeated games with other partners and if they could easily detect cheating, reciprocity-based cooperation (based on a "tit-for-tat" strategy) could emerge over time. International regimes and institutions could enhance the prospects for international cooperation by reinforcing the expectation of repeated engagement ("lengthening the shadow of the future") and by reducing the costs of transactions and monitoring. The relatively low costs of maintaining existing international institutions implied that cooperation could outlast hegemony,

---

[28] Barry J. Eichengreen, "Hegemonic Stability Theories of the International Monetary System," in Richard N. Cooper, ed., *Can Nations Agree? Issues in International Economic Cooperation* (Washington, D.C.: Brookings Institution, 1989), 255–98; Joanne S. Gowa, *Closing the Gold Window: Domestic Politics and the End of Bretton Woods* (Ithaca, N.Y.: Cornell University Press, 1983); Lake, "Leadership, Hegemony"; Timothy McKeown, "Hegemonic Stability Theory and 19th Century Tariff Levels in Europe," *International Organization* 37:1, 1983, 73–91; Andrew Walter, *World Power and World Money* (New York: St. Martin's, 2nd ed., 1993); Michael C. Webb and Stephen D. Krasner, "Hegemonic Stability Theory: An Empirical Assessment," *Review of International Studies* 15:2, 1989, 183–98.

[29] Webb and Krasner, "Hegemonic Stability Theory"; Joseph S. Nye, *Bound to Lead: The Changing Nature of American Power* (New York: Basic Books, 1990).

[30] Robert Axelrod, *The Evolution of Cooperation* (New York: Basic Books, 1984); Robert O. Keohane, *After Hegemony* (Princeton, N.J.: Princeton University Press, 1984).

even if hegemony might be crucial for the initial establishment of such institutions.

The neoliberal argument that international institutions could provide public goods was vulnerable to realist criticisms. Powerful states might bend international institutions to their own interests, or even discard them if necessary.[31] Furthermore, neorealists like Grieco argued, neoliberals had mistakenly assumed that states pursued only absolute gains and hence had a common interest in economic openness. If, however, states were "defensive positionalists," they would also be concerned with the international distribution of gains, as asymmetric gains across states could undermine national security. Security-conscious states would weight *relative* benefit more than absolute benefit, meaning that they would be willing to forgo greater absolute national wealth if (say) a trade-expanding deal would be of greater benefit to states that were potential enemies.[32] This line of reasoning implied that open trade was more likely within stable defensive alliances and unlikely between enemies.[33] As we shall see, real-world outcomes are not always consistent with this generalization.

PROBLEMS WITH EARLY IPE AND NEW SOLUTIONS

The debate between neorealism and neoliberalism reached a virtual dead end by the early 1990s.[34] The debate itself was partly preoccupied with the empirical problem of how to distinguish between preferences

[31] Stephen D. Krasner, *Structural Conflict: The Third World against Global Liberalism* (Berkeley and Los Angeles: University of California Press, 1985).

[32] Joseph M. Grieco, "Anarchy and the Limits of Cooperation: A Realist Critique of the Newest Liberal Institutionalism," *International Organization* 42:3, 1988, 485–507, and his *Cooperation among Nations: Europe, America, and Non-tariff Barriers to Trade* (Ithaca, N.Y.: Cornell University Press, 1990). For a general discussion of the concept of economic security, see Miles Kahler, "Economic Security in an Era of Globalization: Definition and Provision," *Pacific Review* 17:4, 2004, 485–502.

[33] Joanne S. Gowa, *Allies, Adversaries, and International Trade* (Princeton, N.J.: Princeton University Press, 1995).

[34] David Baldwin, ed., *Neorealism and Neoliberalism: The Contemporary Debate* (New York: Columbia University Press, 1993); Stefano Guzzini, *Realism in International Relations and International Political Economy* (London: Routledge, 1998).

regarding relative gains and those regarding absolute gains. It had also reinforced the system-level focus of IPE and underlined the shortcomings of this abstraction. Treating the state as a unitary actor had closed off an important avenue of theoretical and empirical enquiry. The difficulty encountered by proponents of HST in explaining why hegemons pursued variant policies in different areas, or why the United States did not lead on trade in the 1930s, stemmed from this failure to take into account domestic political factors. The assumption that international economic outcomes were the product of international political variables (hegemony, alliances, international regimes, anarchy, etc.) therefore overlooked two important issues.

The first was that domestic politics and institutions might create further obstacles to international economic cooperation, in addition to those identified by realists and by HST. The "structuralist" or system-level orientation of IPE had abstracted from differences in types of domestic political regimes, yet there was reason to think such variations could have a profound impact on system-level outcomes. Recognition of this conceptual deficit turned academic attention toward work in political science. An example of such work is an important contribution by Downs, who had rejected the standard assumption of economics (and, implicitly, of structuralist IR and IPE) that policymakers were omniscient dictators who sought to implement optimal policies.[35] Downs assumed, rather, that politicians were, like market actors, driven purely by self-interest: their unambiguous goal was to be reelected by maximizing the number of votes they gained. Political parties adopted policies solely to obtain the benefits of office: income, prestige, and power. Political ideologies were employed instrumentally to maximize the votes gained. The "median voter theorem" advanced by Downs held that parties would adopt policies that appealed to the preferences of the median voter; party platforms would therefore converge on precisely the same political equilibrium.[36]

Such rationalist theories of domestic politics could also be applied to foreign economic policymaking, potentially providing the "micro-

---

[35] Anthony Downs, *An Economic Theory of Democracy* (New York: Harper and Row, 1957).

[36] Downs and others provided various reasons why multiparty systems tend in practice to survive, including strategic voting by electors and party concerns that moving to the political center could alienate voters at the extreme of the political spectrum.

foundations" that IPE lacked. In the area of trade policy, for example, one could argue that self-interested politicians weigh maximizing the income of the median voter against ensuring the support of organized interest groups, which provide campaign funds and endorse their preferred policy in circumstances when politicians have imperfect information and therefore cannot identify the optimal policy.[37] On this theory, international economic regimes and institutions provide a means by which governments can resist pressures from organized domestic interest groups. Politicians may also use them to transfer income to important domestic political constituents, at the expense of other domestic or foreign groups.[38] This rationalist approach provided an interpretation of international regimes and institutions very different from that of neoliberalism. Generally, it promised to provide theoretical and empirical innovation by drawing on mainstream political science.

The second problem encountered by early IPE theory was in explaining why states of similar size and economic openness responded differently to international events. Here, comparative politics came into its own, showing how domestic politics and institutions could help explain such patterns of variation.[39] For some scholars, differences in foreign economic policy could be explained by reference to configurations of organized interest groups, following Becker's approach.[40] As we discuss later, the need to specify interest group preferences led these scholars on a foray into macroeconomic and trade theory that would bring

[37] Helen V. Milner, *Interests, Institutions, and Information* (Princeton, N.J.: Princeton University Press, 1997), 35.

[38] Thomas Oatley and Robert Nabors, "Market Failure, Wealth Transfers, and the Basle Accord," *International Organization* 52:1, 1998, 35–54; John E. Richards, "Toward a Positive Theory of International Institutions: Regulating International Aviation Markets," *International Organization* 53:1, 1999, 1–37.

[39] Peter Gourevitch, *Politics in Hard Times: Comparative Responses to International Economic Crises* (Ithaca, N.Y.: Cornell University Press, 1986); Peter A. Hall, ed., *Governing the Economy: The Politics of State Intervention in Britain and France* (New York: Oxford University Press, 1986); Peter J. Katzenstein, ed., *Between Power and Plenty: Foreign Economic Policies of Advanced Industrial States* (Madison: University of Wisconsin Press, 1978); John Zysman, *Governments, Markets, and Growth: Financial Systems and Politics of Industrial Change* (Ithaca, N.Y.: Cornell University Press, 1983).

[40] Frieden, "Invested Interests"; Rogowski, *Commerce and Coalitions*. For Becker's approach, see Gary S. Becker, "A Theory of Competition among Pressure Groups for Political Influence," *Quarterly Journal of Economics* 98:3, 1983, 371–400.

about a convergence between IPE and international economics. For other scholars, domestic political institutions deserved more emphasis because they can channel, facilitate, or block competing interest group demands. Once again, the need for theoretical innovation prompted some IPE scholars to look to domestic and comparative political science for inspiration.[41]

This convergence between international, comparative, and domestic political economy created a new danger, that the pendulum would swing to the opposite extreme—the assumption that state policies are entirely a product of domestic factors—leaving certain phenomena inexplicable. It is difficult, for example, to explain the exchange rate and trade policies of western Europe and Japan in the 1960s and 1970s without reference to supranational factors such as the European integration project and alliances with the United States. One needs to conceptualize both internal and external pressures on governments. If governments are to respond to external factors, they must possess sufficient autonomy vis-à-vis voters and organized interest groups or must persuade domestic interests to share their external goals. The metaphor of the "two-level game" captures this idea: governments are engaged in simultaneous bargaining with both domestic interest groups and foreign governments.[42] Although this notion of bi-level bargaining provided a much-needed source of theoretical and empirical innovation, the turn toward domestic politics raised new problems, not least because political scientists disagree over how to model domestic politics and institutions. It also introduced a greater conceptual complexity that was difficult to handle with existing theoretical tools.

THE NEW MAINSTREAM IPE:
STRENGTHS AND SHORTCOMINGS

As we have seen, problems with early IPE approaches have led scholars more recently to draw on both political science and economics for

---

[41] Keohane and Milner, *Internationalization and Domestic Politics*; Milner, *Interests, Institutions, and Information*.

[42] Peter B. Evans, Harold K. Jacobsen, and Robert D. Putnam, eds., *Double-Edged Diplomacy: International Bargaining and Domestic Politics* (Berkeley and Los Angeles: University of California

theoretical and empirical innovation. Here, we focus on the implications of the recent convergence between IPE and economics. Clearly, this convergence has taken IPE further from its origins in international relations and, especially, its early opposition to economics. This has been particularly true in the United States, where in leading universities positive political economy has become the mainstream approach in IPE. Opposition to economics is no longer a helpful starting point, either for those beginning the study of IPE or for those engaged in research.

From the perspective of its adherents, the virtues of positive political economy are numerous. Positive approaches aim for generalizable propositions that can be applied to numerous cases and tested using appropriate data and methods. Simplification is a virtue, resulting in clear, falsifiable hypotheses that link causal (independent) variables to outcomes (dependent) variables. A standard appeal is to Occam's razor, the rule that for a given amount of explanation, a simple theory is preferable to a more complex one. Simplifying assumptions—for example, that economic actors act rationally (instrumentally) to maximize their personal wealth and that politicians act to maximize the probability of their reelection—help to build testable theories.[43] From this perspective, a good theory is one that is empirically consistent with outcomes in a wide variety of cases; an even better theory is one that is robust where one would least expect it to be. With the adoption of such scientific methods, adherents to positive political economy hope to achieve theoretical progress in IPE by the refinement, corroboration, and falsification of particular theories. Convergence with work on political economy done by economists is another theoretical goal.

In the search for better, testable theories, new positivist approaches to IPE built on Becker's work on the demand for policies by competing interest groups. Using textbook economic theories, authors such as Frieden and Rogowski created models of interest group preferences and cleavages that they used to derive predictions about the private demand

Press, 1993); Robert D. Putnam, "Diplomacy and Domestic Politics: The Logic of Two-Level Games," *International Organization* 42:3, 1988, 427–60.

[43] A strict positivist is usually uninterested in whether in the real world some people act in ways inconsistent with these simplifying assumptions. Hence, any "laws" identified are probabilistic.

for different policies on trade and exchange rates.[44] Although they differed on the question of *which* of the available economic theories were appropriate for modeling interest groups' preferences, Frieden and Rogowski showed that a greater attention to economic theory and its rationalist method could produce theoretical and empirical innovation in political economy.

What are the implications of this positivist approach to IPE? Here, we focus on two of the most important. First, it gives an advantage to scholars and students who are trained in economic theory and quantitative method; those who are not need to increase their knowledge of economics and statistics. This need for an orientation in economics has reopened debates about methodology, especially over quantitative versus qualitative method. Second, this approach has had the effect of diminishing the contribution of political variables, both domestic and international, in models of political economy. We discuss each of these implications in turn.

Not only did the turn to economics give an advantage to scholars trained in the subject, it increased the need for others lacking this background to engage more systematically with economic theory. Many students and scholars with backgrounds in IR and political science now find it difficult to follow the economic theory-intensive literature found in some leading journals. Although the academic subject of IR itself has changed greatly since the 1970s,[45] a background in international relations is no longer a prerequisite for IPE research. By the early 1990s, a background in economics and formal political science was perhaps a better foundation for an academic career in IPE.

The turn to economics as a source of innovation also inspired a growing use of quantitative empirical methods in international and comparative political economy. By the mid-1990s, the gold standard for empiri-

---

[44] For an overview of their approach, see Jeffry A. Frieden and Ronald Rogowski, "The Impact of the International Economy on National Policies: An Overview," in Keohane and Milner, *Internationalization and Domestic Politics*, 25–47.

[45] We often notice that our students acquire from IPE literature a caricatured and outdated image of scholarship in international relations. This view portrays IR as security- and war-obsessed and as ignorant of nonstate actors and transnational forces. Of course, IR itself has undergone an evolution similar to IPE's in recent years, including a convergence with domestic political science and a growing focus on the nature and impact of globalization.

cal work in international and comparative political economy was statistical techniques. For example, Garrett claimed to use "the best available data and the most appropriate econometric techniques to test the empirical merits of my arguments"[46] in his study of globalization's constraints on social democratic policies. He expressly hoped his statistical analysis would attract economists to his work and that of others using similar techniques in comparative political economy. Garrett reflected a desire on the part of many IPE scholars to be taken seriously by the discipline, economics, that enjoyed the highest prestige in the social sciences.[47] This trend toward econometrics in political economy both used and promoted the growing availability of quantitative measures of political variables across countries and over time.[48]

The rise of quantitative method as the gold standard of empirical political economy reopened debates about the pros and cons of quantitative and qualitative evidence. Some authors were concerned to defend the usefulness of qualitative evidence, especially structured case studies.[49] For King, Keohane, and Verba, as long as qualitative research methods observed the same "logic of inference" as good quantitative techniques, they could be useful.[50] For many important questions in political economy, measurement was either impossible or undesirable, so that qualitative evidence developed through good methodological practice was necessary. Detailed qualitative work could also complement statistical analysis, because causation remained difficult to establish even in the best econometric work and because qualitative studies could provide illuminating detail about causal relationships. It might be more accurate, then, to describe the methodological gold standard in political economy as one that combined quantitative and qualitative techniques.

[46] Garrett, *Partisan Politics*, 10.

[47] In a symbolic coincidence, Susan Strange, who had long mocked the scientific pretensions of economists, died in the same year Garrett's book was published.

[48] For a list of the most commonly used quantitative sources, see the section "Further Resources" at the end of this chapter.

[49] Helen V. Milner, *Resisting Protectionism: Global Industries and the Politics of International Trade* (Princeton, N.J.: Princeton University Press, 1988); John S. Odell, "Case Study Methods in International Political Economy," *International Studies Perspectives* 2:2, 2001, 161–76.

[50] Gary King, Robert O. Keohane, and Sidney Verba, *Designing Social Inquiry: Scientific Inference in Qualitative Research* (Princeton, N.J.: Princeton University Press, 1994).

The second result of the turn to economic theory and method is a diminished attention to both domestic and international *political* variables in IPE theory and research. It brought an element of economic determinism into political economy modeling. Domestic actors, organized into interest groups, were assumed to be motivated entirely by the material (income) benefits and costs of alternative economic policies. The competition between these groups for influence, shaped by the constraints of collective action, was assumed to determine, more or less, the government's choice of policy. This model largely ignored early IPE's emphasis on international forces such as security and asymmetries of economic development and interdependence. In some ways, therefore, it retarded integration between domestic and international theories of economic policies.

Furthermore, at the domestic level, this approach was often weak on the supply side of economic policy. Later contributions argued that the Frieden-Rogowski approach ignored political institutions, which often play an intermediating role between economic interests and policy outcomes.[51] Perhaps because political science has a comparative advantage regarding theories of political institutions, economic theory has been less influential in this area. Yet it would be wrong to imply that economics has little to say about the nature and impact of institutions on social conflict and cooperation, even though neoclassical economics largely ignored institutions. As Keohane argued in *After Hegemony* (1984), the transactions cost approach in economics usefully suggested that institutions could reduce the costs of collective action.[52] The "new institutional economics," which has grown rapidly in importance within economics in recent decades, builds on the work of pioneering economists such as Coase and North.[53] The renewed interest in the role of institu-

---

[51] E.g.: James E. Alt and Michael Gilligan, "The Political Economy of Trading States: Factor Specificity, Collective Action Problems, and Domestic Political Institutions," *Journal of Political Philosophy* 2:2, 1994, 165–92; Michael A. Bailey, Judith Goldstein, and Barry R. Weingast, "The Institutional Roots of American Trade Policy: Politics, Coalitions and International Trade," *World Politics* 49:3, 1997, 309–38; Helen V. Milner, "Rationalizing Politics: The Emerging Synthesis of International, American and Comparative Politics," *International Organization* 52:4, 1998, 759–86.

[52] Keohane, *After Hegemony*.

[53] For surveys, see Douglass C. North, "Institutions," *Journal of Economic Perspectives* 5:1, 1991, 97–112, and his *Institutions, Institutional Change, and Economic Performance* (Cambridge: Cambridge University Press, 1990); Oliver E. Williamson, "The New Institutional Economics: Taking Stock, Looking Ahead," *Journal of Economic Literature* 38:3, 2000, 595–613.

tions in economic development, for example, has been responsible for a growing attention to political factors by many economists, including those in institutions such as the World Bank.

Even so, the heavy lifting in positivist approaches is often still done by the economic theory rather than by models of domestic politics.[54] Such approaches usually assume that economic interests make demands on political institutions, which in turn channel and privilege some demands over others. The economic interests themselves are beyond the scope of political manipulation or modification, leaving unexplained the ways in which politicians use policies to restructure societal cleavages and actors' perceptions of self-interest.[55]

The new positivist approach was perhaps most neglectful of the role of ideas in shaping actors' identity and in motivating behavior. It appears that actors' preferences bear no simple relationship to actors' material economic position (a criticism traditionally directed at orthodox Marxism). As we have noted, much depends on which economic theory one chooses to specify interests.[56] The positivist approach also abstracts from questions of actors' knowledge: if societal actors are rational, do they also understand and use the theories we use to specify their interests? If so, which theories? Might broader ideologies (e.g., socialist ideologies that emphasize class interests) or time-bound national cultures shape actors' self-conceptions of their interests?

For constructivists, who emphasize the importance of ideas in shaping actors' perceptions of their self-interest, this is a key weakness of economic determinism. Constructivists argue that ideas or ideologies help actors to identify where their interests lie and motivate groups to organize for political purposes, particularly when policies are complex.[57] In explaining changes in policy, rationalists usually focus on

[54] We are grateful to an anonymous reviewer for this phraseology.

[55] For an empirical example of the way in which elites can construct interest coalitions, see Strom C. Thacker, *Big Business, the State, and Free Trade: Constructing Coalitions in Mexico* (Cambridge: Cambridge University Press, 2nd edition, 2006).

[56] In chapter 4, for example, we outline how Frieden's choice of a specific factors model led to quite different predictions about trade politics to Rogowski's, which was based on a model of class cleavages.

[57] Mark Blyth, *Great Transformations: Economic Ideas and Institutional Change in the Twentieth Century* (Cambridge: Cambridge University Press, 2002); John Gerard Ruggie, "International Regimes, Transactions, and Change: Embedded Liberalism in the Postwar Economic Order," *International Organization* 36:2, 1982, 379–415.

shifts in the relative power of different societal actors, on the assumption that actors' preferences are stable. Constructivists instead focus on the potential for changes in preferences caused by shifts in actors' worldviews. Although these two approaches are not incompatible, the preeminence of economic theory in rationalist political economy has meant that the effects of ideational change have been explored less often. From the other side, rationalists have been skeptical of the ability of constructivists to identify clear causal links between ideas and behavior.[58] Such skepticism is probably justified when ideational claims have been allied to a postmodernist rejection of social science. However, as we will see in later chapters, there is a growing body of "moderate" constructivist literature that exhibits a strong desire to elaborate clear, empirically testable theories.[59]

A final consequence of the turn toward economics and to formal approaches in political science has been that other potential sources of theoretical and empirical innovation have been overlooked. Constructivists have argued that minds are shaped in important ways by culture and ideology, but largely ignored in their debate with rationalists is the claim of evolutionary biologists that minds (and perhaps also culture) have been powerfully shaped by millions of years of evolution. From the perspective of many natural scientists, the social sciences, including most economics, have so far missed the opportunity to build on insights from the rapidly converging disciplines of evolutionary biology, anthropology, and cognitive neuroscience.[60] Whether these disciplines will inform our subject in coming years remains to be seen, but the possibility suggests that there even more work to be done than is generally recognized.

---

[58] Even Keynes's admiring biographer, Robert Skidelsky, appears unsure how much difference Keynesian ideas really made: "Keynes's *General Theory* was one of the most influential books of the twentieth century. Yet it is impossible to demonstrate conclusively that economic conditions would have been very different had it never been written" (Robert Skidelsky, *John Maynard Keynes*, vol. 3, *Fighting for Britain, 1937–1946* [London: Macmillan, 2000], xxii). On the methodological difficulties involved, see Peter A. Hall, ed., *The Political Power of Economic Ideas: Keynesianism across Nations* (Princeton, N.J.: Princeton University Press, 1989), chap. 14.

[59] On the varieties of constructivism and their attitudes to social science, see Peter J. Katzenstein, Robert O. Keohane, and Stephen D. Krasner, *Exploration and Contestation in the Study of World Politics: An International Organization Reader* (Cambridge: MIT Press, 1999).

[60] For arguments along these lines, see Edward O. Wilson, *Consilience: The Unity of Knowledge* (London: Little, Brown, 1998); Steven Pinker, *How the Mind Works* (London: Penguin, 1997); Eric D. Beinhocker, *The Origin of Wealth* (Cambridge: Harvard Business School Press, 2006).

OUR APPROACH TO INTERNATIONAL
POLITICAL ECONOMY

In our view, the convergence of international, comparative, and domestic political economy in recent years is a positive development. Perhaps most importantly, it helps to prevent disciplinary biases from excluding potential explanations of phenomena. It also reflects the process of globalization, which has softened distinctions between domestic and international politics.[61] As is now well recognized, the relationship between domestic politics and the international system is complex, with causality proceeding in both directions. The importance of international factors in domestic decisions on policy is especially significant for weaker actors in the international system, including most developing countries. Conversely, we should expect domestic interests and institutions to be of most *systemic* importance in the most powerful states, such as the United States and China.

Of course, capturing this real-world complexity in theoretical models has costs. Often it is necessary to work sequentially rather than try to capture all important variables affecting a particular outcome. In the end, distinguishing causal relationships is a matter of theoretical focus and the tractability of empirical analysis. It is almost always necessary to hold some variables constant, but it is also necessary to question our explanatory variables. To illustrate, much of the literature on economic growth in developing countries suggests that the exceptional growth of many East Asian countries since the 1970s was due to "good policies."[62] But what produced good policies in some states and not others? Were domestic factors decisive, that is, "strong" states were able to set good policies independently of pressures by interest groups, while "weak" states succumbed to them? Or were international factors, such as external security threats, or US aid and preferential trade policies, more important determinants of East Asian policy choices?

Either possible answer, the domestic or the international, is plausible and interesting, though we must also investigate how these two levels

---

[61] We postpone to the final chapter the question of whether globalization is an adequate description of the current state of the world.

[62] E.g., World Bank, *The East Asia Miracle: Economic Growth and Public Policy* (Washington, D.C.: World Bank, 1993).

of analysis interact. Good methodology is largely a matter of being open to different possible explanations and being clear about how they can be tested empirically. In this book, we approach our three main subjects—the political economy of trade, money and finance, and production—with this standard in mind. Neither a domestic nor an international explanation of outcomes is privileged, though we generally treat them sequentially.

In terms of methodology, we are primarily interested in causal explanation, which we see as a precondition of answering the *cui bono* question. We are open to the possibility that both material and ideational forces are important. Generally, method should be appropriate to the questions posed and the causal hypotheses one wishes to investigate. The scholarly consensus, in which we share, is that both quantitative and qualitative empirical evidence is important in IPE; each kind can usefully complement the other.[63] In other words, methodology is derivative rather than a matter of faith.

As for the turn to economic theory in modeling, we have discussed how economic theory has clarified competing claims about the material interests of social actors. Students of political economy need to be alert both to the strengths and to the shortcomings of this approach. We should be open to the possibility that actors' preferences can be manipulated (within limits that are poorly specified by most existing social science) by political entrepreneurs who wield ideas as weapons in the battle for influence.

As long as students of political economy are sensitive to the assumptions made in economic approaches, they have many potential benefits. After all, the difficulty of observing the relationships between actors' beliefs, intentions, and behavior means that one must often proceed by

---

[63] The standard statement of this position is King, Keohane, and Verba, *Designing Social Inquiry.* However, many argue that these authors mistakenly claim that qualitative case studies (with the emphasis on the plural) are of value only to the extent that they approximate the methods of "large-*N*" quantitative methods. For more recent arguments that case study evidence, including single cases, can provide different but still highly useful evidence in social science, see James Mahoney and Gary Goertz, "A Tale of Two Cultures: Contrasting Quantitative and Qualitative Research," *Political Analysis* 14:3, 2006, 227–49; James Mahoney, "Nominal, Ordinal, and Narrative Appraisal in Macrocausal Analysis," *American Journal of Sociology* 104:4, 1999, 1154–96; and H. E. Brady and David Collier, eds., *Rethinking Social Enquiry: Diverse Tools, Shared Standards* (Lanham, Md.: Rowman and Littlefield, 2004).

a process of elimination. For example, one explanation of the shift in US foreign economic policy toward multilateralism in the 1940s is that the previously dominant voice in the American political economy was weakened by economic depression and war in the 1930s and 1940s.[64] Other explanations of this shift focus on reforms to US policymaking institutions in the 1930s.[65] Perhaps only after we have explored the strengths and limitations of these explanations are we in a position to assess the importance of the cognitive factors.

Even those who criticize the turn toward rationalist economics in political economy must first understand and appreciate its benefits.[66] Hence our call for an active but critical engagement between economics and political economy.[67] In the rest of this book, we investigate the political economy of international trade, money and finance, and production. Our focus is on the different analytical approaches to major questions within these three core topics in the field of political economy. We hope that this approach will provide students from different academic backgrounds with the basic theoretical tools they will need in their further studies in IPE.

FURTHER RESOURCES

Further Reading

Peter J. Katzenstein, Robert O. Keohane, and Stephen D. Krasner. *Exploration and Contestation in the Study of World Politics: An International Organiza-*

[64] Jeffry A. Frieden, "Sectoral Conflict and US Foreign Economic Policy, 1914–1940," *International Organization* 42:1, 1988, 59–90.

[65] E.g., I. M. Destler, *American Trade Politics* (Washington, D.C.: Institute for International Economics, 3rd ed., 1995).

[66] Miles Kahler, "Rationality in International Relations," *International Organization* 52:4, 1998, 919–41.

[67] Rationalism remains a controversial topic for many scholars. Some reviewers of this book believed we were hostile to rationalist approaches, others that we were excessively rationalist. In practice, we see the use of simplifying assumptions to generate testable theories about social causation as necessary. One of the standard simplifying assumptions, especially in economics, is actors' rationality, but it is hardly the only one. Our only claim is that students need to be sensitive to the generally close relationship between simplifying assumptions and the predictive power of (rival) theories.

tion Reader. Cambridge: MIT Press, 1999. The introduction provides a good summary of the trend toward convergence between international, comparative, and domestic political economy, and between IR and IPE. Other contributions provide overviews of important areas of research.

Benjamin J. Cohen. "The Multiple Traditions of American IPE." 2007. Available at http://www.polsci.ucsb.edu/faculty/cohen/working/pdfs/Handbook_text.pdf. This article and the following one by Cohen are two useful recent overviews of the state of IPE by a leading scholar.

———. "The Transatlantic Divide: Why Are American and British IPE So Different?" *Review of International Political Economy* 14:2, 2007, 197–219.

Martha Finnemore and Kathryn Sikkink. "Taking Stock: The Constructivist Research Program in International Relations and Comparative Politics." *Annual Review of Political Science* 4:1, 2001, 391–416. A good overview of the constructivist research program.

Useful Websites

- http://www.indiana.edu/~ipe/ipesection/. The IPE section of the International Studies Association, with a variety of useful links and resources.
- datasets with quantitative data on political events, actors and institutions:
- Polity IV: http://www.cidcm.umd.edu/polity/
- World Bank Governance Indicators: http://info.worldbank.org/governance/wgi2007/
- World Bank Database of Political Institutions and other "investment climate" datasets: http://go.worldbank.org/V588NQ0NC0

2 | The Emergence of a Multilateral Trading System

Chapters 2 and 3 discuss the political economy of international trade. We consider how the literature in political economy has answered two broad questions. The first is what explains the shift, over the past century, from an informal, noninstitutionalized trading system to a "multilateral" trading system characterized by rules and formal institutions (chap. 2). The second question is why most countries practice protectionism, despite economists' advocacy of free trade as optimal policy for all countries (chap. 3).

In this chapter, we begin our consideration of the first question with a brief overview of the evolution of the trading system since the nineteenth century. We then argue that the shift toward multilateral institutionalization reflects a combination of ideational and material factors: a process of social learning and the rise of American hegemony in the mid-twentieth century. Most governments accepted that international trade was important to the achievement of national economic and political goals, but the bitter experience of the 1930s demonstrated that the international trading system was fragile and needed to be supported by multilateral rules and institutions. The United States, by then the world's major economic and trading power, adopted a new trade policy after the Great Depression and took the lead in promoting the new system. Today, this multilateral system is subject to challenges, and whether it can be sustained is an open question.

The fragility of the international trading system has much to do with the fact that domestic interests and institutions often lead governments to restrict trade. We postpone a detailed consideration of explanations of protectionism to the following chapter. However, in the second part of this chapter, we show that economists have not in practice been unanimous about the optimality of free trade policies under all circumstances. This lack of unanimity has helped to justify departures from free trade policy. In contrast to international monetary relations (discussed in chapter 4), international trade has always been highly politicized, and economists willing to challenge the orthodoxy of free trade have gotten the ear of policymakers in various places and times.

FROM TRADE UNILATERALISM TO A MULTILATERAL TRADING SYSTEM

In the mercantilist era in the seventeenth and eighteenth centuries, the trade policies of the major European countries were mostly highly protectionist, promoting exports and discouraging imports as a means of achieving a positive national balance of trade. Despite the apparently self-defeating nature of these policies, they persisted for more than two centuries.[1] The Industrial Revolution, which began in Britain, gradually altered this system. Many years after Adam Smith and David Ricardo advocated unilateral free trade policies, Britain finally adopted a free trade policy with the abolition of the mercantile-era Corn Laws in 1846.[2] This policy was widely interpreted at the time and ever since as an attempt to capitalize on and entrench Britain's dominant position in world manufacturing trade.[3] No other major country has ever followed Britain down the path of unilateral free trade, for reasons we discuss later. In the mid-nineteenth century, British policy did prompt some

---

[1] Jacob Viner, "Power versus Plenty as Objectives of Foreign Policy in the Seventeenth and Eighteenth Centuries," *World Politics* 1:1, 1948, 1–29; Ronald Findlay, Rolf G. H. Henriksson, Håkan Lindgren, and Mats Lundahl, eds., *Eli Heckscher, International Trade, and Economic History* (Cambridge: MIT Press, 2007).

[2] For discussion of the reasons for this shift in British trade policy, see David M. Rowe, "World Economic Expansion and National Security in Pre–World War I Europe," *International Organization* 53:2, 1999, 195–231; Cheryl Schonhardt-Bailey, *From the Corn Laws to Free Trade: Interests, Ideas, and Institutions in Historical Perspective* (Cambridge: MIT Press, 2006). John V. C. Nye, *War, Wine, and Taxes: The Political Economy of Anglo-French Trade, 1689–1900* (Princeton, N.J.: Princeton University Press, 2007), rejects the conventional wisdom that Britain was a free trader from this time.

[3] Krasner, "State Power."

relaxation of protectionist policies in Germany, France, and other major countries, but Britain's openness was exceptional. Newly emerging economies such as the United States and Russia were highly protectionist. Trade grew rapidly not because of any decline in protectionism but because of falling transportation costs.[4]

By the standards of the mid-twentieth century, there was very little institutionalization of trading rules and procedures. This informality reflected Britain's unilateralism as well as disagreements on policy among the major countries.[5] Britain's lack of interest in promoting free trade abroad has been seen as inconsistent with the predictions of hegemonic stability theory (HST), on which we comment later.[6] Trade negotiations were not entirely unimportant. The Cobden-Chevalier treaty of 1860 resulted in liberalized trade between Britain and France, but it did not significantly institutionalize international trade rules. In the 1870s, France, Germany, and many other European countries retreated from liberal trade policies as agricultural prices fell in response to rising production in Russia and America. Although Britain was overtaken in the production of some key industrial products by the United States and Germany and ran an increasing trade deficit in the years before 1914, it stuck to a free trade policy. It ran a trade surplus with its empire, but resisted the temptation to give preference to imperial territories, in part because their markets for British exports were not large enough to justify granting them preferential access to the British market.[7] Britain's free trade policy also persisted while the British Admiralty devised plans for war with Germany in the late nineteenth century.[8] When war came in 1914, free trade was temporarily abandoned, but it was not until 1932 that Britain decisively moved toward protectionism.

---

[4] Michael D. Bordo, Barry J. Eichengreen, and Douglas Irwin, "Is Globalization Today Really Different Than Globalization a Hundred Years Ago?" NBER Working Paper, 7195, June 1999, 16–18.

[5] Relatively small countries gain more proportionately from trade liberalization because it overcomes the size constraints they face in domestic markets; therefore, they tend to adopt more open trade policies than larger countries (Krasner, "State Power"). However, at the system level it is the policies of the larger countries that matter most.

[6] McKeown, "Hegemonic Stability Theory."

[7] Barry Turner, *Free Trade and Protection* (London: Longman, 1971).

[8] Paul Kennedy, *The Rise of the Anglo-German Antagonism* (New York: Humanity Books, 1988).

The Collapse of International Trade in the 1930s

The failure of the United States to promote an open international economy during the 1930s, and to stabilize it during its consequent collapse, is often regarded as the paradigmatic—indeed, the only—instance of failure by a hegemon to play the role HST predicts. From this perspective, a declining Britain was no longer capable of performing a hegemonic role to preserve open trade, and an ascendant United States failed to assume leadership.[9] An alternative interpretation is that misguided US domestic monetary policies produced domestic recession, which led to the Hawley-Smoot tariff, passed by Congress in 1930. Britain responded by adopting the system of Imperial Preference in 1932.[10] To this monetary explanation, Kindleberger added (in his *World in Depression*) the argument that US international monetary policies also demonstrated America's unwillingness to assume the burdens of international leadership. With many countries adopting more protectionist policies and deflation spreading throughout the world economy, international trade collapsed.

Within a few years, it became evident that the Hawley-Smoot tariff had failed to relieve pressure on domestic producers and had probably had perverse effects. In 1934, Congress passed the Reciprocal Trade Agreements Act (RTAA), which devolved authority over trade policy to the president and helped to insulate Congress from domestic protectionist pressures. Under this act, the United States had by 1945 concluded 32 bilateral agreements to liberalize trade.[11] However, this shift in policy was achieved by accommodating rather than defeating domestic protectionist pressures. An escape clause in the RTAA allowed the United States to withdraw negotiated trade concessions if they caused serious injury to domestic producers. This same clause was later inserted in the international trading system after 1945, underlining America's ambivalent commitment to trade liberalization after the Great Depression.

[9] Gilpin, "Politics of Transnational Economic Relations"; Krasner, "State Power."

[10] Milton Friedman and Anna Schwartz, *A Monetary History of the United States, 1867–1960* (Princeton, N.J.: Princeton University Press, 1963); Peter Temin, *Did Monetary Forces Cause the Great Depression?* (New York: W. W. Norton, 1976).

[11] See John H. Jackson, *The World Trading System* (Cambridge: MIT Press, 1997), 35–36.

This account of American behavior suggests that HST, which predicts that hegemony produces openness in the international trading system, suffers from important shortcomings. Contrary to this key prediction, the US hegemony after 1945 did not credibly commit to provide the global public good of a wholly open market because of the unwillingness of Congress to accept unconditional free trade. The operating principle of the RTAA and US trade policy, both before and since 1945, has been *reciprocity* rather than free trade, or the idea that trade liberalization should be roughly balanced between negotiating parties. Pressure from domestic protectionist interests has meant that specific sectors have also been excluded from reciprocal liberalization. In 1955, the United States asked to exclude agricultural trade from multilateral trade talks because domestic subsidies originating in the prewar depression were considered too politically sensitive. In 1958, restrictions were placed on imports of textiles and clothing.

The reciprocity principle implies conditional openness, or liberalization of domestic markets in return for liberalization of foreign markets. In theory, reciprocity made it more difficult for other countries to "exploit" the hegemon by benefiting from its open trade policy while pursuing protectionist policies at home. However, as we discuss further in chapter 3, with the emergence of the Cold War the United States had security-driven incentives not to insist on strictly reciprocal conditions of trade with its military allies.[12] This stance eventually produced a protectionist backlash from import-competing interests that suffered from growing penetration in the US manufacturing sector by competitors abroad.

Although the United States never adopted a free trade policy along nineteenth-century British lines, after 1945 it supported a multilateral, rule-based trading system. This aspect of US trade policy is not always emphasized by advocates of HST because it makes the American and British cases less comparable. Nonetheless, American leadership was a crucial factor in the shift toward institutionalized multilateralism in the international trading system after 1945. After World War II the United

---

[12] The important role of security incentives in intra-allied trade relations after 1945 also makes the US case fundamentally different from that of Britain in the nineteenth century, another shortcoming of HST.

States was the chief protagonist in the Anglo-American negotiations over the International Trade Organization (ITO) and the General Agreement on Tariffs and Trade (GATT) of 1947.

The importance of US preferences for the modern international trade order can be seen in its core concepts, reciprocity, unconditional most-favored nation (MFN) status, and safeguards, which originated in established US practice.[13] European governments accepted such ideas in part because they were considered essential to US participation in the postwar economic order, even though unconditional MFN (or non-discrimination) was intended to end European preferential trade arrangements. The US government also played a decisive role in the trade negotiations conducted under the auspices of the GATT, notably the successful Kennedy Round in the 1960s, which resulted in large tariff cuts on manufactured goods. In the Tokyo Round the United States sought to address nontariff barriers, which had become widespread following the tariff cuts of the Kennedy Round. Though initially skeptical, the United States exercised decisive influence over the accord that emerged from the Uruguay Round, which created the World Trade Organization (WTO) and brought agriculture, textiles, and services under multilateral rules.

The elaboration of rules for the conduct of multilateral trade and for negotiated liberalization represented a major shift from earlier global practice. Trade rules and information sharing (policy transparency) reduced the scope for defection, reinforcing overall economic openness. In the face of US relative decline, this regime also made systemic openness less vulnerable than predicted by HST.[14] Indeed, as table 2.1 suggests, both the coverage and membership of multilateral agreements in the GATT increased considerably from the 1970s in spite of growing concerns about relative US decline.

Even though the United States was the main promoter of institutionalized multilateralism, it did not always favor strong multilateral trade institutions. The failure of the ITO in 1950 and its mutation into the GATT standing conference and secretariat occurred because Congress

---

[13] Carolyn Rhodes, *Reciprocity, U.S. Trade Policy, and the GATT Regime* (Ithaca, N.Y.: Cornell University Press, 1993), 71–77.

[14] Keohane, *After Hegemony.*

TABLE 2.1
GATT Rounds and Subjects Covered

Year(s)	Place/Name	Subjects Covered	Countries
1947	Geneva	Tariffs	23
1949	Annecy	Tariffs	13
1951	Torquay	Tariffs	38
1956	Geneva	Tariffs	26
1960–61	Geneva Dillon Round	Tariffs	26
1964–67	Geneva Kennedy Round	Tariffs and antidumping measures	62
1973–79	Geneva Tokyo Round	Tariffs, nontariff measures, "framework" agreements	102
1986–94	Geneva Uruguay Round	Tariffs, nontariff measures, rules, services, intellectual property, dispute settlement, textiles, agriculture, creation of WTO, etc.	123

Source: World Trade Organization.

rejected what it regarded as excessive obligations placed on the United States. This episode demonstrated the increasingly central importance of America's domestic political institutions and its constitutional design for the global economic system. The GATT's exclusion of sensitive sectors also pushed developing countries to the margins of the multilateral trade regime. The GATT regime's lack of a legally binding enforcement mechanism was also consistent with congressional preferences. All this pointed to the way in which the academic debate over HST had deflected attention from the *style* of leadership offered by the hegemonic state.

The World Trade Organization: Toward Stronger Multilateral Rules or a Step Too Far?

The Uruguay Round agreement (URA), reached in Marrakesh in 1994, was the culmination of negotiations that took almost a decade (1986–94). The agreement strengthened multilateral institutionalism by placing new issues and sectors under multilateral rules, bringing many developing countries into the system, and creating a stronger mechanism for the settlement and enforcement of trade disputes. It also established the WTO, which reflected this strengthening of multilateral rules.[15] The result had unprecedented implications for the domestic policies of member countries, changing voluntary compliance into treaty obligation in many areas.[16] The new dispute settlement mechanism (DSM) is crucial in this regard, since rulings can only be rejected by consensus, whereas past rulings by GATT panels could be vetoed by the losing party. A trade policy review mechanism also subjects countries' policies to enhanced multilateral surveillance.

As with any major international agreement, there were compromises on all sides. Although the United States and France wanted to include labor standards, the opposition of developing countries meant that jurisdiction in this area was temporarily given to the International Labor Organization (ILO). The inclusion of environmental standards, which the United States also strongly favored, was also resisted by developing countries. As a quid pro quo for the acceptance by developing countries of service sector liberalization, a key US objective, the anomaly of excluding trade in textiles and clothing from GATT/WTO discipline was ended. Protectionist quotas limiting the export of textiles and clothing by developing countries to industrialized countries, through the Long-Term Arrangement and the Multi-Fibre Arrangement, were to cease in 2005. Such nontariff barriers as voluntary export restraints were also ended by advanced countries. Finally, the EU was able to resist initial US demands for sweeping cuts to agricultural price supports, among other things.

As in the past, US leadership and power was crucial in shaping the outcome. Most of the new issues brought under the remit of the WTO were largely consistent with US preferences. The General Agreement on Trade in Services (GATS), the agreement on Trade-Related Aspects of Intellectual Property Rights (TRIPS), that on Trade-Related Invest-

---

[15] On the WTO, see Bernard Hoekman and Petros C. Mavroidis, *The World Trade Organization: Law, Economics, and Politics* (London: Routledge, 2007); Anne O. Krueger, ed., *The WTO as an International Organization* (Chicago: University of Chicago Press, 1998); John H. Jackson, *The World Trade Organization: Constitution, and Jurisprudence* (London: Royal Institute of International Affairs, 1998), and his *World Trading System*.

[16] Commitments remain voluntary in the area of government procurement.

ment Measures (TRIMS), and further tariff reductions were common objectives of the United States, the EU, and Japan, consistent with their shifting comparative advantage. The major targets of these agreements were developing countries that protected relatively inefficient services sectors such as finance, telecommunications, and consultancy, failed to give strong legal protection to foreign patents, copyrights, and trade-marks, and imposed such measures as minimum local content rules on foreign investors. The EU and Japan also failed to stop the United States from bringing agriculture under WTO rules.[17] The desire of the EU to include competition and investment policy also failed because of lack of US support.

Many developing countries concluded that the overall shape of the URA was biased against their interests. The TRIPS regime in particular has been seen as shifting rents from developing countries to exporters of intellectual property, primarily the United States, Europe, and Japan.[18] The regime's protection of patent rights was also perceived to increase the pricing power of multinational pharmaceutical companies over developing countries and the needs of poor people suffering from AIDS and other treatable diseases. The special and differential rights (preferential market access and exemptions from obligations) histori-cally granted to developing countries also became more conditional. They also acquiesced in the multilateralization of the disciplines of the Tokyo Round and accepted the GATS, which they had initially opposed. Trade in agriculture, of great interest to many developing countries, was only partially liberalized. Tariff escalation and high tariff "peaks" also continue to affect exports from developing countries to advanced countries. Finally, the URA provisions on antidumping action and

[17] The agreement on agriculture sought to eliminate export subsidies, lower subsidies in the domestic market, and change discriminatory import quotas into tariffs in the interests of transpar-ency. The "Cairns Group" of agricultural commodity exporting countries also pushed for the inclusion of agriculture, but the final negotiations on the issue were dominated by the United States and EU.

[18] The extent to which this is true depends, among other things, on the degree to which intellec-tual property (IP) is protected in practice. In the case of China, which is not unusual, the copying of brands and theft of the IP of developed country firms has been extensive and remains so despite efforts to reduce it (see James Kynge, *China Shakes the World: The Rise of a Hungry Nation* [Lon-don: Weidenfeld and Nicolson, 2006], chap. 3).

countervailing duty codes allow developed countries to use them as tools for controlling imports.[19]

The disaffection of many developing countries with the outcome of the URA prompted their opposition to the launch of a new round of trade negotiations in Seattle in 1999. They demanded full implementation of prior commitments by advanced countries before negotiations on new areas such as competition and investment policy could commence. An apparent breakthrough in 2001 launched the so-called Doha Development Round, but negotiations broke down at a subsequent meeting at Cancún in 2003 (see box). Agricultural trade remained a major source of disagreement, but, ironically for a trade round premised on the idea of promoting development, development itself remained controversial because of advanced countries' resistance to the idea that lower-income countries should continue to enjoy special privileges. Reconciling the aspirations of the poorest countries, more successful developing countries, and the advanced countries within an open world economy remains an elusive objective.

THE DOHA DEVELOPMENT AGENDA (HONG KONG MINISTERIAL MEETING, DECEMBER 2005)

Agriculture

Comprehensive negotiations, incorporating special and differential treatment for developing countries and aimed at substantial improvements in market access; elimination of all forms of export subsidies, as well as establishing disciplines on all export measures with equivalent effect, by a credible end date; and substantial reductions in trade-distorting domestic support. Special priority is given to cotton.

Services

Negotiations aimed at achieving progressively higher levels of liberalization through market-access commitments and rule-making, particularly in areas where developing countries are exporters.

---

[19] Antidumping and countervailing duties are widely considered protectionist in practice and a threat to the integrity of the international trade system. However, they are attractive to policymakers as tariffs become marginal, and their selective character enables them to be targeted with precision at competitive threats, avoiding powerful adversaries and isolating particular exporters and national or regional sources. They also create an environment in which exporters are alert to the dangers of antidumping actions and adjust their behavior accordingly.

Nonagricultural products

Negotiations aimed at reducing or, as appropriate, eliminating tariffs, including the reduction or elimination of tariff peaks, high tariffs, and tariff escalation, as well as nontariff barriers, in particular on products exported by developing countries.

Rules

Negotiations aimed at clarifying and improving disciplines dealing with antidumping, subsidies, countervailing duties, regional trade agreements, and fisheries subsidies, taking into account the importance of this sector to developing countries.

Trade facilitation

Negotiations aimed at clarifying and improving disciplines for expediting the movement, release, and clearance of goods, and at enhancing technical assistance and support for capacity-building, taking into account special and differential treatment for developing and least-developed countries.

Intellectual property

Negotiations aimed at creating a multilateral register for geographical indications for wines and spirits; negotiations aimed at amending the TRIPS Agreement by incorporating the temporary waiver that enables countries to export drugs made under compulsory license to countries that cannot manufacture them; discussions on whether to negotiate extending to other products the higher level of protection currently given to wines and spirits; review of the provisions dealing with patentability or nonpatentability of plant and animal inventions and the protection of plant varieties; examination of the relationship between the TRIPS Agreement and biodiversity, the protection of traditional knowledge and folklore.

Dispute settlement procedures

Negotiations aimed at improving and clarifying the procedures for settling disputes.

continued on page 38

Trade and environment

Negotiations aimed at clarifying the relationship between WTO rules and trade obligations set out in multilateral environmental agreements; and at reducing or, as appropriate, eliminating tariff and nontariff barriers to environmental goods and services.

Special and differential treatment

Review of all S&D treatment provisions with a view to strengthening them and making them more precise, effective, and operational.

Source: WTO, Hong Kong Ministerial Briefing Notes, http://www.wto.org/english/thewto_e/minist_e/min05_e/brief_e/brief02_e.htm.

The Seattle meeting also encountered vocal opposition from nongovernmental organizations (NGOs) and violent street protests from opponents of the WTO system.[20] For many NGOs, the new DSM has created an asymmetry between relatively strong protection of multilateral trade rules and weak protection of labor rights, environmental protection, and other nontrade aspirations. There is a widespread concern that when trade rules conflict with these other aspirations, the former tend to triumph, giving priority to (Western) business interests over the interests of citizens, the environment, and developing countries.

From the perspective of developing countries, the relative strength of the DSM in protecting market access rights and its relative weakness in protecting the concerns of environmentalists and labor rights activists is a major advantage. In contrast to the GATT panel system, the DSM has meant that weaker countries are more able than in the past to defend their market access rights against the most powerful actors, the United States and EU. Since 1995, developing countries have been complainants in over one-third of all dispute settlement cases brought to the WTO.[21] Developing countries have generally been opposed to

---

[20] Mike Moore, *A World without Walls: Freedom, Development, Free Trade, and Global Governance* (New York: Cambridge University Press, 2003).

[21] Chad P. Bown and Bernard M. Hoekman, "WTO Dispute Settlement and the Missing Developing Country Cases: Engaging the Private Sector," *Journal of International Economic Law* 8:4, 2005, 861–90.

proposals to allow outside parties access to dispute panels or to provide *amicus curiae* ("friend of the court") briefs.

But the DSM also has disadvantages from the perspective of developing countries. As we have seen, the WTO has allowed the Western countries to defend rights acquired in the URA that have been viewed as systematically biased against development, notably TRIPs. There is also an uneven playing field in the greater legal resources available to most developed countries (here, assistance from development NGOs can be helpful to developing countries). The poorest countries almost universally fail to act as either complainants or interested third parties in the DSM process, even in disputes that concern their access to markets.[22] Weaker countries are also disadvantaged by their relative inability to take effective retaliatory action in the event that the losing party does not comply, and the Dispute Settlement Body authorizes the complaining country to take retaliatory measures.

A good illustration of some of the controversies surrounding the new DSM is the well-known "Shrimp-Turtle" case, brought in 1997 by India, Malaysia, Pakistan, and Thailand against the United States.[23] The complainants argued that the US ban on the importation of certain shrimp and shrimp products was inconsistent with multilateral trade rules. The US Endangered Species Act of 1973, which listed five species of sea turtles as endangered or threatened, had long required US shrimp trawlers use "turtle excluder devices" (TEDs) in their nets when fishing in areas inhabited by sea turtles. In 1989, responding to pressure from domestic environmental groups, the US government also imposed a ban on the importation of shrimp and shrimp products from countries whose fishing fleets endangered sea turtles because they did not use TEDs. In 1998, the WTO panel found against the United States, a ruling later broadly confirmed by the WTO's Appellate Body. Although the objective of the US ban (the protection of sea turtles) was deemed legitimate under GATT Article XX(g), its application was held to have resulted in arbitrary and unjustifiable discrimination against WTO members.[24]

---

[22] Bown and Hoekman, "WTO Dispute Settlement."

[23] This and other DSM cases can be accessed on the extensive WTO website. See http://www.wto.org/english/tratop_e/envir_e/edis08_e.htm, accessed March 5, 2007.

[24] In contrast to its treatment of the four Asian countries, the United States had provided some Caribbean countries with technical and financial assistance as well as longer transition periods for

One interpretation of this case was that it demonstrated that developing countries could use the WTO's DSM to force changes in the trade policies of major developed countries. But for environmental NGOs it demonstrated the fundamental flaws and dangers of the WTO system. The central GATT principle that member countries should not discriminate between "like product[s] originating in or destined for the territories of all other contracting parties" (Article I.1) effectively meant that from the perspective of the multilateral trade regime, a shrimp was a shrimp, whether caught by a process that killed turtles or not. For environmental groups, the power of WTO trade law effectively undermined the ability of governments to adopt policies they deemed necessary to protect endangered species. And because technologies such as TEDs were costly, the WTO was evidently favoring (foreign) producers with lower environmental standards over (domestic) producers with higher standards. The end result, they claimed, would be a "race to the bottom" in environmental standards.

In one sense, however, the WTO presented an opportunity for environmental NGOs. If the like-products rule could be overturned to allow discriminatory but environmentally friendly trade policies, the WTO's powerful DSM might be harnessed to promote their goals. Such sentiments confirmed the general view of developing countries that including environmental goals in the WTO would favor protectionist interests in developed countries.[25]

Similar lines of conflict have opened up in debates over the protection of "core labor standards." Organized labor in advanced countries argues that domestic employment is adversely affected by low labor standards in developing countries. The curtailment of trade union rights, child labor, and production for export by prisoners are said to provide some countries with an unfair cost advantage. To what extent employment in developed countries has been harmed by competition from countries with a comparative advantage in unskilled and semiskilled labor remains

---

their fishermen to begin using TEDs. This discriminatory aspect of the US law made it inconsistent with the "chapeau" of Article XX, as well as Article XI.2(c), which prohibits restrictions on "like" agricultural or fisheries products.

[25] Jagdish N. Bhagwati, *Writings on International Economics*, ed. V. N. Balasubramanyam (New Delhi: Oxford University Press, 1998), 476–504.

a matter of debate among economists.[26] Developing countries, believing that unions in developed countries are using such arguments to justify restrictions on imports, argue that labor standards should be promoted through the ILO, a relatively weak organization.

Regionalism, Bilateralism, and Multilateralism

Alongside the post-1945 multilateral trading system, bilateral and regional trading arrangements continued to coexist, though initially in a subdued manner. The creation in 1958 of the European Economic Community (EEC) customs union was widely emulated, though far less successfully, by many developing countries. With the emergence of a large European trading bloc, the GATT became less dominated by the United States; multilateral negotiations were now primarily dependent on US-EEC agreement. A striking characteristic of this period was that the United States itself largely abstained from pursuing regional or bilateral arrangements outside of the GATT, though, for security reasons, the United States had actively promoted the integration of western Europe. In the 1980s, US policy shifted to a "multitrack" strategy that pursued bilateral and regional trade agreements alongside multilateral negotiations. Since the 1990s, preferential trade agreements (PTAs) such as bilateral and regional integration schemes have proliferated rapidly, raising concerns about the demise of multilateralism.

From the perspective of economics, the proliferation of PTAs is a puzzling outcome, since they are inherently discriminatory and are a second-best alternative to the welfare improvements possible at a global level.[27] From the perspective of political economy, PTAs may be explained by a range of factors. Most obviously, many PTAs, including the European Union, have been driven primarily by political rather than

[26] Adrian Wood, "Globalization and the Rise in Labour Market Inequalities," *Economic Journal* 108:450, 1998, 1463–82; Jeffrey Sachs and Howard D. Shatz, "Trade and Jobs in US Manufacturing," *Brookings Papers on Economic Activity* 1, 1994, 1–84; Matthew Slaughter and Phillip Swagel, "Does Globalization Lower Wages and Export Jobs?" *IMF Economic Issues*, 11, 1997.

[27] As Jacob Viner (*The Customs Union Issue* [London: Stephens and Sons, 1950]) pointed out, the net welfare gains from PTAs depend on the balance between trade creation (welfare gains due to production and consumption changes) and trade diversion (putting cheaper producers outside the PTA at a disadvantage). See also Richard Lipsey, "The Theory of Customs Unions: A General

economic goals. Governments and some protectionist interest groups may also prefer PTAs over multilateralism precisely because they are discriminatory. The North American Free Trade Agreement of 1993 (NAFTA) was justified by some in Washington, D.C., as a signal to the EU and Japan that the United States had alternatives to the GATT if the Uruguay Round should fail. PTAs may also be subject to a "snowball" effect, as other countries respond by forming defensive PTAs. Competitive firms in knowledge-intensive sectors may also favor both PTAs and multilateral liberalization agreements if they allow firms to achieve greater economies of scale.[28] Labor unions may pose fewer objections to such PTAs, since they can attract inward foreign direct investment (FDI), which can strengthen rather than erode the position of workers. For related reasons, smaller groups of countries may also find it easier to achieve quicker and deeper liberalization agreements than are possible in the complex negotiations that take place at the WTO.

Is the recent proliferation of PTAs a threat to multilateralism? Article XXIV of the GATT has long permitted the formation of customs unions and free trade areas between contracting states on the condition they satisfy a few loose criteria. The largest regional arrangements, the EU and NAFTA, appear to have created more trade than they have destroyed. The creation of the EEC's common external tariff in the 1960s also seems to have had a dynamic positive effect on multilateralism, by prompting the US government to engage Europe in deeper multilateral tariff cuts than had previously been attempted.

Yet the recent growth of trade bilateralism and regionalism and the concurrent stalling of WTO negotiations have raised new doubts about the relationship between PTAs and multilateralism. In mid-2007, the WTO estimated that the number of operational regional trade agreements (in which it includes bilateral agreements) will reach 400 by 2010. Most of them have been negotiated since the early 1990s. The proliferation of PTAs may have diverted limited negotiating resources

Survey," in Jagdish N. Bhagwati, ed., *Selected Readings International Trade* (Cambridge: MIT Press, 1987), 357–76.

[28] Helen V. Milner and Edward D. Mansfield, "The New Wave of Regionalism," *International Organization* 53:3, 1997, 589–627.

and domestic political capital away from the multilateral system. On the other hand, the stake of the developing countries in the multilateral system has arguably never been higher given the trend toward export-led growth. Multilateral trade negotiations have always been subject to periodic breakdowns and brinkmanship, so it is too early to write off the WTO as irrelevant.

Conclusion: Explaining the Emergence of a Multilateral Trading System

The rise of multilateral institutionalism from the mid-twentieth century reflects a combination of collective learning from the experiences of the interwar period and the rise of American hegemony. By 1945, most governments of developed countries accepted that expansion of international trade was necessary to achieve national economic and political goals. The experience of the 1930s suggested that stronger multilateral constraints needed to be placed on national trade policies. Reciprocal trade liberalization within the GATT, initially confined to manufacturing between the developed countries, had the political advantage for governments of mobilizing export-oriented domestic interests that could counter protectionist lobbies who opposed liberalization. Pro-trade interests could also be reassured that tariff "binding," whereby countries agree not to raise tariffs in the future, and period reductions would gradually expand their access to foreign markets. Over time, as increased trade produced growth in incomes and employment, this political consensus widened. Additional sectors were brought into the multilateral system, and interest in the system on the part of developing countries increased dramatically from the end of the 1980s.

US hegemony was a second factor supporting multilateralism after World War II. The United States provided crucial leadership in the early decades of the GATT and remains central to the success of the system today. Of course, US preeminence also allowed it to set much of the trade agenda, though various factors have acted as a counterbalance. The rise of a second major trade power, the EU, significantly constrained US policy, though the multilateral system has also been the chief means by which the United States has limited the negative consequences (for itself) of discriminatory European regionalism. Another constraint on the ability of the United States to use the multilateral trade system for its own purposes has been the alternatives available to other countries, including bilateral and regional trade arrangements. The rapid growth in country membership of the GATT/WTO in recent decades may suggest that the system offers benefits even to the weakest. One indication of this distribution of power is that the strengthened legal framework of the WTO has been used by other countries success-fully to challenge US policies.

Today, the multilateral system created after World War II is subject to serious stresses, perhaps more serious than any in half a century. As interest in the system on the part of developing countries has increased, the commitment of governments in advanced countries, including the United States, has faltered. The continued rapid expansion of devel-oping countries' exports of manufactures and services may further threaten this commitment. In part for this reason, organized labor in advanced countries and environmental and human rights activists have opposed some key aspects of the WTO system. Regionalism and bilater-alism may continue to grow if governments find that these alternatives can avoid the political difficulties raised by the opponents of multilater-alism.[29] Other factors push in the opposite direction. Most importantly, the growth of FDI and of outsourcing of manufacturing processes to developing countries by large firms in developed countries provides corporate support for an open trading system. The evolving balance between these competing political forces will be a key determinant of the stability of the global trading system over time.

ECONOMIC IDEAS AND INTERNATIONAL TRADE

Economists have generally supported, although not explained, the post-war trend toward multilateralism we have described. However, they have been less unanimous about the optimality of free trade than is

---

[29] In practice, regional arrangements like the EU and NAFTA do not avoid the difficulties raised by economic integration between rich and poor countries, though they have been able to harmo-nize region-wide environmental, labor, and other standards at relatively high levels.

often supposed. This diversity of opinion has sometimes helped governments to justify departures from free trade practices, though the influence of economists over most countries' trade policy is probably quite limited. Many economists otherwise convinced of the benefits of free trade have also accepted that reciprocity-based trade liberalization may be more effective and sustainable than unilateral free trade policies. They have done so mainly for reasons of political economy, since reciprocity has little justification in mainstream trade theory.

Classical Trade Theory

Adam Smith's advocacy of international specialization, based on the absolute advantage of each country, was an extension of his argument that the domestic division of labor increased productivity. Smith argued that it was better to buy abroad what was more expensive to produce at home, and exchange with foreigners goods that enjoyed lower production costs at home. The scope of possible international exchange between countries would, he believed, be limited by whether or not they possessed an absolute advantage in a particular commodity. Smith argued that the generalized protectionism of his time was the result of "merchants' conspiracies" (interest group pressure), though he accepted that under certain circumstances protection could enhance national security. He also argued that the question of whether liberalization was best undertaken unilaterally or negotiated reciprocally should be determined by examining empirical evidence.[30]

David Ricardo developed a deeper justification for trade liberalization—international specialization based on comparative advantage. In Ricardo's celebrated model of two countries, two commodities, and one factor of production (labor), voluntary exchange between them was beneficial to both even if one country enjoyed an absolute advantage in both commodities, because it could profitably specialize in the commodity in which it enjoyed the greatest comparative (cost) advantage. Similarly, the less absolutely productive country would benefit from

[30] Edward M. Earle, "Adam Smith, Alexander Hamilton, Friedrich List: The Economic Foundations of Military Power," in Peter Paret and Gordon A. Craig, eds., *Makers of Modern Strategy: From Machiavelli to the Nuclear Age* (Princeton, N.J.: Princeton University Press, 1986), 217–61.

specializing in the production of the other commodity, in which it enjoyed a comparative advantage. In other words, trade should be based on national specialization in the production of commodities that each country could produce relatively efficiently using domestic labor. In practice, Ricardo argued that England should specialize in the production of manufactures and unilaterally remove agricultural protections, which penalized the poor via high prices and mainly benefited the rentier class.

Neoclassical Trade Theory

Ricardo's theoretical justification for free trade policies, though substantially extended since then, remains the cornerstone of modern international trade theory.[31] But Ricardo had not adequately explained why different countries had different comparative advantages. During the interwar years, Hecksher and Ohlin extended the theory to include capital and land as additional factors of production. Subsequently, Paul Samuelson used capital and labor endowment alone to provide a more elegant account of international specialization that became the standard neoclassical model of the theory of trade. The key result held: specialization and free trade would be optimal for national and global welfare.

Under various restrictive assumptions, the Heckscher-Ohlin-Samuelson (H-O-S) theory, as it became known, predicts that a country's comparative cost advantage will lie in goods in which it uses its abundant factor intensively in production.[32] Industries can in principle be ranked according to their relative capital-labor ratios. International specialization between countries would then depend on the relative endowment of the two factors of production within them. Thus, countries that were capital rich would specialize in the production of capital-

[31] On neoclassical trade theory see Jagdish N. Bhagwati, *Trade, Tariffs, and Growth* (Cambridge: MIT Press, 1969), 3–122.

[32] It assumes that "production functions," or technical productivities, are identical across countries. This contrasts with Ricardo, who assumed that they varied. It also assumes, among other things, constant returns to scale (i.e., that unit costs remain constant as production increases), an assumption that has gained greater significance in recent years. See Edward E. Leamer, "The

intensive goods, and those abundantly endowed with labor would produce more labor-intensive ones.[33]

These predictions about the likely pattern of international trade have
been extensively investigated. One debate was sparked by Leontieff's
study of US international trade (1953), which found that the United
States, more capital-abundant than its trading partners, was exporting
products more labor-intensive than its imports, contrary to predictions
of the neoclassical model. Among the many interpretations of the
"Leontieff paradox" is that human capital (essentially skills) embodied
in US labor should be construed as a third input incorporated in goods
manufactured in the United States. But the acquisition of human capital
can be affected by government policy, which sits uneasily with the idea
of natural resource endowment, and the trade patterns arising from
it, as "God-given."[34] Others argued that Leontieff's tests were poorly
specified, though respecifications did not entirely remove doubts about
the H-O-S model's predictive capacity.[35]

A second debate concerned the compatibility of the model with the
increasingly important phenomenon of "intraindustry" trade, in which
two countries exchange goods in the same sector or industry (think of
Germany and France exporting cars to each other). Empirical studies
show that intraindustry trade in differentiated manufactures is especially high in western Europe, though it is also of increasing importance
in North-South trade.[36] They also suggest that countries tend to become

---

Heckscher-Ohlin Model in Theory and Practice," Graham Lecture, *Princeton Studies in International Finance*, No. 77, February 1995.

[33] Abba Lerner, "The Diagrammatical Representation of Cost Conditions in International
Trade," *Economica* 12, August 1932, 346–56; Ronald W. Jones, "Factor Proportions and the
Heckscher-Ohlin Theorem," *Review of Economic Studies* 24:1, 1956, 1–10.

[34] Giovanni Dosi, Keith Pavitt, and Luc Soete, *The Economics of Technical Change and International Trade* (London: Harvester Wheatsheaf, 1990), 32–34.

[35] Edward E. Leamer, "The Leontief Paradox, Reconsidered," *Journal of Political Economy* 88:3,
1980, 495–503.

[36] Herbert J. Grubel and P. J. Lloyd, *Intra-industry Trade: The Theory and Measurement of International Trade in Differentiated Products* (London: Macmillan, 1975); Nigel Grimwade, *International Trade. New Patterns of Trade, Production, and Investment* (London: Routledge, 1989), 89–
141. The possibility that intraindustry trade is simply a statistical phenomenon owing to the
aggregation of production and trade data is unconvincing: high levels of intraindustry trade are
observed even when the data is disaggregated.

more similar in economic structure over time rather than increasingly specialized in different products and industries, as the standard trade model predicts. Intraindustry trade also suggests that increasing returns to scale (decreasing average costs as production increases) are important, since constant or decreasing returns would give producers an incentive to supply all varieties of the product. Specialization occurs, instead, because the fixed costs of producing individual goods are sufficiently high to require a substantial volume of production to achieve profitability.[37] This in turn implies the emergence of large firms that compete with rivals in international markets (oligopoly), via product differentiation and (often) technological innovation. The introduction of increasing returns, technology, and oligopolistic competition to explain intraindustry trade can also justify departures from free trade on national welfare grounds, as we discuss later.

An important theorem associated with the H-O-S model is the Stolper-Samuelson theorem concerning the impact of trade on a country's factor prices (and hence incomes). It predicts that trade will improve returns to the abundant factor and decrease returns to the scarce factor.[38] So, for example, trade would increase the wages of skilled workers and reduce the wages of unskilled workers in advanced countries. Protection would have the opposite effect.[39] The Stolper-Samuelson theorem has powerful implications for political economy, since it suggests that trade (and any trade policy) will produce winners and losers even if total welfare increases. This result holds even when some of the standard H-O-S assumptions are relaxed.[40]

---

[37] Products can be differentiated horizontally, vertically, and technologically. Horizontal differentiation arises because of the variety of consumer tastes, or perhaps because firms try to intensify barriers to market entry. Vertical differentiation results from differences in quality that allow consumers to rank individual products hierarchically, among cars, watches, etc. Technological differentiation occurs because of innovation, resulting in the introduction of new products to the marketplace, as in the electronics and pharmaceuticals industries.

[38] Wolfgang Stolper and Paul A. Samuelson, "Protection and Real Wages," *Review of Economic Studies* 9, November 1941, 58–73.

[39] This points immediately to possible demands for trade protection from the losers from trade, a subject to which we return in the next chapter.

[40] The H-O-S theory articulates a long-run equilibrium in which factors of production are free to move across different sectors. Short-run issues like factor immobility, dealt with in the "specific factors model," are discussed in the next chapter. However, it is useful to note here that in this

Such distributional conflicts do not overturn the general prediction of the H-O-S model that trade increases national and global welfare, given its standard assumptions of constant returns to scale and perfect competition. The conventional view is that the basic proposition of neoclassical trade theory about the relationship between free trade and global welfare cannot be faulted on grounds of its internal logic, but its empirical validity is less certain given the restrictiveness of its assumptions. For most economists, gains from specialization and competition remain the central justification for international trade.

Criticisms of Comparative Advantage Theory and the Justification of Intervention

Challenges to Ricardian comparative advantage and successor neoclassical theories of international trade arise from a number of concerns. The first and the oldest of them is the infant industry argument. This criticism was put forcefully by German writers like Friedrich List, who was influenced by Alexander Hamilton, and Gustav Schmoller. List argued that international trade did not guarantee the dynamic convergence of differing national productive capabilities, and he advocated trade protectionism to promote industrialization in latecomer countries.[41] List was not opposed to international trade as such, but argued that it was only beneficial between equally advanced nations. The basic claim is that without initial protection, potentially competitive firms may never emerge or survive because of existing dominant producers. The intellectual antecedents of this view were mercantilist, though the infant industry argument was a continuing subject of debate in Britain and was accepted, most notably, by John Stuart Mill.[42] Today, developing countries are the principal defenders of this view, although List believed that international specialization in the world economy as a whole was

---

model, protection will still raise the real return of factors specific to the import-competing sector and lower the real return of factors specific to the export sector.

[41] Friedrich List, *The National System of Political Economy*, trans. Sampson S. Lloyd (London: Longmans, Green, 1909).

[42] Douglas A. Irwin, *Against the Tide: An Intellectual History of Free Trade* (Princeton, N.J.: Princeton University Press, 1996), 116–37.

predicated on climatic conditions that made temperate zones suited to manufacturing, and the tropics to agricultural and primary production.

In practice, there was extensive government involvement in the economies of virtually all nineteenth-century European latecomer countries, Japan, and the United States, including trade protection. Government economic intervention generally remained substantial in capitalist countries after 1945, especially in developing countries, in varieties of trade and "industrial" policies.[43] The mixed results of infant industry protection lead many economists to argue that the argument in favor of it overlooks the greater potential failure of government policy. As many governments in developing countries discovered, protected industries could remain infantile for decades and reduce efficiency as well as growth. This objection is practical rather than theoretical, and this exception to the free trade doctrine remains a standard one in economics texts. It has probably weakened the appeal of free trade prescriptions in many latecomer countries.[44]

A range of other, less well supported challenges to neoclassical prescriptions have been made. One of the better known is the claim that large countries could use "optimal tariffs" to reduce global demand and to force import prices down, thereby gaining at the expense of other countries. The standard objection to this theory is that it does not take into account the possibility of protectionist retaliation by other countries, which could leave all worse off. Some have argued that a very large (hegemonic) country could still obtain net benefits if the cost of retaliation by others is high.[45] In the period after World War II, many developing countries also highlighted the so-called balance-of-payments constraint on growth, using it to justify generalized trade protection. However, currency devaluation is usually a more appropriate response to declining foreign exchange reserves, and the balance-

[43] Raymond Vernon, ed., *Big Business and the State* (London: Macmillan, 1974); Steven J. Warnecke, ed., *International Trade and Industrial Policies* (London: Macmillan, 1979).

[44] A more subtle argument is that if successful graduation from infant status is simply a matter of time, failures in the system of industrial finance might be the key source of the problem. If so, government intervention in finance rather than trade policy might be the appropriate response to this market failure. But the potential for government policy failure remains.

[45] John A. C. Conybeare, *Trade Wars: The Theory and Practice of International Commercial Rivalry* (New York: Columbia University Press, 1987).

of-payments argument has received diminishing support. Another justification for protection, especially after 1945, is the impact of trade on domestic employment. The argument is that imports may cause rising unemployment in the presence of inflexible wages, justifying protection against imports and subsidies for exports. It is commonly argued, however, that such trade protection deals with the symptoms rather than the ultimate cause of the problem and thus creates additional inefficiencies.

Two other important and related criticisms of the neoclassical theory and its advocacy of free trade focus on the role of technology and of increasing returns to scale, respectively, factors ignored by the neoclassical model. The effects of technology provide a plausible explanation for patterns of international specialization, an alternative to the H-O-S theory of factor proportions.[46] In particular, specialization based on "technology gaps" may depend on history and accident rather than on factor endowments. First-comer firms and countries can exercise a "competitive exclusion" by appropriating technological advantages before latecomers do. Technological capability, or the skills and knowledge necessary to innovate, develop, produce, and sell, can have a man-made, institutional basis and be self-sustaining. In turn, patterns of international specialization can be products of country-specific institutional organization, policies, and chance. Technology gaps between countries may produce, under conditions of free trade, increasing polarization of industrial structures and of economic performance. Some sectors are said to possess greater potential for future growth in demand and for future product and process innovation.[47] Analogous convictions informed nineteenth-century continental European fears of the potential consequences of engaging in unfettered international trade with a more technologically advanced England.

Theories of product cycles explain trade along similar lines, introducing FDI as a key aspect of the market structure within which technological advances occupy a critical role.[48] The key issue in product cycle

[46] Dosi, Pavitt, and Soete, *Economics of Technical Change.*

[47] Dosi, Pavitt, and Soete, *Economics of Technical Change*, 250–53.

[48] Seev Hirsch, "The US Electronics Industry in International Trade," *National Institute Economic Review* 34, 1965, 92–107; Raymond Vernon, "International Investment and International Trade in the Product Cycle," *Quarterly Journal of Economics* 80:2, 1966, 190–207; Gary C. Hufbauer, "The Impact of National Characteristics and Technology on the Commodity Composition

theory is the relative distance of each country from the technological leader. The latter will initially sell its technically superior goods in its domestic market. As the product matures and mass production develops, the leader exports these goods to other countries, first other relatively advanced countries and subsequently developing countries. In other words, trade takes place as a consequence of technological gaps, before other countries catch up to the technological leader.[49] Eventually, the product and related technology becomes standardized as it diffuses to countries further down the technological hierarchy. Developing countries become manufacturers of the good as advanced economy firms export the now old technology via FDI. As the home and export markets for the good shrink, these firms renew sales and profits via innovation that produces new products. Ultimately, these new products and related technologies in turn diffuse throughout the global economy in yet another product cycle. Technological diffusion produces a cycle of shifting comparative advantages in which, eventually, the technological leader may even import these goods from developing countries (as the United States and United Kingdom import television sets today from China).

Technological theories of international trade focus our attention on the dynamics of comparative advantage and the potential gains in income and growth from the acquisition and absorption of technology. By contrast, in the standard neoclassical model trade results in one-off gains in welfare, the product of moving from a hypothetical position of autarky to a position of openness in which international trade and economic specialization occur. There has been a growing recognition of the role of technology in modern economies. The ability to generate and apply knowledge through research and development (R&D) can be the decisive factor in determining the location of particular economic activities.

First-comer advanced industrial economies, enjoying the advantages of being established manufacturers of complex products, become a bar-

---

of International Trade in Manufactured Goods," in Raymond Vernon, ed., *The Technology Factor in International Trade* (New York: Columbia University Press), 175–231.

[49] M. V. Posner, "International Trade and Technical Change," *Oxford Economic Papers* 13:3, 1961, 323–41.

rier to the entry of latecomer countries, effectively constituting a form of exclusion that may reduce national and global welfare.[50] This can provide a justification for the state in latecomer countries to intervene, extending the old infant industry argument.[51] In terms of economic policy, the crucial question is the time it takes technology to diffuse from the leading country to other countries. Domestic institutions condition innovative capacity and R&D, as well as knowledge gained through experience (learning by doing). Countries able to import and use technology more quickly than others may gain an advantage, through technology licensing, FDI, or even technological piracy. Given their potential impact on trade, growth, and jobs, it is hardly surprising that technology policies are often highly politicized and that the protection of technological advantages became an important objective of advanced countries in the Uruguay Round.

So-called new trade theories initiated in a series of articles by James Brander and Barbara Spencer in the early 1980s, focused on the issue of trade under circumstances of international oligopoly, in which excess profits were up for grabs.[52] The key argument was that a "strategic trade policy" by governments, such as a tariff or subsidy that favored the national champion, could alter market outcomes. "Strategic" in this context referred to the game-theoretic interaction between firms in oligopolistic market structures, not to be confused with the use of *strategic* to designate defense-related industries or industries of unusual technological or economic importance. Conceivably, such interventions might shift excess profits to the domestic firm, thereby raising domestic welfare and diminishing foreign welfare, in a fashion analogous to an optimal tariff. The eye-catching battle in the civilian aircraft industry between Boeing and Airbus, for which the US and European governments

---

[50] Ralph E. Gomory and William J. Baumol, *Global Trade and Conflicting National Interests* (Cambridge: MIT Press, 2000), 1–22.

[51] Sanjaya Lall, "Imperfect Markets and Fallible Governments: The Role of the State in Industrial Development," in Deepak Nayyar, ed., *Trade and Industrialization: Themes in Economics* (New Delhi: Oxford University Press, 1997), 43–87.

[52] For an accessible overview of this body of work, see Barbara J. Spencer and James A Brander, "Strategic Trade Policy," in Steven N. Durlauf and Lawrence E. Blume, eds., *The New Palgrave Dictionary of Economics* (Basingstoke: Palgrave Macmillan, 2008).

provided implicit or explicit financial support, respectively, provided a standard illustration for this argument.

Despite its prominence, strategic trade theory produced few practical results.[53] Oligopolistic industries producing excess profits turned out to be relatively unattractive industries such as tobacco. The theory also assumed much about the ability of governments to choose both appropriate industries and appropriate interventions, which depended on detailed knowledge of the global market conditions in every industry. As with other theoretical arguments for exceptions to the free trade principle, the argument for strategic trade policy could be exploited by well-organized interest groups to capture taxpayer subsidies. Brander and Spencer subsequently retreated to the view that since strategic trade "mentalities" on the part of governments risked producing a mutually destructive subsidies war, international trade agreements should focus on restraining export subsidies. This merely confirms the decades-old GATT ban on export subsidies. Others emphasized the importance of positive externalities from particular industries due to knowledge spillovers and learning, which might produce dynamic growth effects for the rest of the economy.[54]

Although arguments for strategic trade policy turned out to be less compelling than their proponents had hoped, the engagement of prominent economists in the debate helped to foster the general impression that when economists relaxed the unworldly assumptions of the neoclassical model, justifications for restrictions on trade could easily be found. For example, Paul Krugman, in a statement he probably came to regret, asserted that government protection (preferably subsidization) of strategic sectors could be theoretically justified and that "the case for free trade is currently more in doubt than at any time since the 1817 publication of Ricardo's *Principles of Political Economy*."[55] In the case of the United States in the 1990s, the new trade theory provided ammunition to vigorously ideological commentators, who were able to claim that economists were only belatedly coming to understand what

---

[53] Gene M. Grossman, "Strategic Export Promotion: A Critique," in Paul R. Krugman, ed., *Strategic Trade Policy and the New International Economics* (Cambridge: MIT Press, 1986), 47–68.

[54] Paul R. Krugman, *Re-thinking International Trade* (Cambridge: MIT Press, 1996).

[55] Paul R. Krugman, "Is Free Trade Passé?" *Journal of Economic Perspectives* 1:2, 1987, 131–32.

those with common sense had known all along: that the ideology of free trade had allowed America's allies to undermine its high-technology competitiveness.[56] Some commentators argued that not comparative advantage but "competitive advantage," which stressed institutions, human capital, infrastructure, and other national characteristics, was the appropriate focus of policy.[57]

Most economists, including Krugman, continued to insist that the practical case for free trade remained very strong and that the idea of national competitiveness (rather than firm- or sectoral-level competitiveness) lacked meaning, since Ricardo's theory of comparative advantage remained valid. But their reasons for rejecting interventionism often included arguments concerning the dangers of policy "capture" and of foreign retaliation. (We turn to these considerations of political economy in the next chapter.) In the meantime, the idea of national competitiveness has prospered, with national competitiveness rankings attracting much attention from media and policy analysts.

In recent years strategic trade policy has been applied to the setting of technical standards. States or regional groupings that are able to establish their favored technical standard among several competitors as the global standard can provide strategic advantages to their own firms. Europe's attempt to establish GSM as a global mobile telephony standard suggests what is at stake in this area, especially for European advocates of strategic interventionism.[58] The strategic advantages may be greatest in high-technology sectors where there are substantial economies of scale. Although this strategy may avoid some of the standard problems with strategic trade policy, it may still entrench relatively inferior technologies and firms. It is also unclear how much economic theory drives such policy initiatives. Europe has also attempted to promote International Financial Reporting Standards rather than America's national accounting standards as a global norm. Although doing

[56] Robert Kuttner, *The End of Laissez Faire* (New York: Knopf, 1991); Clyde V. Prestowitz Jr., *Trading Places: How We Allowed Japan to Take the Lead* (New York: Basic Books, 1988).

[57] Michael E. Porter, *The Competitive Advantage of Nations* (New York: Free Press, 1992); Prestowitz, *Trading Places*.

[58] For a discussion of the strategic aspects of standard setting, see Walter Mattli and Tim Büthe, "Setting International Standards: Technological Rationality or Primacy of Power?" *World Politics* 56:1, 2003, 1–42.

so may provide advantages to European firms listed in non-EU stock exchanges and provide a marginal advantage to EU financial markets, the economic benefits to be gained from such strategies are uncertain. The most significant benefits may derive from the ability of a global standard setter to avoid renegotiating difficult domestic or regional political bargains.

CONCLUSION

We have argued in this chapter that the rise of an institutionalized, multilateral trade regime in the mid-twentieth century reflected both collective learning by governments from the experiences of the interwar period and the rise of American hegemony. The collapse of international trade during the 1930s provided a powerful justification for stronger multilateral constraints on trade policies, as did the more positive experience of the early postwar years. The shift in US attitudes toward trade was crucial, given America's increased importance in the global economy and its ambivalence toward submitting to such multilateral constraint. As the memory of the interwar experience faded, as the role of technology in international trade and specialization increased, and as developing countries became increasingly integrated into the global economy, the multilateral consensus weakened among the advanced countries. The United States, whose role in promoting the multilateral system in the mid-twentieth century was pivotal, has itself been affected by doubts, fed in part by perceptions of American decline relative to Europe, Japan, and now China. Doubts about multilateral trade can also be a source of leverage. The major countries have used the threat of their potential defection from the multilateral system to obtain greater concessions from other countries, including developing countries. Controversial issues such as labor and environmental standards have been placed on the agenda, and it remains difficult to assess the future consequences for the multilateral system.

We have also argued that debates over international trade within the economics discipline over the past two centuries have favored trade liberalization. But the history of trade protection, which has hardly been one of steady, progressive liberalization since the early nineteenth century, implies that the effect of mainstream economic ideas on trade policy outcomes has been weak. One reason for this, we have suggested, is that even mainstream economists have long argued that departures from free trade can be justified under certain circumstances. Traditional infant industry arguments have received support from more recent theories that investigate the implications of imperfect competition and technology for trade and trade policy. The resulting potential for conflicting national protectionist policies can help justify the multilateral constraints provided by the GATT and WTO since 1947. From another perspective, these multilateral constraints simply entrench the position of the advanced countries, which already have a lead in high-technology industries.

International trade raises fundamental issues of political sovereignty and procedural justice that are commonly ignored within economics. Most countries commonly set national minimum standards relating to child labor, workplace safety, the use of prison labor, pollution, and so forth. To those who see such standards as essential aspects of democracy, even of civilization, it seems odd that countries might be obliged to allow open trade with other countries in which companies are not obliged to adhere to such (possibly costly) standards. As Dani Rodrik has argued, trade and other forms of economic globalization can conflict with our basic understandings of procedural justice.[59] It is generally inadequate, for example, to say that a net addition to income (national or global) is justified, if it involves some gaining more than others lose; generally we want to know about the means by which the net increase was achieved (was it achieved through deception, criminal activity, or the exploitation of child labor, or was it the result of hard work by the winners?). The question Rodrik poses is whether it should be "immaterial to our story if the gains from trade are created, say, by a company shutting down its factory at home and setting up a new one abroad using child labor." One of the standard objections to this line of argument and its implication that some restrictions on trade are

---

[59] On this and a range of other related issues, see the posting (and related debate) by Dani Rodrik on his web blog: http://rodrik.typepad.com/dani_rodriks_weblog/2007/04/trade_and_proce.html, accessed January 28, 2008.

justified is that we would not expect the government to restrict commerce when technological change creates losers. Since most agree that technological change, to the extent it is separable from globalization, on average has more powerful redistributive effects than does international trade, this seems to be a powerful argument in favor of laissez-faire.[60] Rodrik counters, however, that most people would judge the results of technological change produced by innovation and hard work as procedurally different from the results of practices that are commonly abhorred and outlawed.

It seems clear that the assessment of the net gains from trade cannot be a simple matter of determining the balance of material economic gains and losses. Perhaps for this reason, trade policy has never been entirely an economic matter in practice. Even if most economists believe that free trade remains the best practical policy, the history of international trade suggests that it is extraordinarily difficult to sustain, either in autocracies or in democracies. In the following chapter, we consider in more detail why governments in practice have diverged from economists' standard prescriptions.

FURTHER RESOURCES

Further Reading

Bernard M. Hoekman and Petros C. Mavroidis. *The World Trade Organization: Law, Economics, and Politics.* London: Routledge, 2007. An accessible overview of the institutions, politics, and economics of global trade.

Michael John Trebilcock and Robert Howse. *The Regulation of International Trade.* London: Routledge, 3rd ed., 2005. A comprehensive discussion of the legal and institutional aspects of global trade.

Douglas Irwin. *Against the Tide: An Intellectual History of Free Trade.* Princeton, N.J.: Princeton University Press, 1996. A nontechnical history of the trade debate among economists.

---

[60] For a recent analysis of the respective distributive effects of technological change and openness, see IMF, *World Economic Outlook, September 2007* (Washington, D.C.: IMF, 2007), chap. 4.

Useful Websites

- www.wto.org: the WTO website provides a large range of resources, including texts on international trade agreements, data on trade flows, dispute settlement cases, and individual country commitments.
- http://www.llrx.com/features/trade3.htm: a helpful guide to international trade law resources on the Internet.
- http://www.cid.harvard.edu/cidtrade: a useful site for news and academic publications on trade.
- www.worldbank.org/trade: the World Bank's Trade Research Group site, with an emphasis on its development aspects and a large amount of trade data.

3 | The Political Economy of Trade Policy

This chapter focuses on the political factors that lead governments to put restrictions on trade, as they do to varying degrees across countries and over time. Here we can safely leave aside the theoretical possibility that protectionism may raise aggregate economic welfare in some circumstances (discussed in the previous chapter). Since governments often enact protectionist policies even when doing so seems to reduce aggregate welfare, political economists face a puzzle. In the previous chapter we argued that debates among economists about the possible justifications for protection have favored governments seeking reasons to adopt such policies. Since it is unlikely that economists' views alone explain governments' decisions to protect, we focus here on the two most common theories of protectionism: political interests and political institutions. Interest-based theories divide into two main forms: statist and domestic societal. Institutional explanations consider how domestic institutions privilege certain interests and policies.

INTEREST-BASED THEORIES OF TRADE POLICY

Interest-based explanations of trade policy outcomes generally do three things. First, they identify the key actors in the making of trade policy. Governments make trade policy, but it may be the product of "statist" objectives, of the "aggregation" of the preferences of societal actors, or of some combination of the two. Second, interest-based theories specify the trade-related preferences of these actors, usually by drawing on other economic or political theories that generate predictions about their preferences. Third, they make explicit or implicit assumptions about whose preferences prevail in creating trade policy. In what follows, we discuss statist and societal interest versions of this approach.

State Interests in Trade Policy

The realist tradition in international relations regards the state as a rational, unitary actor concerned to maximize power or security. For this tradition, international trade can have significant effects on the international distribution of wealth, power, and military capabilities.[1] The presence of these "security externalities," realists argue, means that governments cannot remain indifferent to the results of international trade. In effect, they claim that economists' arguments for free trade have too narrow a foundation, based as they are on considerations of economic welfare alone. The security externalities of trade can be separated into sectoral, technological, and aggregate economic outcomes.

DEFENSE INDUSTRIES: SECTORAL ARGUMENTS FOR PROTECTION

Realist concerns about the sectoral effects of trade often lead to justifications for departures from laissez-faire policies. Some sectors are considered especially significant for national defense. Since the Industrial Revolution, concerns about the viability of the manufacturing sector under conditions of open international competition have driven many to argue that the state must protect strategic sectors such as transport and other heavy machinery, machine tools, and, more recently, high technology. Henry Kissinger has decried outsourcing from the United States, viewing it in terms of national power: "I don't look at this from an economic point of view but the political and social points of view. The question really is whether America can remain a great power or a dominant power if it becomes a primarily service economy, and I doubt that. A country has to have an industrial base in order to play a signifi-

---

[1] Gilpin, *War and Change*; Gowa, *Allies, Adversaries*; Grieco, *Cooperation among Nations*; Rowe, "World Economic Expansion"; Gautam Sen, *The Military Origins of Industrialization and International Trade Rivalry* (London: Pinter, 1984).

cant role in the world."[2] If national defense is a priority, it may seem to give reasons to protect sectors that provide autonomy in crucial defense goods, even if doing so results in an economic welfare loss. This argument has a venerable tradition even in liberal political economy: Adam Smith himself justified sectoral exceptions to free trade on the grounds that "defense is more important than opulence."[3]

However, this justification of a trade-off between national wealth and national self-sufficiency does not tell us where protective lines should be drawn, or why states opt for different trade-offs in different circumstances. Sweden, for example, once a highly militarized European great power, is today a relatively open trader with very modest military ambitions. Self-sufficiency in many sectors, from agriculture to textiles to computer chips, might plausibly be justified on defense grounds. Where does this argument for protection stop? For reasons of security, a state may choose to be less prosperous and less economically specialized, but if it goes too far, the loss to economic welfare can be so great that both national wealth *and* national security are diminished. If protection lowers long-run growth, the harm to national security can be greater than that caused by dependence on other countries for strategic goods.

Beyond this general consideration, there are other limits to the realist argument for protection. The growing importance of intraindustry manufacturing trade reduces the likelihood that open trade will result in the wholesale loss of manufacturing, though there are doubts about whether this trend will continue. At present, Kissinger certainly exaggerates the economic importance of outsourcing. Offshored inputs are so far relatively unimportant in total trade, making up only about 5% of average gross output in developed countries in 2003, and only 2%-3% in the United States and Japan.[4] Furthermore, for most countries, self-sufficiency is more feasible in civilian industries than in defense

<hr>

[2] "American Jobs Must Not Be Lost, Says Kissinger," *Times News Network*, July 16, 2003. On outsourcing, see chapter 6.

[3] Andrew Walter, "Adam Smith on International Relations: Liberal Internationalist or Realist?" *Review of International Studies* 22:1, 1996, 5–29.

[4] IMF, *World Economic Outlook, April 2007* (Washington, D.C.: IMF, 2007), 164; Edward E. Leamer, "A Flat World, a Level Playing Field, a Small World after All, or None of the Above? A Review of Thomas L. Friedman's *The World Is Flat*," *Journal of Economic Literature* 55:1, 2007, 83–126.

hardware. Much of the latter is technology- and capital-intensive, which keeps it out of the reach of most countries. To the extent that defense production occurs at the technological frontier, it is harder to imitate. Increasing returns to scale in defense output also affect procurement costs, making military goods much cheaper to buy from a producer already selling to its own government. Importing from a range of foreign suppliers can lessen the risks involved, and the stockpiling of strategically important commodities such as fuel can be more efficient than protectionism. Overall, we can conclude that unless we classify most industries as defense-related, the defense industry argument amounts to an a priori claim about the need to protect some sectors rather than a plausible general theory of the actual outcomes of trade policy.

TECHNOLOGY: DUAL-USE TECHNOLOGIES AND EXTERNALITIES

Arguments for protection in technology-related sectors often overlap with concerns about specific defense goods, but they can be distinguished by their claim that technology can provide positive externalities to the rest of the economy. From this perspective, the trade-off we have described between national wealth and national autonomy may not apply in high-technology sectors. The goods produced by such sectors, it is said, are often of a "dual-use" nature, being important for both the defense sector and the national civilian economy. Moreover, innovation increasingly occurs in the civilian sector and is then applied to defense industries, rather than the reverse.[5] We addressed the argument about the importance of technology in international trade in the previous chapter. As employed by realists, it links defense goods and the need for national capability in dual-use technologies to the idea that leading-edge technologies, especially in manufacturing, allow countries to achieve dynamic gains in global competition, ensuring long-run economic and military security. Countries that succeed in leading-edge industries achieve higher productivity growth and larger long-run increases in national wealth and power. In many cases, such arguments

[5] Wayne Sandholtz, Michael Borrus, John Zysman, Ken Conca, Jay Stowsky, Steven Vogel, and Steve Weber, *The Highest Stakes: The Economic Foundations of the Next Security System* (New York: Oxford University Press, 1993).

have been used to justify government promotion of particular sectors through a combination of trade and industrial policy.[6]

Once again, such arguments tend to identify "strategic" industries, though this time in the sense of sectors that are technology intensive and that generate positive externalities for the whole economy. For example, computer software and integrated circuits may have significant implications for productivity growth in a range of industries that use them. The applied technology and skills acquired in the manufacturing of these high-technology components may also be important and might push the entire economy onto a path of higher long-run growth.[7] The argument that governments should be concerned about such national capabilities usually relies on claims that learning-by-doing is crucial in manufacturing. In addition, governments may have concerns about relying on key components imported from potentially unreliable trading partners. The need for self-sufficiency has also been used to justify restrictions on foreign acquisition of firms in designated strategic sectors. Patents can also slow the rate of international diffusion of technology, which may be one reason why advanced countries have since the 1980s insisted on the protection of their intellectual property.

Many economists dispute the size of the externalities claimed by proponents of strategic trade policies and argue that open trade is the best path to national security. Relying on domestic industries may condemn domestic users to the purchase of second-rate products, constricting technological diffusion and growth. Moreover, as we saw in chapter 2, the argument for intervention to promote high-technology industries assumes much about the ability of governments to pick winners and to resist the demands of vested interests. How influential such ideas on strategic trade protections have been remains an open question, though they have been important in some cases.[8] In any case, these sophisti-

---

[6] For example, in the 1990s such arguments were used to justify protection against Japanese high-technology imports in the United States and Europe as well as subsidies to promote private sector research in dual-use technologies. See Andrew Walter, "Globalization, Corporate Identity, and European Technology Policy," *Journal of European Public Policy* 2:3, 1995, 427–46.

[7] Stephen S. Cohen and John Zysman, *Manufacturing Matters: The Myth of the Post-industrial Economy* (New York: Basic Books, 1987).

[8] Laura D'Andrea Tyson, *Who's Bashing Whom? Trade Conflict in High-Technology Industries* (Washington, D.C.: Institute for International Economics, 1992). Tyson was named as President

cated arguments for government intervention cannot explain the persistence of protectionist policies in less exciting, relatively low-tech industries. As with the argument on defense-related industries, this is less a theory of trade protection than a normative argument for selective intervention. Only if one could explain why these ideas become important in particular times and places could it help to build a political economy theory of trade policy.

NEOREALISM AND RELATIVE GAINS IN INTERNATIONAL TRADE

In contrast to the arguments for protection of defense industries and technological capacity, another theory associated with the realist school does claim to explain general patterns of protection. This theory is based on an argument about relative gains associated with neorealism. Its proponents argue that the security externalities associated with trade mainly derive from the asymmetric distribution of the standard gains from trade. Thus, even trade in non-defense-related and low-technology sectors may produce an imbalance of gains that threatens the security of a country, resulting in a protectionist response from the state. This line of argument does not contest standard neoclassical trade theory, but like the other arguments based on the strategic interests of the state, it claims that economists have too narrow a conception of national welfare.[9]

The neorealist argument on trade derived from Grieco's critique of the neoliberal assumption that rational, egoistic states maximize aggregate gains from trade.[10] In the neoliberal view, greater economic openness is possible if international institutions reinforce commitments and contracts, so that defection and cheating by individual countries are less likely. According to Grieco, neoliberals took for granted the claim of mainstream economists that open trade was an optimal policy for all

---

Clinton's first head of the President's Council of Economic Advisors, and this administration launched an expansion of government-funded high-technology programs in the early 1990s.

[9] On the complexities that arise in determining the gains from trade, see the summary in the *New Palgrave Dictionary of Economics*, ed. John Eatwell, Murray Milgate, and Peter Newman (London: Palgrave, 2001), 2:453–54; and Elhanan Helpman, "The Noncompetitive Theory of International Trade and Trade Policy," in World Bank, *Proceedings of the World Bank Annual Conference on Development Economics, 1989* (Washington, D.C., World Bank, 1990), 193–230.

[10] Grieco, "Anarchy and the Limits of Cooperation."

countries because it would produce absolute gains. In an anarchical international political system, states are, for Grieco, "defensive positionalists" rather than maximizers of absolute welfare and power. That is, if open trade between two countries produced greater relative gains for one, the other's security would be threatened, justifying trade protection.

The importance of national security need not mean that states in all circumstances prefer autarky to trade. Avoidance of trade reduces national economic welfare and long-run growth, compromising security over time. States will also be more willing to trade openly with allies than with adversaries, since gains from trade by a state's allies can enhance its national security. Because security alliances may shift, however, states might be cautious about unequal trade with allies. Gowa accordingly argued that open trade is likelier in bipolar than in multipolar international systems, since the probability of defection from an alliance is generally lower in the former.[11]

Criticisms of this neorealist theory have been various.[12] First, like all realist theories of protectionism, it ignores the role of domestic anti-trade interests, a factor we discuss later. Second, it may exaggerate the salience of relative gains for most governments.[13] Trade has limited effects on national income in most large countries (China being today's prominent exception), and even large differences in the relative gains from bilateral trade would be unlikely to have great effects on national capabilities and growth, except perhaps in the very long run. For most countries, increased inputs of domestic labor, capital, education, and technological advances have been more important for growth since 1945, though it is difficult to separate technology completely from trade and FDI.[14] As for China, even though its total trade-to-GDP ratio was nearly 70% by 2005, net exports still contributed much less to its rapid growth of output than did investment and improvements to productivity. Trade is on average more important for smaller countries, but they

[11] Gowa, *Allies, Adversaries.*

[12] See Guzzini, *Realism in International Relations,* chap. 11.

[13] See various contributions to Baldwin, *Neorealism and Neoliberalism*; and James D. Morrow, "When Do 'Relative Gains' Impede Trade?" *Journal of Conflict Resolution* 41:1, 1997, 12–37.

[14] See Edward F. Denison, *Accounting for United States Economic Growth, 1929–1969* (Washington, D.C.: Brookings Institution, 1974); Angus Maddison, *Phases of Capitalist Development* (Oxford: Oxford University Press, 1982).

are generally not a threat to major powers. Nor is it clear whether the possession of nuclear weapons alters the relationship between trade and relative gains. If a country can achieve deterrence through existing stocks of nuclear weapons, it may have less concern about relative gains abroad (this may not apply to nonnuclear nations). Finally, it is not obvious why democratically elected governments will make the long-run effects of trade a priority, given that political elections generally shorten the "time horizon" of incumbent governments and lead them to focus on trade's short-run, domestic political effects.

We discuss these domestic political considerations later. In the meantime, it is clear that the strength, but also the weakness, of the neorealist model lies in its singular emphasis on the effects of international security on trade. Consistent with the theory, among other things, is the pattern of trade between the Western allies after 1945, which liberalized much more rapidly than did East-West trade or, for example, India-Pakistan trade. But even if we take the neorealist theory on its own terms, ignoring domestic politics, why must security considerations push in one direction only, toward constraints on trade? A country could trade with an enemy state in the hope of promoting prosperity and interests in it that favor peaceful cooperation. Trade might also foster homegrown political opposition to the enemy's incumbent government, as West Germany hoped would happen as a result of its *Ostpolitik* strategy toward East Germany in the 1970s. Or should governments avoid all trade with enemy states so as not to enrich them and bolster the incumbent government? Neorealist theory throws little light on such subtle diplomatic questions. Nor, most importantly for our purposes, does it explain the details of trade policy, such as why many countries' openness to trade varies by sector and by product. Attributing all such variations to hypothetical effects on the balance of international gains from trade is implausible; it appears that we need to take account of domestic political factors.

Societal Models of Choices in Trade Policy

For some of the reasons just given, many scholars agree that the simplifying assumption that the state is a unitary actor, adopted by realism and neoliberalism alike, is problematic when it comes to explaining trade policy outcomes. In contrast to realism's focus on the international distributive consequences of trade, they argue that domestic distributional effects are often far more important for trade policy choices. In societal models of trade policy, domestic interests are divided into winners and losers. Politicians are assumed to be motivated primarily by their concern to be (re)elected. Specific outcomes are a product of competition for political influence between groups with divergent interests.[15] Note that most societal approaches assume free trade to be the economically rational policy in all circumstances; politics is the reason why protectionism is so common in practice. Protectionist outcomes reduce aggregate economic welfare, but they redistribute income toward particular societal groups. Politicians favor these groups because they are well organized and provide electoral support, producing a structural bias toward protectionism. The majority of ordinary voters (consumers) lose in the process, but consumer interests are poorly represented because the costs of protection are spread relatively thinly across society and because of collective action problems.[16]

A significant body of work by economists has modeled the process of trade policymaking to explain how the preferences of voters and interest groups influence politicians and outcomes. It assumes that economic actors have incentives to pursue rents that can be delivered by government intervention. The most important of these scholarly efforts is *endogenous tariff theory*, which models the political "market for tariffs."[17] This body of work includes electoral competition, societal demands for protection, and public policy goals as factors shaping trade

[15] Milner, *Interests, Institutions, and Information*, 2–29; John S. Odell, "Understanding International Trade Policies: An Emerging Synthesis," *World Politics* 43:1, 1990, 139–67.

[16] Collective action problems refer to the difficulty that large groups have in organizing to pursue common goals, primarily because of the incentive for any one actor to free ride on others who may be willing to bear the costs of such organization. For a classic account, see Mancur Olson, *The Logic of Collective Action: Public Goods and the Theory of Groups* (Cambridge: Harvard University Press, 1965).

[17] Stephen P. Magee, "Endogenous Tariff Theory: A Survey," in David C. Colander, ed., *Neoclassical Political Economy, The Analysis of Rent-Seeking and DUP Activities* (Cambridge: Ballinger, 1984), 41–55; Gene M. Grossman and Elhanan Helpman, *Interest Groups and Trade Policy* (Princeton, N.J.: Princeton University Press, 2002); Elhanan Helpman, "Politics and Trade Policy," in Richard E. Baldwin et al., eds., *Market Integration, Regionalism and the Global Economy* (Cambridge: Cambridge University Press, 1999), 86–116.

policies. Most of these models assume that governments are interested in maximizing their chances of retaining political office. According to Magee, "tariffs are an equilibrating variable in political market, which balance opposing forces in redistributional battles."[18] Political parties compete by adopting commitments on trade that maximize their chances of appealing to domestic interest groups. A variant of this approach employs the attributes of the median voter rather than interest groups to determine policy outcomes.[19] When the economy imports labor-intensive goods, if the median voter has a higher endowment of labor per unit of capital than the economy as a whole, the political equilibrium is positive tariffs, the revenues of which are redistributed to the public in proportion to income. By contrast, Magee assumes that informational costs put interest groups in a better position than voters to identify policy options.

Grossman and Helpman posit a different version of the tariff-formation function, focusing on attempts by interest groups to influence political incumbents. In this model, "the incumbent politician's objective is to maximize a weighted sum of total political contributions and aggregate social welfare."[20] They assume that interest groups initiate the political interaction by offering campaign contributions to incumbent politicians in order to influence their stance, instead of the latter anticipating interest group preferences and articulating appropriate policies. Politicians choose policies that will increase campaign contributions, and again, positive tariffs result. Evidence from US congressional elections lends some support to this view, since incumbents of both parties are disproportionate beneficiaries of campaign contributions.

The extent of concentration of the sector[21] is also likely to affect the lobbying process because high concentration means that the gains from protections against imports will go to fewer actors and their costs of lobbying will be more easily borne. This increases the likelihood that a coalition can be organized to lobby government. Small and medium-

---

[18] Magee, "Endogenous Tariff Theory," 42.

[19] Wolfgang Mayer, "Endogenous Tariff Formation," *American Economic Review* 74:5, 1984, 970–85.

[20] Grossman and Helpman, *Interest Groups and Trade Policy*, 115.

[21] A highly concentrated sector is one in which a few firms together hold a large proportion of total market share.

sized firms may be less well placed to influence decision makers unless they are geographically concentrated. Once the costs of setting up a lobbying group have been defrayed, lobbyists are likely to make ongoing efforts to influence trade policy.

A government's autonomy to pursue broader goals, including the maximization of aggregate welfare, is greater if voters have interests in many issues between which trade-offs are possible. That is, there is no reason to assume that governments are mere impassive aggregators of (protection-biased) societal interests. Without that assumption, statist and domestic societal approaches may be compatible. Societal demands for relief from imports may be reinforced when incumbent governments combine them with concerns for national political or strategic trade policy. At the same time, international trade regimes, about which approaches focused on security or domestic politics often say little, may help governments to deflect domestic pressure for protectionism and to obtain a degree of autonomy in setting policies.

An initial problem for interest group theories lies in deciding how to model conflicts of interest. There are three main approaches. The first, a long-run model, uses the Stolper-Samuelson model discussed in the previous chapter to derive class-based cleavages of interest on trade. The second, associated with the specific factors approach, predicts that societal divisions follow sectoral rather than class lines. The third model suggests that interest cleavages will occur at the level of the firm, with relatively large internationalized firms supporting more open trade policies. We discuss these three approaches in what follows.

FACTOR (CLASS) INTERESTS IN TRADE POLICY

Given its clear distributional implications, the Stolper-Samuelson theorem on the equalization of factor returns through trade was an obvious choice for political economists wanting to specify interest cleavages. The main lines of conflict in this model are class based, though the rural-urban divide also receives significant attention.[22] According to Rogowski, increases (or decreases) in international trade are equivalent to lower (or higher) tariffs that increase (or lower) trade. As we saw in the previous chapter, Stolper-Samuelson showed that abundant factors

---

[22] Rogowski, *Commerce and Coalitions.*

gain income as international trade increases, and relatively scarce factors lose. On this basis, Rogowski classifies economies into four simplified, exclusive types: capital and land rich and labor poor (type I); capital and labor rich and land poor (type II); capital and labor poor and land rich (type III); and capital and land poor and labor rich (type IV). His model predicts two main cleavages: a class conflict with two types of endowment and a rural-urban cleavage in two others.

In a type I advanced economy, class conflict results as capitalists and landowners favor trade while labor opposes it. In an advanced type II economy, landowners and rural workers (depending on the extent of their mobility) lose from increased trade, whereas capitalists and workers, who comprise the entire urban sector, gain and push for trade liberalization. Similar urban-rural conflict is predicted in a more backward type III economy, in which landowners favor increased trade against the opposition of urban capital and labor. In a backward type IV economy, class conflict is likely between labor, on the one hand, and landowners and capitalists, on the other.

Rogowski's parsimonious model illuminates some of the classic cases of trade policy, such as the capital-labor coalition for free trade in nineteenth-century Britain that successfully overcame resistance from the landed elite. Unfortunately, however, the model does not always fit important cases. In the capital- and land-abundant United States after 1945, labor did not consistently oppose liberalization of trade; in fact, organized labor, with some sectoral exceptions, largely supported liberalization until the 1970s. In addition, segments of US industry have opposed liberalization since the mid-1970s in spite of capital abundance. Similarly, significant segments of European capital opposed free trade during the same period, contrary to the expectation that a coalition of protrade capital and labor would be in conflict with a politically insignificant agricultural sector opposed to it. These examples suggest that Rogowski's model may sometimes be helpful in identifying broad lines of societal conflict over trade, but it fails to capture important intraclass conflicts of interest.[23]

---

[23] Midford argues that Rogowski's model can be salvaged if labor is treated as a nonhomogeneous factor (Paul Midford, "International Trade and Domestic Politics: Improving on Rogowski's Model of Political Alignments," *International Organization* 47:4, 1993, 535–64).

SECTORAL INTERESTS IN TRADE POLICY: THE SPECIFIC FACTORS MODEL

The H-O-S theory used by Rogowski assumes that factors of production are fully mobile across different sectors within (though not across) countries. However, if intersectoral factor mobility is low, societal interests are likely to divide along sectoral rather than class lines. Factor immobility is plausible since capital equipment is typically fabricated for a specific purpose and skilled labor can be highly trained to perform specific tasks. Shifting such factors to uses in other sectors is difficult and costly.

The *specific factors*, or Ricardo-Viner, model is the usual means of analyzing the case of factor immobility.[24] In its standard form, capital is sector-specific and hence immobile, while another factor is mobile across sectors (usually unskilled, "generic" labor). The model predicts that trade will have positive effects on capital income in export sectors and negative effects on capital income in import-competing sectors. The return to capital in import-competing sectors falls as labor moves from that sector into the expanding export sector. By contrast, the return to capital in the export sector improves as it expands and attracts labor.[25] The outcome for labor depends on the intensity of factor use in the two sectors as well as consumption patterns (note that the prices of imported goods will fall).

The specific factors model predicts that the main line of conflict over trade policy falls between import-competing sectors and exporting sectors. Trade increases the real price of factors specific to exporting sectors and lowers the real price of factors specific to importing sectors. Note that if labor itself is sector-specific (or if it divides into relatively immobile skilled labor and relatively mobile unskilled labor), its interests in trade will depend on where it is located (i.e., in exporting or import-competing industries). In other words, sector-specific capital and labor will share common interests: firms and unions in an exporting sector will gain from trade liberalization, whereas those "stuck" in an import-

---

[24] Frieden, "Sectoral Conflict."

[25] The implications of the specific factor approach are complicated if capital in exporting and import-competing sectors is owned in a stock portfolio by the same principal. This suggests that the trade policy preferences of owners of capital may thus depend in part on the structure of ownership of industry in each country.

competing sector will lose. Relatively mobile factors will have ambiguous interests, which may prevent them from mobilizing to influence trade policy.

There is a good deal of evidence in favor of the specific factors approach. Writing in the 1930s, for example, Schattschneider showed that a plethora of industry groups in the United States lobbed intensively and successfully during the Depression for trade protection, the end result being the Hawley-Smoot tariff of 1930.[26] Similarly, in recent decades, in advanced countries both firms and unions in declining industries such as textiles, footwear, steel, and shipbuilding have supported protection against imports. The theory also helps to explain why tariff rates often vary substantially across different product groups, an outcome that is difficult for realist or class-based theories to explain.

It is tempting, though ultimately unsatisfying, to assume that one should adopt Frieden's specific factors approach when discussing the political short run, when factors are relatively immobile, and Rogowski's class-based approach for discussions of the political long run. However, as Hiscox points out, these two models represent polar opposites on a spectrum of factor mobility; in practice, most real-world situations fall between them. Thus, in order to analyze a particular case we must consider the actual degree of intersectoral factor mobility.[27] Hiscox argues that in early phases of economic development factor mobility is relatively high, whereas in more advanced stages factor mobility declines as more differentiated forms of human and physical capital emerge and as technology comes to play a more important role. This may help to explain, for example, why a broad capital-labor coalition in favor of free trade existed in mid-nineteenth-century Britain, whereas in Britain and other advanced countries in more recent decades, intraclass cleavages have spread, producing a mixed pattern of open trade in some sectors and heavy protection in others.

Hiscox also argues that a class-based partisan divide is more likely to facilitate growth by allowing protagonists in trade policy to reach an overarching social compact, providing joint gains. The Scandinavian model sought broad-based cooperation between capital and labor to

[26] E. E. Schattschneider, *Politics, Pressures, and the Tariff* (New York: Prentice Hall, 1935).
[27] Hiscox, *International Trade.*

ensure greater joint gains, whereas more fragmented political systems that are more responsive to sectoral differences over trade policy tend to produce more damaging rent-seeking competition between societal agents. Although this is unlikely to be the last word on the subject, the argument shifts attention to political institutional factors, generally acknowledged as a weakness of interest-based approaches and discussed later.

Firm-Level Interests in Trade Policy

A third approach assumes that interests divide at a much lower level than that assumed by either of the two theories previously outlined. From this perspective, the degree of intersectoral factor mobility matters less for preferences on trade than does the degree of internationalization of individual firms.[28] In the Stolper-Samuelson model, capital is assumed to be mobile within but not between countries. In addition, it takes little account of the source and volatility of demand for a firm's output. Indeed, it is striking that the two main political economy theories of trade policy say little about the impact of business cycles, since relief from imports is most likely to be sought during economic downturns, when unemployment and excess capacity are higher.[29]

According to Milner, much depends on the combination of export dependence and multinationalization exhibited by each firm. Firms that are neither export dependent nor multinationalized (i.e., with no foreign operations—type I firms) are likely to support protectionist policies in national economic downturns. By contrast, export-dependent (type II) firms will favor policies that open markets abroad. Export-oriented multinational corporations (MNCs) with high levels of cross-border intrafirm trade (type III firms) will favor an open trade policy even in the face of increasing competition at home from imports, because protectionism could provoke foreign retaliation and undermine their intrafirm trade strategy (and hence their global corporate competitiveness). Firms that are not export dependent but are multina-

---

[28] Milner, *Resisting Protectionism*.

[29] Overvalued exchange rates also tend to foster protectionist demands, but this additional complication is rarely modeled in theories of trade politics.

tionalized (type IV) will favor selective protectionism, since foreign retaliation will not undermine their competitive position.

Milner argues that the protectionist response to economic downturn
in the 1970s was much more muted than in the 1930s because of the
much higher proportion of type III firms in the later period. Over time,
as more firms have constructed highly integrated multinational production networks with high levels of intrafirm trade, corporate support for protectionist trade policies has fallen. The result has been a
weakening of the relationship between national economic downturns
and trade protection.

Matters may be even more complicated than this, since firms with
activities in more than one sector may experience internal conflict over
trade policy. Imports of intermediate goods (those used in production)
are often traded intrafirm. Even when this is not the case, users of
intermediate goods may lobby against import protection.[30] Furthermore, firms may shift from one category to another. So, for example,
if firms based in import-competing sectors can shift production to
lower-cost countries and export back to their original home base, as
posited in the product cycle theory, they will be unlikely to favor protection against foreign imports. As we discuss in chapter 6, type IV MNCs
appear to be in decline, and export orientation is on the rise. Often,
however, many such firms with branded products are outsourcing the
production process to cheaper locations such as China, managing the
supply-chain and distribution process. These MNCs should have strong
preferences for open trade.

Much may also depend on the degree of mobility enjoyed by firms
in particular sectors, bringing us back to the issue of intersectoral factor
mobility. If firms do favor protection, an import tariff could also raise
the costs for firms in other sectors (for example, by bidding up the
price of intersectorally mobile labor), triggering demands for additional
interventions. As a result, Hiscox suggests, the relationship between
capital mobility and trade policy interests is more complicated than
Milner argues.[31] We could add that foreign corporate ownership and

---

[30] E.g., Destler, *American Trade Politics*, 194–95.

[31] Michael J. Hiscox, "International Capital Mobility and Trade Politics: Capital Flows, Coalitions and Lobbying," *Economics and Politics* 16:3, 2004, 253–85.

control might also affect corporate preferences. A foreign-owned and foreign-controlled type I firm might be less likely to favor protection in a recession than a domestically owned and controlled type I firm. This might be because the foreign owners reside in a country that is a potential target of trade barriers, but foreign owners might also be reluctant to overtly lobby a host country government out of concern not to jeopardize their domestic political position. More research is needed in this area to assess these possibilities.

General Criticisms of Interest-Based Approaches

As we noted earlier, interest-based approaches suffer because there are competing economic interpretations of material interests in trade policy. Hiscox's approach has the advantage of specifying under what circumstances the assumptions of the specific factors model rather than the Stolper-Samuelson model apply. But international capital mobility introduces further complications that push against any simple, clear predictions about the trade preferences of economic actors. Nor do the main models investigate the consequences of increasing returns to scale for the preferences of domestic interest groups. Alt and others note that introducing increasing returns to scale produces ambiguous distributional outcomes. The end result may be that there is simply no parsimonious means of deriving societal preferences on trade policy from economic theory.[32]

This is a major problem for interest-based approaches, since their analytical leverage derives from their deployment of economic theory to predict actors' preferences. If material economic interests are ambiguous even in economic theory, it leaves open the possibility that actors' interests and related preferences may be influenced by other factors, such as ideology. As the uncertainty of actors regarding their interests increases, ideas may provide "focal points" that help them to clarify their preferences. Garrett and Weingast argue that the role for ideas is likely to be more important the higher is the degree of uncertainty and

---

[32] Alt et al., "Political Economy of International Trade." See also Krugman, *Rethinking International Trade*, 80.

the lower are both distributional and power asymmetries.[33] The more radical notion that ideas largely determine actor interests has yet to receive substantial empirical support in the area of trade policy.[34]

Ideas may matter most to those actors for whom the standard distributional issues of trade policy matter least. In recent years developmental and environmental NGOs have become increasingly active on trade policy in ways that the standard models do not predict. Although traditional interest-based models may help to explain why unions are concerned about the impact of trade on labor and environmental standards, it is less obvious how the models can account for other NGO activism on trade. Instead, these NGOs are apparently motivated by concerns about the negative consequences of trade and international trade regimes for global development and the environment. These are material factors, but different from those emphasized in traditional interest models.[35] Such groups may countervail the influence of protrade business lobbies in particular, and their long-term impact on the international trade system is as yet unclear.

As we have seen, the analytical leverage of domestic societal approaches is mainly a product of the economic models they deploy; they tend to say little, however, about how governments actually go about setting trade policy in response to competing demands from domestic interests. This problem was recognized in Schattschneider's classic analysis of the US Hawley-Smoot tariff of the 1930s. He argued that the tariff was the product of overwhelming pressure from protectionist industry interests: "the pressures supporting the tariff [were] made overwhelming by the fact that the opposition [was] negligible."[36] The

[33] Geoffrey Garrett and Barry R. Weingast, "Ideas, Interests, and Institutions: Constructing the European Community's Internal Market," in Judith Goldstein and Robert O. Keohane, eds., *Ideas and Foreign Policy: Beliefs, Institutions, and Political Change* (Ithaca, N.Y.: Cornell University Press, 1993), 173–206.

[34] For reviews of the ideas literature, see John Kurt Jacobsen, "Much Ado about Ideas: The Cognitive Factor in Economic Policy," *World Politics* 47:2, 1995, 283–310; and Odell, "Understanding International Trade Policies."

[35] Margaret E. Keck and Karen Sikkink, *Activists beyond Borders: Advocacy Networks in International Politics* (Ithaca, N.Y.: Cornell University Press, 1998). However, Susan Sell and Aseem Prakash ("Using Ideas Strategically: Examining the Contest between Business and NGO Networks in Intellectual Property Rights," *International Studies Quarterly* 48:1, 2004, 143–75) argue that business groups and NGOs are similar in that both are motivated by material and normative concerns.

[36] Schattschneider, *Politics, Pressures, and Tariff*, 285.

outcome was largely the result of "effective demands upon the government." Schattschneider recognized that outcomes also had an institutional aspect, and that it was important to understand why the institutions of the American political system so favored one set of interests over others.[37] Societal models generally predict a protectionist bias in trade policy because losers from increased trade have a much greater incentive to organize than do winners. This does not explain why, in practice, levels of protection vary widely across countries. This poses a challenge not only to interest-based models, but also to institutionalist models, which we discuss in what follows.

INSTITUTIONAL THEORIES OF TRADE POLICY

Institutions are commonly seen as an intervening variable between the preferences of interest groups, which we have already discussed, and the formation of trade policy.[38] Constitutional provisions and the functioning of the institutions encountered by interest groups matter. Political institutions structure the constraints and opportunities of interest groups and usually are crucial in determining eventual policies. Notably, they help to overcome a major problem faced by domestic societal approaches, which is that they often overpredict the level of protection.

Two issues have received most attention in the literature. The first is the distribution of authority and decision-making powers between the executive and legislature, both in general and for particular issues (i.e., constitutional authority). The second is the electoral system, because the ability of interest groups to influence legislators may vary between majoritarian and proportional representation systems of pluralist democracy.[39] We discuss both of these factors next.

[37] Schattschneider, *Politics, Pressures, and Tariff,* 5–6.

[38] Witold J. Henisz and Edward D. Mansfield, "Votes and Vetoes: The Political Determinants of Commercial Openness," *International Studies Quarterly* 50:1, 2006, 189–212; Susanne Lohmann and Sharon O'Halloran, "Divided Government and US Trade Policy: Theory and Evidence," *International Organization* 48:4, 1994, 595–632; Bailey, Goldstein, and Weingast, "Institutional Roots."

[39] Majoritarian electoral systems are generally based on the first-past-the-post method, favoring single-party governments. Proportional electoral systems are often associated with consensual democracies and coalition governments.

Constitutional Authority and Policy Outcomes

The institutional setup in democratic polities is usually either parliamentary or presidential. In parliamentary systems, the executive assumes office symbiotically and simultaneously with the election of parliament, and his or her authority depends on the continuing confidence of the legislature. In presidential systems, both executive and legislature can be elected contemporaneously, but the authority of the former is separable from that of the legislature. In most circumstances, the legislature cannot force the executive to resign.[40]

According to Milner, there are five distinctive elements in the institutional decision-making process of pluralist democracies: agenda setting, amendment, ratification or veto, referendums, and side payments.[41] If all these decision-making powers are concentrated in the hands of a single actor or group, domestic politics become unimportant because the state is effectively unitary. However, if the institutional structure gives different actors influence over these parts of the decision-making process, institutional arrangements and practices can have a crucial bearing on the ability of interest groups to achieve their policy preferences. The assumption that the state is nonunitary is generally valid even for most highly authoritarian regimes.

As regards the distribution of constitutional authority between the executive and the legislature, control over the agenda often sets the terms of the debate. The authority to set the agenda usually resides with the executive (i.e., the prime minister) in a parliamentary system and varies considerably in presidential forms of government, though foreign policy is often the province of the president. Presidents with authority over trade policy may help to overcome the protectionist bias of democracies predicted by societal models, since their national mandate may allow them to pursue the national good and to form protrade coalitions with legislators.[42] When other actors possess the

---

[40] For further discussion, see Arendt Lijphart, ed., *Parliamentary versus Presidential Government* (Oxford: Oxford University Press, 1992).

[41] Milner, *Interests, Institutions, and Information.*

[42] Daniel L. Neilson, "Supplying Trade Reform: Political Institutions and Liberalization in Middle-Income Presidential Democracies," *American Journal of Political Science* 47:3, 2003, 470–91.

authority either to amend the agenda, or to ratify proposed legislation, the agenda-setter's autonomy is restricted. In some circumstances, the legislature may constrain its own power to amend the details of a policy proposal, such as in the US "fast track" authority (since the Trade Act of 2002, this has been called the "trade promotion authority"). Such arrangements exist when complex, distributive agreements that cannot survive amendment are involved and delay is costly. At least in the case of the United States, these devices are generally believed to favor less protection.

A further institutional arrangement that affects policymaking is a constitutional provision for ratification, which means the ability to veto. The power to ratify may reside with either the legislature or the executive, depending on who plays the role of agenda-setter. In foreign economic policymaking, the executive usually initiates, and the legislature has the power either to amend or to ratify. The agenda-setter must anticipate the support of the executive, legislature, or the public for the proposed policy and craft it accordingly. The power to ratify, which raises the cost of rejection, is likelier for international negotiations because the power to amend would undermine the executive's credibility with foreign governments during negotiations.

Another constitutional device that influences policymaking is the provision for referenda. The executive may refer a policy to the public by resorting to a referendum, bypassing the legislature and effectively curbing its authority. If referenda are called, they can shift influence from interest groups to voters, who collectively fulfill the ratification function. Examples of referenda on trade policy are difficult to find, so generally the executive branch seeks support for its trade policy in the legislature.

Finally, institutional mechanisms for making side payments are also relevant to outcomes in trade policy. The use of side payments depends on the ability of policymakers to identify the potential for trade-offs between concessions on trade policy and concessions in other areas (or trade-offs between different areas of trade policy). Thus, one group of legislators might support demands for bilateral trade liberalization in exchange for support for an agreement by the executive to demand other concessions from the beneficiary. For example, US trade policy toward China in the 1990s, before the latter's entry into the WTO, often involved linking trade liberalization with demands for an improvement in Chinese policy on human rights. Similarly, the ratification of the NAFTA treaty by the US Congress in 1994 also depended on Mexico's willingness to offer concessions on environmental and labor standards.

Although such distinctions provide nuance to explanations of outcomes on trade policy in particular cases, it is not at all clear that they explain broad patterns of trade policy. In particular, there is no systematic difference in the policies of presidential and parliamentary systems. Similar political systems can also produce quite different policies on trade, as is evident in the cases of presidential systems in France and the United States.[43] Nor can institutional models explain within-country differences in protection across sectors as easily as interest-based models.

Voting Systems and Policy Outcomes

Electoral institutions can affect trade policy outcomes in a variety of ways. Larger electoral districts tend to subsume sectoral interests within a wide voting constituency, potentially weakening their impact. They can, however, facilitate the emergence of broader, interregional and national class-based political coalitions. In the same way, proportional representation (PR) systems, in which party leaders choose candidates, reduce the scope for sectoral interest group influence because these groups must compete with a wide constituency of voters. This produces the claim that PR systems favor more open trade.[44] By contrast, small electoral constituencies in majoritarian systems can give disproportionate influence to sectoral or firm-level interest groups and create alliances with their political representatives.

Geographical factors can also be important. To the extent that electoral districts coincide with the geographical location of particular industries, this congruence may increase the responsiveness of political

[43] Sean D. Ehrlich, "Access to Protection: Domestic Institutions and Trade Policy in Democracies," *International Organization* 61:3, 2007, 575.

[44] Ronald W. Rogowski, "Trade and the Variety of Democratic Institutions," *International Organization* 41:2, 1987, 203–23.

representatives to lobbying on trade by these industries. For example, an electoral system that gives greater representation to rural districts, as in Japan, can entrench protectionist policies in agriculture. Geographically concentrated sectoral alliances between labor and capital are most likely to have an impact on parliamentary representatives and decision-makers. Studies of the Hawley-Smoot tariff show that logrolling allowed each individual lobby to advance its own protectionist claims in Congress, and that it was rational for everyone to jump on the bandwagon to seek protection from imports in a shrinking market.[45]

Electoral institutions can also affect the coherence and discipline of political parties.[46] Strong political parties tend to be less susceptible to protectionist demands from multiple sectoral interests. PR systems favor coalition government and can weaken party discipline, which implies a greater susceptibility to such demands. But PR systems can also encourage broad, stable coalitions between capital and labor that favor open trade (as in Scandinavia). There are also no clear relationships between particular electoral systems on the one hand and numbers of constituencies and levels of party discipline on the other. As a result, there is considerable ambiguity in the predictions that flow from electoral models of trade policymaking. Unsurprisingly perhaps, the data show no strong relationship between the trade policies of PR and majoritarian political democracies.[47] Nor, as with presidential versus parliamentary institutions, can electoral institutions explain variation in protection between countries with the same kind of electoral system, or variations between sectors within individual countries.

In the long run, institutions themselves are politically endogenous, and interest groups can mobilize to influence political institutions in ways that increase or entrench their influence. But this does not mean that interest cleavages will determine long-run trade outcomes. Since trade is hardly the only salient political issue and rarely the most important, political institutions (including political parties) are quite un-

---

[45] Barry J. Eichengreen, "The Political Economy of the Smoot-Hawley Tariff," *Research in Economic History* 1:2, 1989, 1–43.

[46] See Gary W. Cox, *Making Votes Count: Strategic Coordination in the World's Electoral Systems* (Cambridge: Cambridge University Press, 1997).

[47] Ehrlich, "Access to Protection," 575.

likely to reflect interest cleavages on trade.[48] In most countries, electoral systems are permanent, and this institutional inertia suggests that endogeneity is not an acute problem for this form of institutional analysis.

CONCLUSION

Modern theories of international trade remain anchored in the theoretical contributions of classical and neoclassical economics. These standard economic theories have been most conspicuously deployed in domestic societal models of trade politics, whereas approaches to trade policymaking based in political science have been more associated with statist theories of international relations. Both approaches help to explain why protection in practice generally exceeds the level that most economists believe maximizes economic welfare. However, both approaches probably exaggerate the protectionist bias in trade policy, and they find it difficult to account for variations in protectionism across countries and sectors. This appears to have much to do with the fact that neither takes sufficient account of the role of domestic political institutions in determinations of trade policy. More recently, political economists have shown increasing appreciation of the way in which interests interact with institutions and ideas to produce such outcomes. Yet it would be too much to claim that these initial attempts at consolidation have produced a robust theory of trade policymaking. The focus of the literature on interest-based models has meant that institutionalist and ideational models are comparatively underdeveloped.

Despite these weaknesses, there have been some important theoretical results. The roles of technology and asset specificity in trade have been increasing in recent decades, and these developments are linked to the rising incidence of increasing returns to scale in production, intraindustry trade, and FDI. This relationship seems to have had the effect of eroding old class-based political trade coalitions that were evident before the early twentieth century. Hence, although intraindustry trade and FDI are often said to reduce conflicts between trading part ners, they may increase the propensity for societal interests to engage

[48] Hiscox, *International Trade*, 37.

in rent-seeking competition. Most modern political economies thus continue to be finely balanced between political demands for protection and those for open trade, though much depends on their political institutions. In addition, new political actors such as environmental and developmental NGOs are now active in trade politics in ways that are not predicted by traditional models of political economy. Whether these developments bode well or ill for the maintenance of a relatively open international trading system is an open question.

FURTHER RESOURCES

Further Reading

Ronald Finlay and Kevin H. O'Rourke. *Power and Plenty: Trade, War, and the World Economy in the Second Millennium.* Princeton, N.J.: Princeton University Press, 2008. An examination by two economists of the close relationship between trade and geopolitics over the long run.

Michael J. Hiscox. *International Trade and Political Conflict: Commerce, Coalitions, and Mobility.* Princeton, N.J.: Princeton University Press, 2002. A useful synthesis of domestic societal theories of trade policy outcomes.

Sean D. Ehrlich. "Access to Protection: Domestic Institutions and Trade Policy in Democracies." *International Organization* 61:3, 2007, 571–605. A critique of existing accounts of the role of domestic political institutions in trade policy, arguing that the number of institutional access points available to lobbies matters most.

Useful Websites

- http://r0.unctad.org/trains_new/index.shtm: the UNCTAD Trains Database provides data on trade policy for most countries. Unfortunately, subscriptions are required.
- http://www.bis.doc.gov/about/index.htm: The US Department of Commerce's Bureau of Industry and Security is responsible for investigating the links between trade policy and national security.
- http://go.worldbank.org/2EAGGLRZ40: the World Bank's Database of Political Institutions provides detail by country and over time on electoral systems, executive and legislative powers, etc.

4 | The Evolution of the International Monetary System

Chapters 4 and 5 discuss the political economy of international money and finance. In chapter 2 we discussed the reasons for the evolution of the international trade system toward institutionalized multilateralism. Similarly, in this chapter we consider how the literature in political economy has tried to explain the evolution of the international monetary system. As for international trade, the international monetary system also became characterized by institutionalized multilateralism by the mid-twentieth century, for a similar combination of material and ideational reasons. In contrast to trade, however, multilateralism in international monetary arrangements peaked in the 1960s and has been in retreat since then. We emphasize the rise of private financial markets and associated political changes in explaining this trend.

Although international monetary arrangements in the nineteenth century were much less politicized at the domestic level than were those for international trade, over the course of the twentieth century this became less true. And at the international level, international monetary arrangements have always been politically controversial. This has much to do with the strong tendencies toward hierarchy in global monetary and financial markets and the asymmetric consequences this has for the distribution of costs and benefits across countries. The conflict between national macroeconomic stabilization policies and international monetary commitments has become more acute with the reemergence of open financial markets since the 1970s. We postpone to chapter 5 a discussion of the consequences of this conflict.

In order to address the question of how to explain international monetary evolution, we must first consider some preliminary issues concerning the balance between adjustment and financing in international monetary organization. After this, we go on to argue that the rise of domestic macroeconomic management in the twentieth century, itself the result of new ideas and of democratization, has had profound effects on this balance and on the international monetary system in general. These effects include the growing politicization of international monetary and financial arrangements compared to the nineteenth century, the gradual undermining of an anchor role for gold, and a shift toward greater exchange rate flexibility and from public to private international finance.

FINANCING AND ADJUSTMENT IN THE BALANCE OF PAYMENTS

The central organizational problem for any international monetary system concerns the mechanism of adjustment to balance-of-payments disequilibria between countries.[1] The fundamental issue from the perspective of political economy is that the costs of adjustment to disequilibria are typically distributed asymmetrically across countries and across different groups within countries. International financing mechanisms are a means of sustaining balance-of-payments deficits and thereby avoiding (at least temporarily) such adjustment pressures. Thus, the nature of the international adjustment mechanism(s), and the balance between financing and adjustment, constitutes the core of the politics of international monetary arrangements.

To see this more clearly we need to understand the balance of payments (BoP). This measures a country's transactions with nonresidents over a given period of time (e.g., monthly, quarterly, or yearly). It categorizes different kinds of cross-border "flow," and it balances by defini-

---

[1] Standard analyses emphasize the three interrelated problems of adjustment, liquidity, and confidence, but the second two are largely derivative of the first. The first two are addressed below; the "confidence problem" relates to the confidence of private and public actors in the adjustment rules and in the liquidity mechanism, notably the assets that play the role of international mone-

tion. The sum of the balances on current, capital, and financial accounts, the "overall balance" (line 5 in table 4.1), must equal the change in reserve assets (which consist of a country's monetary reserves and its credit balance at the International Monetary Fund, or IMF).[2] Unless otherwise specified, when referring to a BoP deficit or surplus, we mean the overall balance.

Although one country's balance-of-payments deficit is matched by foreign surpluses, in practice there is often more pressure on deficit countries to adopt adjustment measures. This is because deficit countries must either "adjust" to eliminate their deficit, or sell assets to foreigners or accumulate liabilities to foreigners to "finance" ongoing deficits. Both strategies, as we will see, are costly. By contrast, surplus countries can sometimes simply accumulate net claims on foreigners (including official reserves).[3] The limits to deficit-financing mechanisms vary greatly by country. The sale of assets to foreign residents often hits political limits earlier than economic limits: witness the political controversy in the United States in the 1980s over Japanese investments in the United States and more recently over Chinese investments. Financing deficits by borrowing abroad can also be costly, and these costs often rise as more is borrowed. Some foreign creditors may also impose preconditions on the borrower that are politically or economi-

---

tary reserves. See Benjamin J. Cohen, *Organizing the World's Money* (New York: Basic Books, 1977), 37–38.

[2] Notice that in line 6a of table 4.1, an increase in monetary reserves takes a negative sign. Note also that the overall balance includes "errors and omissions," a balancing item. The definitions employed here follow the new IMF format, agreed on in 1996. In this new format, what was formerly the current account is split into two, the (new) current account and the (new) capital account, while the old capital account becomes the "financial account." The main change involves moving unilateral transfers (including debt forgiveness) from the old current account to the new capital account. See Christopher Bach, "U.S. International Transactions, Revised Estimates for 1982–98," *Survey of Current Business* (US Department of Commerce, Bureau of Economic Analysis), 79, July 1999, 60–74, and IMF, *Balance of Payments Textbook* (Washington, D.C.: IMF, 1996), available at http://www.imf.org/external/np/sta/bop/BOPtex.pdf. However, since the literature continues to refer to the "capital" account rather than the financial account, we use these terms interchangeably later in this chapter.

[3] The main cost of doing so is reduced consumption and investment compared to potential, but these costs are more hidden than those that accrue to deficit countries. However, as we will see, large surplus countries (Germany and Japan since the 1960s and 1970s, and China more recently) can come under heavy pressure to adjust from deficit countries, especially the United States.

TABLE 4.1
South Korean Balance of Payments, 1996 to 1999:1, by Quarter (US$ millions)

	1996				1997				1998				1999
	I	II	III	IV	I	II	III	IV	I	II	III	IV	I
1. Current account	-4,358	-5,127	-7,249	-6,272	-7,353	-2,723	-2,053	3,962	10,919	11,118	9,823	8,692	6,193
A. Goods and services	-4,020	-4,455	-7,007	-5,662	-6,837	-1,879	-1,402	3,739	10,339	11,625	10,410	9,881	6,658
a. Goods	-2,383	-3,125	-5,526	-3,931	-5,401	-806	-27	3,056	9,717	11,458	10,596	9,856	6,779
Exports	31,948	32,918	30,110	34,992	31,058	35,960	34,864	36,739	32,675	34,406	31,428	33,613	31,477
Imports	-34,331	-36,043	-35,636	-38,923	-36,459	-36,766	-34,891	-33,683	-22,958	-22,948	-20,832	-23,757	-24,698
b. Services	-1,637	-1,329	-1,482	-1,731	-1,435	-1,073	-1,374	683	622	167	-185	25	-121
Services receipts	5,486	5,933	5,990	6,004	6,016	6,547	6,696	7,043	5,856	6,002	6,069	6,653	5,949
Services payments	-7,123	-7,262	-7,472	-7,735	-7,451	-7,620	-8,070	-6,360	-5,234	-5,835	-6,254	-6,628	-6,070
B. Income	-362	-648	-227	-579	-417	-796	-566	-677	-705	-1,266	-1,114	-1,969	-1,019
Income receipts	860	843	952	1,011	1,002	911	893	1,072	992	834	725	720	886
Income payments	-1,222	-1,491	-1,179	-1,590	-1,419	-1,707	-1,459	-1,749	-1,697	-2,100	-1,839	-2,689	-1,905
C. Current transfers	24	-24	-15	-30	-99	-47	-85	899	1,285	760	527	780	555
2. Capital account	-127	-181	-136	-153	-178	-155	-145	-131	-50	350	-65	-64	-84
Capital account credit	4	4	6	5	4	4	5	3	2	432	23	7	3
Capital account debit	-131	-185	-142	-158	-182	-159	-150	-134	-52	-82	-88	-71	-87
3. Financial account	5,378	9,847	2,103	6,593	4,215	6,728	763	-20,901	-5,687	147	-3,922	1,025	3,191
A. Direct investment	-1,181	-396	-590	-178	-507	-225	-661	-212	-334	347	491	114	618
Direct investment abroad	-1,586	-1,076	-846	-1,163	-1,131	-1,016	-1,272	-1,031	-839	-821	-1,671	-1,468	-789
Inward direct investment	405	680	256	985	624	791	611	819	505	1,168	2,162	1,582	1,407
B. Portfolio investment	2,139	5,759	3,252	4,034	2,594	5,829	5,444	428	3,806	568	-3,878	-2,374	952
a. Equity securities	760	2,458	879	1,204	536	2,543	505	-1,380	2,890	-17	-224	1,248	2,805
Assets	-80	-170	-185	-218	-150	47	-249	31	136	-2	-28	-65	43
Liabilities	840	2,628	1,064	1,422	686	2,496	754	-1,411	2,754	-15	-196	1,313	2,762
b. Debt securities	1,379	3,301	2,373	2,830	2,058	3,286	4,939	1,808	916	585	-3,654	-3,622	-1,853
Assets	-829	-645	-1,726	-2,146	-159	-325	329	2,483	1,078	-1,164	-57	-1,485	-170
Liabilities	2,208	3,946	4,099	4,976	2,217	3,611	4,610	-675	-162	1,749	-3,597	-2,137	-1,683

Source: IMF, International Financial Statistics, February 2000.

TABLE 4.1 (cont'd)
South Korean Balance of Payments, 1996 to 1999:1, by Quarter (US$ millions)

| | 1996 | | | | 1997 | | | | 1998 | | | | 1999 |
	I	II	III	IV	I	II	III	IV	I	II	III	IV	I
C. Other private investment	4,623	4,697	-333	3,162	2,236	1,220	-3,961	-25,838	-12,265	-902	-544	1,964	1,130
a. Banks	570	1,470	391	-654	806	422	-1,734	-17,615	-3,517	1,775	463	2,015	1,329
Assets	-1,534	-688	-2,373	-3,579	-414	-1,242	-555	-6,125	-139	2,220	2,693	2,196	382
Liabilities	2,104	2,158	2,764	2,925	1,220	1,664	-1,179	-11,490	-3,378	-445	-2,230	-181	947
b. Other sectors	4,053	3,227	-724	3,816	1,430	798	-2,227	-8,223	-8,748	-2,677	-1,007	-51	-199
Assets	-1,505	-1,443	-852	-970	-966	-1,609	-1,337	-1,084	-1,030	-749	383	1,202	933
Liabilities	5,558	4,670	128	4,786	2,396	2,407	-890	-7,139	-7,718	-1,928	-1,390	-1,253	-1,132
D. Other public investment	-203	-213	-226	-425	-108	-96	-59	4,721	3,106	134	9	1,321	491
a. Monetary authorities	-19	-1	-10	0	-41	-1	-3	-18	-2	-1	-6	-3	-2
b. General government	-184	-212	-216	-425	-67	-95	-56	4,739	3,108	135	15	1,324	493
4. Net errors and omissions	207	-1,173	1,601	462	6	143	-1,151	-4,006	135	-2,226	-1,282	-2,983	-890
5. Overall balance	1,100	3,366	-3,681	630	-3,310	3,993	-2,586	-21,076	5,317	9,389	4,554	6,670	8,410
6. Reserves and related items	-1,100	-3,366	3,681	-630	3,310	-3,993	2,586	21,076	-5,317	-9,389	-4,554	-6,670	-8,410
a. Reserve assets	-1,100	-3,366	3,681	-630	3,310	-3,993	2,586	9,972	-9,357	-11,265	-5,534	-4,812	-6,321
b. Use of IMF credit and loans								11,104	4,040	1,876	980	-1,858	-2,089

Source: IMF, *International Financial Statistics,* February 2000.

cally costly. Foreign borrowing can also be risky, since the willingness of foreign creditors to extend finance can be volatile. Nevertheless, because borrowing does not normally transfer ownership of national assets to foreigners, deficit countries often rely heavily on this form of financing over long periods of time.

This fact also suggests that adjustment policies sufficient to eliminate deficits are often even more costly for governments. Adjustment measures work primarily by reducing domestic consumption, investment, and growth in the short term. To illustrate, consider South Korea's BoP from 1996 to early 1999 (table 4.1).

To simplify the discussion, we leave aside the relatively insignificant (at least for Korea) capital account. In the absence of adjustment measures, to avoid running down monetary reserves, any deficit on current account must be financed by a corresponding surplus on financial account. Korea's current account deficit meant it was spending considerably in excess of its national income through foreign borrowing. Over 1996, Korea achieved this by selling equities to foreigners and by borrowing heavily from international banks. As is now well known, this financing choice proved unsustainable once private foreign creditors drew down or sold their Korean assets. In 1996, before the crisis hit, the Korean economy was growing rapidly, though its exports were not, resulting in a rising current account deficit (5.9% of GDP). The financing problem was greater than this, as Korean firms were investing heavily abroad, while foreign firms had found it difficult to invest in many sectors in Korea (line 3A, table 4.1). For 1996 as a whole, foreign financing included net portfolio (equity and debt) inflows of $15.2 billion, net corporate (nonbank) borrowing of $10.4 billion, and net bank borrowing of $1.8 billion.

When these financial inflows reversed in the wake of the Thai crisis of July 1997, reserves fell quickly and the economy was plunged into a BoP and financial crisis, necessitating rapid, deep, and politically costly adjustment measures in return for IMF assistance. Over 1998, GDP fell by 7%, unemployment rose, and many firms and banks went into bankruptcy. The adjustment costs are apparent in the current account change, from a large deficit to an unprecedented surplus of 9% of GDP in 1998. As table 4.1 shows (lines 1Aa), export receipts continued to stagnate despite the large fall in the value of the currency. The burden of adjustment fell on imports, which fell by one-third from late 1997 to early 1998, indicative of the collapse in domestic consumption and investment. Nevertheless, the large current account surpluses this deep adjustment produced allowed Korea to rebuild its reserves rapidly over 1998–99 (line 6a, table 4.1) and to repay its IMF borrowings early.

The role of official reserves also emerges clearly from this story. These enable countries to finance temporary deficits without more borrowing or adopting costly adjustment measures. Stocks of reserves are accumulated over time, so that past economic performance and policies affect a country's ability to draw on them in times of difficulty. The accumulation of large stocks of monetary reserves is itself costly in terms of forgone consumption and investment, and after some point governments will prefer to finance BoP deficits by inducing private capital inflows or by borrowing from foreigners. The availability of such private and official finance, and a country's desire for political autonomy from foreign creditors, will be crucial factors in national decisions about how large monetary reserves need to be. Since the crisis, Korea, along with many other developing countries, decided that its precrisis reserves ($34 billion in June 1997) were insufficient given the demonstrated vulnerability of the country to large and rapid shifts in private capital flows. This has led to an unprecedented accumulation of foreign exchange reserves since the mid-1990s—essentially a form of insurance against future crises. As figure 4.1 shows, developing countries (in marked contrast to developed countries) on average have recently accumulated reserves well in excess of the traditional rule of thumb of three months' import coverage.

Adjustment in Theory and Practice

Economics textbooks often outline how, in principle, both perfectly fixed and perfectly flexible exchange rate systems[4] can facilitate automatic adjustment processes that eliminate BoP imbalances. In both

[4] "Fixed" and "pegged" exchange rates are interchangeable terms. In practice, the government commits to maintain the nominal "peg" value against another currency (or "basket" of currencies) within a limited fluctuation band. "Flexible" exchange rates describe the situation in which the government allows the foreign exchange market to determine the nominal exchange rate against

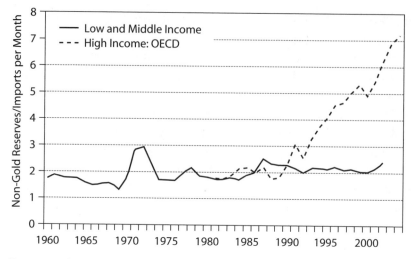

Figure 4.1. Monetary Reserves as a Multiple of Monthly Imports, High- and Low/Middle-Income Countries, 1960–2004
Source: World Bank, *World Development Indicators* database.

models, the real exchange rate adjusts to remove either external surpluses or deficits.[5] Assuming Korea needed a real depreciation of the won (the Korean currency) before the crisis to promote net exports, how might this have occurred?

In the case of a fixed nominal exchange rate and a current account deficit, stagnating exports and rising unemployment in Korea's export sector could reduce real wages, eventually reducing domestic prices to the point where international competitiveness would be restored.[6] A second "semiautomatic" adjustment mechanism may operate if Korean residents sell won for foreign currencies because they expect a won devaluation, obliging Korea's central bank to sell its foreign exchange reserves to buy won in the foreign exchange markets. This would reduce

other currencies. In practice, actual exchange rate policies fall between perfectly fixed and perfectly flexible exchange rates.

[5] The real exchange rate is the real "price" for which a currency exchanges for other currencies, and is different from its observable "nominal" exchange rate. A country's real exchange rate R is equal to $S(P^* / P)$, where S is the nominal "spot" exchange rate, P the average domestic price level, and P^* the average foreign price level. Note that a *lower* value of R implies a higher real exchange rate, making the country's exports *less* competitive.

[6] Note these effects depend on the level of intersectoral factor mobility, an issue discussed in chapter 3.

the domestic money supply, reducing total expenditure and pushing down prices, helping to restore competitiveness.[7] These two mechanisms supposedly operated in the ideal world of the gold standard.[8] In the real world of the 1990s, prices and wages in Korea were not flexible downward (in part because of its labor unions), so that adjustment was insufficiently rapid, or Korea's reserves were inadequate.

The obvious alternative for Korea was simply to float its currency, allowing the *nominal* exchange rate of the won to depreciate against other major currencies, restoring competitiveness. Economists such as Milton Friedman claimed flexible exchange rates could automatically eliminate external deficits in this way.[9] It had the great advantage of bypassing the two mechanisms previously mentioned and could obviate the need for domestic price and wage flexibility altogether. In practice, flexible exchange rates rarely work in this stabilizing manner. In fact, the real value of the won was sustained by continued large capital inflows from abroad before 1997. Even with exchange rate depreciation, total export values may take a long time to recover to close the external deficit.[10]

Since automatic adjustment is often not forthcoming, governments wishing to undertake active adjustment measures have three main options: trade protection, "expenditure-reducing," and "expenditure-switching" policies. Higher tariffs or quotas on imports increase the relative price of imported goods, but these measures are generally disparaged by economists. Increased trade protection would also have been incompatible with Korea's GATT membership and its relations with major countries like the United States and Japan.

Expenditure-reducing policies include restrictive monetary and fiscal policies, but growing capital mobility means that which of them is

[7] This is the case of "unsterilized" foreign exchange market intervention, in which the central bank does not offset the expansionary impact on the domestic money supply by selling bonds to the financial sector.

[8] A pure "currency board" leads to an equivalent outcome, since all exchange market interventions by the currency board are also unsterilized.

[9] Milton Friedman, "The Case for Flexible Exchange Rates," in his *Essays in Positive Economics* (Chicago: University of Chicago Press, 1953), 157–203.

[10] Because of "J-curve" or "hysterisis" effects: see Paul R. Krugman and Maurice Obstfeld, *International Economics: Theory and Policy* (Reading, Mass.: Addison-Wesley, 5th ed., 2000), 466–68.

effective depends on a country's exchange rate policy. This was outlined in the standard Mundell-Fleming (MF) model of the early 1960s.[11] *Under fixed exchange rates,* monetary policy contraction raises the domestic interest rate, attracting speculative capital from abroad. The central bank must resist currency appreciation by selling domestic for foreign currency, reversing the initial decrease in the money supply and rendering monetary policy powerless to affect prices or output. This result has been termed the "impossible" or "unholy" trinity, since it implies that a government must choose only two of the following three things: a fixed exchange rate, monetary policy autonomy, and capital account openness.[12] The power of fiscal policy, however, remains intact and is even enhanced under fixed rates. Fiscal contraction reduces domestic output and interest rates (by reducing government borrowing). Lower interest rates threaten currency depreciation, requiring monetary contraction by the central bank, thus enhancing the effect of fiscal contraction.[13]

Expenditure-switching policies are simply another term for exchange rate changes. Real currency devaluation "switches" domestic expenditure away from imported goods toward domestic production by altering relative prices. As we discuss later, concerns about policy credibility and costs to domestic consumers often deter governments from devaluing.

One major problem with macroeconomic policymaking is that governments have multiple policy targets but possess limited policy instruments. In practice, a combination of macroeconomic policy adjustment

[11] The MF model relied on then-standard Keynesian assumptions. See Robert Mundell, "The Monetary Dynamics of International Adjustment under Fixed and Floating Exchange Rates," *Quarterly Journal of Economics* 74:2, 1960, 227–57, and "Capital Mobility and Stabilization Policy under Fixed and Flexible Exchange Rates," *Canadian Journal of Economics and Political Science* 29, 1963, 475–85; J. Marcus Fleming, "Domestic Financial Policies under Fixed and Floating Exchange Rates," *IMF Staff Papers*, 9, November 1962; Jacob Frenkel and Assaf Razin, "The Mundell-Fleming Model a Quarter Century Later: A Unified Exposition," *IMF Staff Papers*, 34, December 1987.

[12] Benjamin J. Cohen, "The Triad and the Unholy Trinity: Problems of International Monetary Cooperation," in Richard Higgott, Richard Leaver, and John Ravenhill, eds., *Pacific Economic Relations in the 1990s: Cooperation or Conflict?* (London: Allen and Unwin, 1993), 133–58.

[13] Conversely, under *floating* exchange rates, only monetary policy is powerful (because fiscal contraction results in currency depreciation). Later we address the problem that MF analysis exaggerated the power of activist fiscal and monetary policy even under these conditions.

and exchange rate changes is often necessary. For example, if a country is suffering from both high unemployment and an excessively large external deficit, under an open capital account and a pegged exchange rate, fiscal expansion is the only available macroeconomic policy option to reduce unemployment. Fiscal expansion by itself would also worsen the external deficit, so the government would need to combine it with exchange rate devaluation to restore both external and internal equilibrium.[14] Further complications and policy dilemmas often arise. For example, unions in sectors sheltered from international trade competition may have little concern for the competitiveness of industries in the traded goods sector. If they dominate national wage-setting and respond to devaluation with increased wage demands, unemployment might coexist with both "cost-push" inflation and an external deficit.[15]

Note also that when governments have multiple objectives, a "credibility problem" can emerge. It can arise, for example, from a contradiction between an exchange rate commitment and an internal inflation or unemployment objective. Italy in the early 1990s suffered from high unemployment and large external deficits. As noted above, devaluation was part of the textbook solution to this problem (fiscal expansion was made difficult by Italy's existing high levels of fiscal deficit and public debt). However, the government had made a public commitment not to devalue the lira against other currencies in the European Monetary System (EMS). For this promise to be credible to the private actors in the foreign exchange markets, they would have had to believe that the government was willing to tolerate persistently high levels of unemployment (given the inflexibility of the labor market). Market actors were right to judge that as unemployment grew, the exchange rate commitment became increasingly incredible because the democratically elected government was highly sensitive to unemployment. This is an example of what is often termed a "time inconsistency" problem, in which the credibility of a particular policy commitment declines when policymakers face changed circumstances. The problem arises when a policymaker commits *ex ante* to following a certain policy rule (such as a

---

[14] The correct policy combination depends entirely on the nature of the initial disequilibrium.
[15] See Wendy Carlin and David Soskice, *Macroeconomics and the Wage Bargain* (Oxford: Oxford University Press, 1990).

given exchange rate peg) in the future, but has an *ex post* incentive to defect from the rule.[16]

Note that if the authorities can credibly signal to private market actors that they possess no internal objective and only desire a stable exchange rate, no doubt about their credibility arises. This may approximately describe the situation enjoyed by governments and monetary authorities in the classical era of the gold standard in the late nineteenth century. Since then, many factors have eroded the credibility of exchange rate commitments for most countries. The trend toward democratization, the growth of unions, and new understandings about the power of macroeconomic policy and associated expectations of government have all caused foreign exchange markets to become more skeptical of government promises to maintain "fixed" exchange rates.[17] These factors also alter the credibility of exchange rate commitments in an asymmetric way. Countries with low unemployment and current account surpluses, such as Germany enjoyed for many years after 1950, are less vulnerable to collapses of market confidence than countries with high unemployment and external deficits. Developing countries can also exhibit weak taxation bases, fiscal subsidies for basic commodities, and weak social safety nets, making it difficult to undertake policy adjustments in response to changed circumstances, further undermining the credibility of their exchange rate commitments.

International Interdependence and Adjustment

So far, we have considered the adjustment problem from an individual country's perspective. Since economic policies, especially those of large countries, affect other economies, we also need to consider adjustment from a systemic perspective. This is obviously true when a country undertakes exchange rate adjustment, which creates a potential for in-

---

[16] Finn Kydland and Edward S. Prescott, "Rules Rather Than Discretion: The Inconsistency of Optimal Plans," *Journal of Political Economy* 85:3, 1977, 473–92.

[17] Barry J. Eichengreen, *Golden Fetters: The Gold Standard and the Great Depression, 1919–1939* (New York: Oxford University Press, 1992); and Beth A. Simmons, *Who Adjusts? Domestic Sources of Foreign Economic Policy during the Interwar Years* (Princeton, N.J.: Princeton University Press, 1994).

ternational conflict.[18] When all governments have domestic policy objectives, the problem can become acute. How far can or should policy
coordination go under a fixed exchange rate system? At a minimum,
given free movement of capital between two countries A and B, the
maintenance of a fixed exchange rate between them requires the same
level of real interest rates in both countries, and hence perfectly coordinated monetary policies. This is because if market actors expected currency B to depreciate against A in the future, they would require an
interest rate premium over and above what they could obtain by holding assets in currency A, equal to the amount of *expected* depreciation
of currency B over the period (the "interest parity theorem").

If the world economy only consisted of A and B, a payments imbalance between them raises the question of who will adjust first, the deficit or the creditor country. Since the loss of monetary reserves is more
difficult to sustain than is acquiring reserves, deficit countries often
come under market pressure to adjust first. If A is the deficit country
and the threat of reserve depletion forces it to devalue, this raises the
price of imported goods from B and reduces standards of living in A
(at least in the nontraded sector). This does not mean that B escapes
adjustment costs, since A's devaluation amounts to a currency revaluation for B, which could hurt its export sector. In a more realistic world
in which there are many countries, most of the costs of adjustment may
fall on the devaluing country.

In a world economy in which all countries peg their exchange rates,
there will be $n - 1$ exchange rates (where n is the number of countries).
For the system to be stable, there can only be $n - 1$ exchange rate policies: the nth country *must* adopt a passive attitude toward its exchange
rate. This can create an additional deep asymmetry within a pegged
exchange rate system, since the nth country is in the position of being
able to focus on internal economic objectives. The classic example is the
Bretton Woods exchange rate system in which other countries pegged
to the US dollar, allowing the American authorities to concentrate on
domestic (and foreign policy) objectives. For many years, this asymmet-
rical bargain worked reasonably well, providing the basis for the expan-

[18] Paul De Grauwe, *International Money* (Oxford: Oxford University Press, 2nd ed., 1996),
chap. 3.

sion of trade and security for the Western alliance. From 1966, the Johnson administration's simultaneous pursuit of the Vietnam War abroad and the extension of social welfare at home led to growing fiscal and current account deficits. This prompted exchange market speculation against the dollar and in favor of the German mark, given Germany's growing current account surplus. Germany's partial controls on short-term capital inflows and the Bundesbank's sterilization of the effects of its purchases of foreign currency provided some relief from the inflationary effects of these inflows, but these ultimately proved insufficient to maintain the exchange rate peg.[19] Since it was evident that the US government would not substantially reduce the fiscal deficit, from 1968, the German government reluctantly accepted a series of mark revaluations; ultimately, it allowed the mark to float temporarily in 1971 and permanently after March 1973. Currency revaluations were politically costly because of resistance from the important financial and export sectors in West Germany.[20] The ability of the United States to shift the costs of adjustment onto others, including the most important payments surplus country, stemmed from the position of the dollar in the international monetary system and America's relatively low dependence on trade.

This kind of leader-follower relationship, where $n - 1$ countries accept the nth country as the monetary standard-setter, will only work if the leader's market is dominant in global trade and if its policies provide reasonable stability. Such stability usually means that the center country pursues a relatively low inflation monetary policy. The United States acted in this stabilizing manner from about 1950 until the mid-1960s, and West Germany did the same in the EMS until 1990. In both cases, however, these center countries eventually exploited their dominant systemic position to pursue destabilizing policies that shifted the costs of adjustment onto other countries.[21]

[19] The Bundesbank sterilized the expansionary effects of these purchases on the money supply by selling government bonds to the banking sector. There are limits to sterilization policies, as selling more bonds will eventually require higher yields, which encourages more capital inflows.

[20] C. Randall Henning, *Currencies and Politics in the United States, Germany, and Japan* (Washington, D.C.: Institute for International Economics, 1994), 182–83.

[21] Andrew Walter, "Leadership Begins at Home: Domestic Sources of International Monetary Power," in David M. Andrews, ed., *International Monetary Power* (Ithaca, N.Y.: Cornell University Press, 2006), 51–71.

One might conclude that the obvious solution is to abandon pegged exchange rates altogether for floating rates, as West Germany did in 1973. However, for many reasons countries are reluctant to adopt fully floating exchange rates, including high levels of trade openness, commodity export dependence, foreign indebtedness, low internal inflation-fighting credibility, and regional integration objectives.[22] Nor do flexible exchange rate policies remove the dilemmas that interdependence creates; they merely alter their form. For example, in a floating rate system, national monetary expansion stimulates demand via lower interest rates and exchange rate depreciation, but it can also worsen the bilateral trade balance of other countries with the devaluing country. This could induce competitive devaluations or protectionist retaliation. The negative foreign impact is lower if national monetary expansion raises the rate of growth, or (in the case of a large country) if it lowers *world* interest rates. Expansionary fiscal policy, though less powerful for the home country under floating rates, may affect foreign output positively via exchange rate and output effects, and negatively by raising world interest rates. Hence, the demand from small open economies for policy coordination in a floating rate regime could be higher than under fixed rates. The political problem is that large countries, whose policies have most impact on the rest of the world, have fewer incentives to coordinate macroeconomic policies. Others may simply have to bear the costs of adjustment that emanate from large countries' policies.

INTERNATIONAL FINANCE AND RISK

We noted above that a key determinant of the pressure for adjustment on individual countries is the structure and availability of international finance (often called *liquidity*). The first line of defense for a deficit country is national monetary reserves, though given the size of today's foreign exchange markets these are often inadequate in the face of a concerted market attack. Today, monetary reserves are mainly held in the form of highly liquid government debt denominated in only a few

[22] Guillermo A. Calvo and Carmen M. Reinhart, "Fear of Floating," *Quarterly Journal of Economics* 117:2, 2002, 379–408.

currencies, above all the US dollar.[23] The emergence of such "key currencies" creates a basic asymmetry in the system between key currency countries and the rest, since it can give the former considerable influence over the supply and price of international finance.

There are three main sources of international finance: private international capital markets, key country external deficits, and public international finance provided by bilateral lenders or by international financial institutions (IFIs). The relative sizes of these sources of finance matters greatly, as does the willingness to lend of those who control them.

Before we discuss in more detail the different sources of international finance, it is helpful to consider the different forms of risk that arise in international borrowing, though note that risk categories can overlap and are often interdependent. For borrowers, maturity and currency risk are often emphasized, though we also emphasize here "reversal risk" and "sovereignty risk." Maturity risk occurs when the timing of repayments of interest or principal on financial obligations differs from the timing of cash receipts by the borrower. For example, if a borrower uses the receipts from a loan that must be repaid within three months to invest in assets that will not generate positive cash receipts for some years, the borrower is accepting a maturity mismatch risk ("borrowing short and investing long").[24] Banks specialize in managing this kind of risk. Currency risk arises when the borrower borrows in foreign currency to finance investment in assets (or current consumption) that produce cash receipts denominated in another currency (usually domestic currency).

Reversal risk arises when a borrower is dependent on flows of new external finance that can be stopped or reversed, potentially provoking a recession or even a debt crisis. Such stops and reversals may result

---

[23] In the late nineteenth century, countries came to hold these key currencies, or foreign exchange reserves, in addition to gold—mainly consisting of sterling balances, or deposits held in London (Peter H. Lindert, "Key Currencies and Gold, 1900–1913," *Princeton Studies in International Finance*, 24, 1969). Today, liquid assets (usually in the form of government bonds) denominated in key currencies such as the US dollar, Euro, and yen have come to dominate all other forms of official international reserves, though many countries continue to hold gold reserves.

[24] This risk may be offset by other maturity mismatches in the borrower's portfolio of assets and liabilities, which is why maturity risk is usually applied to whole portfolios rather than individual assets and liabilities.

from policies adopted by foreign creditor governments or multilateral institutions, or from changing attitudes to risk in private financial markets (such as so-called capital strikes and investor panics resulting in "capital flight"). Finally, sovereignty risk occurs when a country obtains finance from an external lender who requires the government to adopt policies it would not otherwise choose ("conditionality"), or when foreign financing reduces national control over important assets, technology, resources, and sources of employment.

From the perspective of lenders, maturity and currency risks also exist and must be managed. For example, investors bear currency risk in the form of the possibility that the exchange rate between the currencies in which the assets are denominated changes relative to the investor's base currency. Additional sources of risk for lenders/investors include credit risk (the risk of borrower default), market risk (the risk that the market value of the assets in their portfolio are uncertain and can fluctuate), liquidity risk (the risk that it may be difficult to sell an asset in the future for cash without accepting a large discount on its original purchase price), legal risk (the risk that the interpretation or application of legal contracts is uncertain), and political risk (the risk that asset values are affected by changes in a country's government or its policies). Note that when lenders take measures to reduce some forms of risk, they may increase risk for borrowers, such as when lenders shift currency risk to borrowers, or if they use conditionality to limit political risk. Moreover, attempts to limit some forms of risk may increase other risks, such as when lenders use conditionality to limit the risk of policy change, but their doing so increases the risk of a change in government and overall credit risk.

Private International Finance

Private lenders lend voluntarily to foreign borrowers only if they expect to be repaid with a profit, which is often seen as the reward for assuming one or more of the risks we have identified. Such lenders include banks making loans, bond and equity investors, and foreign direct investors.[25]

---

[25] Remittances from foreign residents, which are recorded as credits on current account, can also be an important additional source of finance for developing countries.

The borrower may be a foreign government or monetary authority or individual firms or banks, though in aggregate this can allow a country to run a current account deficit. From the perspective of borrowers, the maturity risks of these various forms of capital inflow differ considerably. Long-term debt finance (loans or bonds) and FDI can be more stable than short-term debt or equity inflows (i.e., less subject to sudden stops or reversals).[26] Debt finance also generally requires fixed contractual repayments at specified intervals, whereas the dividends and profits paid to foreign investors on equity inflows and FDI usually involve no such legal guarantees of size or timing. FDI and foreign purchases of shares in domestic listed companies (equities) usually also require foreign investors to bear the currency risk.

By contrast, until very recently most borrowing in the form of bank loans and bonds by developing countries has been denominated in convertible foreign currencies, so that the borrower has borne the currency risk. Why this is so is a matter of debate, since governments of developed countries usually do not find it difficult to borrow from international lenders in their domestic currency. For example, nonresidents held on average 16% of UK sterling-denominated government debt over the period 1990–2002 (of this, 6% was held by foreign central banks and 10% by others, mainly private investors).[27] The comparative historical difficulty that most countries have had in borrowing in their own currency is commonly referred to as the problem of "original sin"—though note that the incidence of own currency borrowing has increased since this became a matter of academic interest.[28] The historical phenomenon may be due to investors' perception of greater currency, political, and liquidity risk in developing countries because of relatively weak domestic institutions, as well as investors' desire to limit

---

[26] As table 4.1 shows, equity flows proved more stable for Korea than did short-term debt issued to Korea's banks and firms.

[27] Calculated from the Bank of England's Monetary and Financial Statistics Tables, http://213.225.136.206/mfsd/iadb/BankStats.asp?Travel=NIx, accessed September 24, 2007.

[28] Barry J. Eichengreen, Ricardo Hausmann, and Ugo Panizza, "Currency Mismatches, Debt Intolerance and Original Sin: Why They Are Not the Same and Why It Matters," NBER Working Paper, 10036, October 2003; Morris Goldstein and Philip Turner, *Controlling Currency Mismatches in Emerging Markets* (Washington, D.C.: Institute for International Economics, 2004).

their portfolio diversification by holding assets in a limited number of currencies. It is too soon to tell whether the recent ability of some developing countries to borrow from foreign investors in their own currencies is a temporary phenomenon or whether the permanent redemption of original sin is possible after all.

Whatever its origins, currency risk can be very costly for borrowing countries because depreciation vis-à-vis the debt denomination currency increases the real external debt burden. At the end of 1997, Korea's liabilities to international banks *maturing within one year* totaled $59 billion, almost three times its monetary reserves of $20 billion.[29] Much more than the problems of competitiveness discussed earlier, it was the growing reluctance of international banks to refinance this short-term debt that precipitated the crisis of late 1997. As the Korean currency collapsed in December 1997 from 1,100 to (at worst) 1,960 won per dollar, the implied won value of Korea's external debt soared. As many of the Korean banks and corporations who had borrowed from international banks were now unable to repay, the currency crisis soon became a corporate and banking crisis as well.[30] The story in Thailand and Indonesia was very similar.

Bonds were historically important in private international financing in the nineteenth century and have become important again since the 1990s. International securities often have deeper secondary markets than bank debt and so can reduce liquidity risk for investors. But sudden reversals of bond investor sentiment can produce payments crises, such as that which followed the panic in the Russian ruble-denominated government debt ("GKO") market in 1998. A similar crisis had occurred in Mexico in 1994, after the Mexican government had tried to reassure investors who had previously purchased peso-denominated short-term government bonds (*cetes*) by issuing US dollar-denominated bonds in their place (*tesobonos*). Once the rising stock of *teso-*

---

[29] These and other figures are taken from the joint BIS-IMF-OECD–World Bank statistics on external debt, available at http://www1.oecd.org/dac/debt/htm/debto.htm, accessed February 27, 2004. The database now includes historical debt statistics from 1990 for many developing countries.

[30] The resolution of the Korean crisis was thus crucially dependent on the willingness of international banks to restructure about $100 billion in Korean debt, which they did in January 1998.

bonos had become larger than Mexican dollar reserves, investors panicked anyway, leading to a severe currency and debt crisis. Mexico's assumption of the currency risk had increased the *credit* risk for investors. The same was true in the more recent case of Argentina, which issued large amounts of dollar-denominated public bonds in the 1990s. The credit risk for investors initially appeared to be limited because of Argentina's currency board system and "hard" peg to the US dollar. When rising indebtedness and recession eventually led to currency crisis, peso depreciation resulted in Argentinean default. Hence, in lending to developing countries there can be a trade-off for creditors between currency risk and credit risk.

As we have noted, portfolio equity inflows or FDI both allow the borrowing country to avoid currency risk and a substantial amount of cash-flow/credit risk (since there are usually no fixed payments liabilities attached to such borrowing).[31] The relative stability of FDI may derive from the illiquidity of the assets compared to relatively small holdings of equity or debt securities, and the possibility that FDI investors take a longer term view compared to bond investors. In the event of currency depreciation, the value of local FDI or equity stakes may even increase if the assets are in the traded goods sector.

These advantages of FDI and (to a lesser extent) portfolio equity inflows have often been outweighed for developing countries by the perceived disadvantages of foreign ownership and control. In Latin America in the 1970s, and Korea in the 1990s, bank debt as a form of deficit financing was generally preferred because it did not entail loss of control over important corporate assets, technology, resources, and sources of employment (see chapter 6). The vulnerability this borrowing created was thus in part the result of these countries' restrictive policies toward inward equity flows and FDI, stemming from their desire to prioritize the reduction of perceived sovereignty risk.[32]

---

[31] Portfolio equity and FDI are often difficult to distinguish in practice, though in theory the difference is that only the latter involves effective control over the corporation and assets acquired. Most countries use 10% ownership of total shares of a given entity as the cutoff point between portfolio investment and FDI.

[32] In the Latin American case, borrowing from foreign banks suffered from an additional source of risk in the form of interest rate risk because the debt was contracted at floating (variable) interest rates.

Key Country External Deficits

To the extent that key currency countries run large overall payments deficits and allow other countries to accumulate their debt as monetary reserve assets, this can provide another source of international finance. Countries that accumulate key currency reserves can use these reserves as a source of emergency finance in the future if their payments position deteriorates, or to pay off existing debts. Triffin pointed out that overall US payments deficits became the most important source of new international liquidity in the international monetary system from the late 1950s.[33] He argued that if the United States were to undertake adjustment measures to reduce its external deficit, this would prompt offsetting policy adjustments by other countries and result in a global recession.

There has been debate over the stability of this form of international finance, since center country deficits can become excessive, resulting in global inflation and exchange rate instability. Foreign exchange reserves are subject to substantial currency risk, as holders of sterling reserves discovered in the early 1930s and holders of dollar reserves have discovered since 1971. When particular countries accumulate large amounts of such reserves predominantly in one currency (usually US dollars), attempts to reduce such currency risk through diversification may backfire if they prompt others to sell dollars. China and other large holders of dollar reserves are in this situation today, as were Japan and Germany in the 1980s. In addition, there is some reversal risk inherent in holdings of dollar reserves, since the center country could conceivably freeze existing foreign asset holdings to render them unusable or even repudiate its outstanding debts.

The strong incentives for other countries to hold key currency monetary reserves can also be a means by which the key currency country can finance its own *current* overall payments deficits. Again, the best-known example is the United States since the 1960s. Other countries' willingness to hold additional US government liabilities (Treasury bills and bonds) as monetary reserves allowed the United States to run con-

---

[33] Robert Triffin, *Gold and the Dollar Crisis: The Future of Convertibility* (New Haven: Yale University Press, 1961).

tinuously large overall payments deficits with apparently little consequence other than rising external liabilities. Although interest is paid to holders of Treasury debt securities, the real return on such debt has historically been very low, suggesting that this source of finance for the United States has been unusually cheap and highly profitable.[34] President de Gaulle of France termed this America's "exorbitant privilege," although his analysis played down the important role of US payments deficits as a source of finance to the system as a whole.

Public International Finance

For the many developing countries that receive low net private capital inflows, outright grants (aid), debt forgiveness, and new loans from foreign governments or international organizations can be important sources of international finance.[35] Occasionally, in the late nineteenth century, central banks in the major countries provided short-term emergency loans to their foreign counterparts, such as when the French and Russian central banks provided emergency loans to the Bank of England in the 1890 and 1907 crises.[36] Balance-of-payments loans were also made by the League of Nations in the 1920s.[37] However, as we argue later, the idea and the bulk of the practice of public international finance is closely connected with the rise of macroeconomic stabilization and welfare objectives in the mid-twentieth century.

In all cases, public international finance is premised on some form of market failure. Today, the IMF is the main international financial institution (IFI) that provides short-term international finance to

---

[34] Pierre-Olivier Gourinchas and Hélène Rey, "From World Banker to World Venture Capitalist: US External Adjustment and the Exorbitant Privilege," NBER Working Paper, 11563, 2005.

[35] Grant aid transfers usually show up as credits in the current account. Debt forgiveness shows up as a credit in the capital account. New loans from other governments or international agencies show up as credits in the financial account. For official financial assistance to classify as aid, it must involve a grant element (for example, a loan at below-market interest rates).

[36] J. Lawrence Broz, "The Domestic Politics of International Monetary Order: The Gold Standard," in David Skidmore, ed., Contested Social Orders and International Politics (Nashville, Tenn.: Vanderbilt University Press, 1997), 53–91.

[37] Louis B. Pauly, Who Elected the Bankers? Surveillance and Control in the World Economy (Ithaca, N.Y.: Cornell University Press, 1997).

countries suffering payments problems. The IMF's role is often justified by the instability of private sector finance. It was originally seen as a means of maintaining the pegged exchange rate system in the face of potentially unstable market speculation. One aspect of this was the policy surveillance function of the IMF, intended to ensure that national economic policies were compatible with systemic exchange rate stability. Another aspect was the IMF's role as provider of short-term public international finance to countries suffering temporary balance-of-payments deficits. Keynes saw this public international finance as a means of avoiding costly deflationary adjustment policies of the kind that occurred in the early 1930s. The justification for long-term public international financial assistance, through international institutions like the World Bank and bilateral aid programs, has also been based on the assumption that private long-term financing will be insufficient to promote economic development in the poorest countries.

In practice, IFI lending, especially in the case of the IMF, has become associated with restrictive policies rather than the maintenance of high levels of domestic demand and employment. This is because of the macroeconomic policy requirements for borrowing countries that are standard preconditions of such loans, commonly referred to as *policy conditionality*. One likely reason for such policy conditionality is that the IMF's resources only consist of the limited pooled contributions of member states, and the major countries have had strong incentives to ensure that borrowers repay the Fund. In addition, there is evidence that IMF staff recruitment and promotion has been biased in recent years toward individuals with non-Keynesian, neoclassical views.[38] We return to this issue later, but it is clear that the governance of the IFIs is of central importance in determining the policy conditionality faced by sovereign borrowers. This can dramatically affect the level of sovereignty risk for borrowing countries and the preferred balance between international financing and adjustment. There is also some reversal risk in borrowing from the IFIs (e.g., in the event of borrower noncompliance with core policy conditionalities), and currency risk (since the IFIs lend in hard currencies)

[38] Jeffrey M. Chwieroth, "Testing and Measuring the Role of Ideas: The Case of Neoliberalism in the International Monetary Fund," *International Studies Quarterly* 51:1, 2007, 5–30.

NATIONAL STABILIZATION POLICY AND
INTERNATIONAL MONETARY ORGANIZATION

We have argued that the balance between adjustment and financing in international monetary organization is greatly complicated when countries adopt domestic stabilization objectives. In this section, we argue that the evolution of international monetary organization over the past century can be seen as an uneven process of adaptation to a dramatic shift in *domestic* monetary organization and economic policy. We postpone the question of "feedback" from the international monetary and financial system to national monetary organization and policy to the next chapter.

The Development of National Money

National monetary systems of the kind assumed in standard modern macroeconomics are a relatively recent historical phenomenon, though the gap between theory and practice has always been considerable.[39] The growing centralization of national monetary organization is strongly associated with the development of the modern state, though only in the twentieth century was the "nationalization" of paper money generally established. The institutions associated with national monetary organization are also of recent vintage. By 1900, only 18 countries had central banks, and all but two (Sweden's and England's) were less than 100 years old.[40] The rise of paper ("fiduciary") money issued by central banks eventually laid the institutional foundations for national monetary management, but this also took some time (and the acceptability of such money initially depended on it being backed by reserves of gold or silver).

The possibilities of "monetary policy" were also limited by intellectual constraints that were only gradually overcome in the early part of the twentieth century. The Bank of England's suspension of gold

---

[39] On the prevalence of within- and between-country competition over currencies in history, see Benjamin J. Cohen, *The Geography of Money* (Ithaca, N.Y.: Cornell University Press, 1998).

[40] Forrest Capie, Charles Goodhart, and Norbert Schnadt, "The Development of Central Banking," in Forrest Capie et al., *The Future of Central Banking: The Tercentenary Symposium of the*

convertibility from 1797 until 1821 mobilized the defenders of orthodox finance, including Ricardo and the "Currency School," who saw in
the emergence of a domestic paper money standard the road to financial ruin.[41] The restoration of the fixed gold convertibility of sterling
was seen as a crucial constraint against inflation. Another was the legal
restriction of the quantity of Bank of England note issuance, notably
in the Bank Act of 1844. But politics pushed in the other direction: the
1844 act also consolidated the emerging monopoly position of Bank of
England notes.[42] The legal and political dependence of central banks
on governments generally rendered them subject to periodic pressure
to provide cheap deficit financing, particularly during national emer-
gencies or when their charters were up for renewal. The issuance of
new notes, the production cost of which was minimal, allowed the state
or central bank to expropriate real private resources ("seigniorage").[43]

The emerging national monetary hierarchy, with central bank notes
becoming "as good as gold," was reinforced by restrictions on the circu-
lation of foreign currencies and the suspension of convertibility for
foreign coins at national mints. Commercial banks increasingly held
their reserves at the central bank. This enabled the central bank to act as
a "lender of last resort" (LLR) when panic spread through the banking
system, although in most countries such LLR responsibilities were accepted only after the 1930s.[44]

The International Gold Standard

The pre-1914 international gold standard was not a product of collective international design of the kind achieved at Bretton Woods in 1944.
There was a clear but gradual trend toward the gold standard in Europe

---

Bank of England: The Tercentenary Symposium of the Bank of England (Cambridge: Cambridge
University Press, 1994), 4–9.

[41] Frank W. Fetter, *Development of British Monetary Orthodoxy 1797–1875* (Cambridge: Harvard University Press, 1965).

[42] Lawrence H. White, *The Theory of Monetary Institutions* (Malden, Mass.: Blackwell, 1999), 82.

[43] While monetary debasement is as old as coinage itself, the emergence of central bank money
provided an opportunity for the technique's more extensive exploitation by the state.

[44] White, *Theory of Monetary Institutions*, 19.

from 1873, led by Germany, the Netherlands, and Scandinavia.[45] Britain's adherence to a gold standard entrenched a growing international role for sterling, with other countries using bills issued by London finance houses to finance international commercial transactions. As both foreign private and public actors accumulated sterling assets for financial purposes, this benefited the City of London, which naturally favored the gold standard.

In theory, there was no room for autonomous monetary policy in the gold standard. The so-called rules of the game (or more accurately, behavioral norms) included the commitment to buy and sell national currency for gold without limit at a fixed price and to allow the free cross-border flow of gold. In practice, central banks diverged in various ways from these norms. The Bank of England relied heavily on the manipulation of its discount rate because of its slim gold reserves; sometimes it even took account of the domestic "state of trade" in setting its level.[46] In France and Germany, central banks used various devices to limit gold convertibility so as to achieve a degree of national monetary autonomy.[47]

Nevertheless, before 1914 there was little pressure for outright inflation in the major countries, allowing their central banks to maintain effective independence in practice. Crucially, in Britain, the external commitment to fixed gold convertibility had priority. The limited appreciation of how interest rates affected the real economy and the limited political influence of Britain's working classes also helped to insulate the central bank from pressure that might have compromised this commitment. The political dominance of the financial bourgeoisie and landed interests, which held a substantial proportion of their financial assets in fixed-income domestic and foreign bonds, reinforced the polit-

---

[45] Capie, Goodhart, and Schnadt, "Development of Central Banking," 10–11; Jeffry A. Frieden, "The Dynamics of International Monetary Systems: International and Domestic Factors in the Rise, Reign, and Demise of the Classical Gold Standard," in Barry J. Eichengreen and Marc Flandreau, eds., *The Gold Standard in Theory and History* (New York: Routledge, 1997), 206–27.

[46] Arthur I. Bloomfield, *Monetary Policy under the Gold Standard, 1880–1914* (New York: Federal Reserve Bank of New York, 1959); Richard S. Sayers, *Bank of England Operations, 1890–1914* (London: King, 1936).

[47] Broz, "Domestic Politics."

ical preference for low inflation and fixed exchange rates.[48] By contrast, in some peripheral countries in Europe and the Americas, persistent fiscal deficits and political instability produced inflation and undermined attempts to peg to gold.[49]

World War I brought similar levels of political and monetary instability to the heart of the European-dominated international monetary system. The gold standard was suspended in the main belligerent countries at the outbreak of the war. After 1918, the widening of the electoral franchise in Britain and other countries and rising political demands from the working classes everywhere undermined the domestic political foundations of the gold standard. However, the postwar monetary turmoil in Europe ensured that political and economic elites looked back to the prewar gold standard as a beacon of economic and political stability. This set the stage for growing political conflict over national and international monetary arrangements in Europe.

A fundamental problem for all the major European countries was the enormous stock of public debt caused by heavy wartime reliance on government borrowing.[50] To make matters worse, in some countries most of this debt was short term. Reducing the level of national debt to sustainable levels required either more tax increases or refinancing the debt at longer maturities and lower interest rates.[51] The distributive implications of these alternatives provoked intense social conflict, hampering the process of monetary and currency stabilization. Debtors (including the state and corporate sector) had an interest in inflation. The working classes, which had made enormous sacrifices during the war and which had few assets, also demanded increased government expenditure on social welfare. Creditors, including savers and the financial sector in particular, had most to lose from inflation and lobbied

---

[48] Broz, "Domestic Politics"; Giulio M. Gallarotti, *The Anatomy of an International Monetary Regime: The Classical Gold Standard, 1880–1914* (Oxford: Oxford University Press, 1995), 151–58.

[49] Marc Flandreau, Jacques Le Cacheux, and Frédéric Zumer, "Stability without a Pact? Lessons from the European Gold Standard, 1880–1914," *Economic Policy* 13:26, 1998, 117–62.

[50] Eichengreen, *Golden Fetters*, 74–75.

[51] For example, in France in 1920, the ratio of short-term public debt to GDP was 65%. The difficulty of refinancing it was a much more serious threat to monetary control than the fiscal deficit of 13% of GDP (Eichengreen, *Golden Fetters*, 81).

strongly for a return to the gold standard, as well as cuts in public expenditures and taxes.

The years of inflationary chaos in the early 1920s strengthened the postwar creditor backlash and bolstered the ideological appeal of the gold standard. This facilitated a general movement back onto the gold standard, the most notable example being Britain's decision to return to gold in 1925.[52] More direct international pressure, particularly from the United States and Britain, was also important in some cases, such as the international stabilization schemes sponsored by the League of Nations in countries like Austria and Hungary. These schemes included new central banking statutes designed to promote monetary orthodoxy.[53] The 1924 Dawes loan, which enabled Germany to return to the gold standard, also included a proviso for the Reichsbank to be formally independent of the government. For a few short years this restored gold standard appeared to be working reasonably well, but by the early 1930s, it lay in ruins. Britain's departure from gold in the crisis of late summer 1931 marked the end of the system, though it was not until 1933 and 1936 that the United States and France, respectively, left gold. Why did this restoration experiment fail?

One argument is that the gold standard was ultimately incompatible with postwar governments' new short-term domestic macroeconomic objectives. These objectives lowered the credibility of the commitment to a fixed exchange rate and raised the cost of maintaining it.[54] In this view, wider enfranchisement and growing political influence of the working classes increased demands on governments to make priorities of domestic output and employment objectives rather than the exchange rate and low inflation. Eventually, domestic politics demanded a choice in favor of these incipient "Keynesian" domestic policy objectives, and the gold standard was abandoned.

[52] Dennis E. Moggridge, *The Return to Gold, 1925: The Formulation of Economic Policy and Its Critics* (New York: Cambridge University Press, 1969).

[53] Governor Norman of the Bank of England adopted the rather extreme personal policy of refusing to visit countries without central banks and refusing all contact with foreign ministers of finance and their officials. The Bank of England was also reluctant to extend financial support to countries with politically subordinate central banks (Richard S. Sayers, *The Bank of England, 1891–1944* [Cambridge: Cambridge University Press, 1976], 160–61, 193–94).

[54] Eichengreen, *Golden Fetters*, 391; Simmons, *Who Adjusts?* 61.

The claim about the impact of the widening of the electoral franchise is more consistent with the British case than with other countries' experiences. A number of European countries had adopted nearly universal male suffrage before the era of the gold standard, with apparently limited cost in terms of monetary credibility and stability (in 1848 in France, and 1871 in Germany). Conversely, restricted franchises in Russia, Austria-Hungary, and Italy coincided with high national debts and long-term interest rates and exchange rate instability.[55] Still, Eichengreen and Simmons are correct to suggest that in many countries leftist political parties were more likely to gain political power after the war than before.

Since Eichengreen and Simmons are also correct that financial markets judged many governments' gold standard commitments as lacking credibility in the interwar years, what was the source of the problem? Although financial markets in the 1920s had no modern economic models to deduce a policy contradiction between employment and exchange rate objectives (the Mundell-Fleming model was developed in the 1960s), it is possible that they possessed inductive knowledge of this contradiction. Another possibility is that financial markets were simply concerned that governments would be tempted to inflate their way out of their fiscal and debt overhang problems (as some had tried in the early 1920s). More research is required to decide between these two explanations, since both are consistent with the fact that financial markets reacted negatively to evidence of fiscal and monetary laxity and departures from gold standard rules.

Both arguments are compatible with the general claim that the process of democratization, reflected in the growing importance of mass politics, was of central importance in undermining the credibility of the commitment to a "hard" exchange rate peg. Central bank independence (CBI) from government could sometimes partially offset this trend: countries like France with highly independent central banks made a more credible commitment to gold despite mounting unemployment, in contrast to countries with more subordinate central banks, such as Britain, Sweden, and Japan.[56] In the years that preceded

---

[55] Flandreau, Le Cacheux, and Zumer, "Stability without a Pact?" 130.

[56] Beth A. Simmons, "Central Bank Independence between the World Wars," *International Organization* 50:3, 1996, 407–44.

the Keynesian revolution in economic theory, the absence of a clear intellectual alternative to the gold standard reinforced elite attachment to a system that eventually produced outcomes dysfunctional from most points of view.[57] From 1932, British policymakers began very tentatively to experiment with cheap money policies that promoted higher levels of employment.

These arguments about the importance of domestic political change in the major European countries in undermining the gold standard are at odds with the standard argument about the absence of hegemony as the prime cause of interwar monetary instability. In this view, British decline and a newly preponderant America's unwillingness to assume the burden of leadership undermined the international gold standard. As Kindleberger famously put it:

> The world economic system was unstable unless some country stabilized it, as Britain had done in the nineteenth century and up to 1913. In 1929, the British couldn't and the United States wouldn't.[58]

This argument has some merits in focusing attention on the shortcomings of international monetary cooperation in the late 1920s and early 1930s, but it has been criticized on many other grounds. It underplays the attempts by Britain and the United States to restore the international gold standard in the 1920s, the role of policy mistakes in Britain and elsewhere, and the destabilizing effects of the war and postwar settlement. It also ignores the domestic political conflict that arose from the financial and economic legacy of the Great War, and the rising importance of socialist politics in undermining the commitment to gold.[59]

A New International Monetary System: Bretton Woods

The Bretton Woods agreement of 1944 was a true watershed, representing an attempt to found a new kind of international monetary order

---

[57] Barry J. Eichengreen and Peter Temin, "The Gold Standard and the Great Depression," NBER Working Paper, 6060, 1997.

[58] Kindleberger, *World in Depression*, 292.

[59] Ruggie, "International Regimes"; Walter, *World Power*, chap. 5.

on the explicit acceptance of new domestic macroeconomic objectives.[60] The establishment of two new international institutions, the IMF and World Bank, introduced a greater element of collective management of international money and finance than in the past. Even so, elements of historical continuity included a pegged exchange rate system, a monetary anchor role for gold, and a reserve role for both gold and major key currencies.

Much IPE literature initially emphasized the importance of US hegemony in the construction of the Bretton Woods system.[61] Although US leadership was indeed crucial to the outcome, hegemony theory does not explain the details of the Bretton Woods system. "Social" democracy and associated new Keynesian thinking about policy combined to ensure that many governments in Europe saw high-employment policies as an essential ingredient of postwar political reconstruction.[62] National demand-management policies and in many cases state-directed industrial policy were seen as the means to achieve these goals. In developing countries, similar policies were pursued for nationalist and developmental reasons even in the absence of democracy. Almost everywhere, national fiat money systems were entrenched and central banks placed under government control. In the Bretton Woods agreement it was accepted that governments would and should use national stabilization policy to manage domestic output, employment, and price objectives. Keynesian ideas were not fully victorious, particularly in the United States, but classical monetary orthodoxy had collapsed almost everywhere, and financial interests were often seriously weakened by the Great Depression and war.[63]

The Great Depression had delegitimized the gold standard because of its association with deflation and mass unemployment. Keynes had

---

[60] Richard N. Gardner, *Sterling-Dollar Diplomacy in Current Perspective* (New York: Columbia University Press, 1980); Harold James, *International Monetary Cooperation since Bretton Woods* (Washington, D.C.: IMF; New York: Oxford University Press, 1996); Armand Van Dormael, *Bretton Woods: Birth of a Monetary System* (London: Macmillan, 1978).

[61] For a discussion, see Walter, *World Power*, chap. 6.

[62] Ruggie, "International Regimes."

[63] On Keynesian ideas, see Hall, *Political Power of Economic Ideas*, especially chapters 2 and 3; and G. John Ikenberry, "A World Economy Restored: Expert Consensus and the Anglo-American Postwar Settlement," *International Organization* 46:1, 1992, 289–321.

famously described the gold standard as a "barbarous relic" and declared its incompatibility with active demand-management policy. Yet the United States, which by the 1940s held most of the world's gold reserves, insisted that gold be retained alongside convertible currencies as a monetary reserve asset and as an anchor for the exchange rate system. The Bretton Woods conference therefore agreed to adopt a more flexible "gold-exchange standard." Since domestic monetary policy autonomy was prioritized, capital controls were allowed (IMF Article VI.3).[64] All currencies would be pegged to gold *or* to the US dollar (IMF Article IV.1.a), but no country would be required to defend an exchange rate that produced a "fundamental disequilibrium" in the balance of payments (IMF Article IV.5). This meant that pegs could be adjusted in such circumstances, though in principle adjustments required consultation with other countries through the IMF to prevent competitive devaluation. The concept of fundamental disequilibrium was left undefined, but the general understanding was that persistent overall payments imbalances would require exchange rate adjustment. These and other ambiguities in the Bretton Woods system played a constructive role in facilitating agreement and in providing for subsequent flexibility.[65]

The postwar international monetary system soon evolved into a gold-dollar system, whereby the United States maintained dollar convertibility into gold at the fixed (1934) price of $35 per ounce. Other countries could freely hold dollar reserves and could, if they wished, sell these reserves for gold at the official price, either in the private gold market, or by presenting them for conversion at the "gold window" of the US Treasury. The emerging Cold War also resolved the decades-long problem of persistently large US payments surpluses by facilitating US acquiescence to large European devaluations over 1948–49 and costly American aid and troop deployments in Europe and Asia. These helped to produce the large US payments deficits from the early 1950s that later became associated with the Bretton Woods system and which provided a large proportion of the new liquidity in the postwar international monetary system.

---

[64] Capital controls are policy measures that restrict cross-border transactions in financial assets.

[65] Jacqueline Best, *The Limits of Transparency: Ambiguity and the History of International Finance* (Ithaca, N.Y.: Cornell University Press, 2005).

The room allowed in the Bretton Woods agreement for domestic macroeconomic activism and the potentially adjustable character of the exchange rate pegs arguably reduced their credibility. As a result, timely changes to currency pegs were encouraged. Furthermore, the IMF was authorized to use its pool of member contributions to make short term loans to members who needed to defend their exchange rate. National quotas were to be comprised of 25% gold and 75% national currency, but countries could borrow up to 125% of this quota (with successive "tranches" having more conditions attached), repayable within three to five years. From the Keynesian perspective, a temporary deterioration in a country's payments position should be financed to counteract the "deflationary bias" in the system that derived from the special vulnerability of deficit countries. As Article 1(v) of the Bretton Woods agreement stated, a key objective was

> To give confidence to members by making the Fund's resources available to them under adequate safeguards, thus providing them with an opportunity to correct maladjustments in their balance of payments without resorting to measures destructive of national or international prosperity.

By late 1947 it had become clear that the IMF's total resources were wholly inadequate to achieve this objective, but the Cold War intervened and the United States provided bilateral financial aid to western Europe in the form of the Marshall Plan. IMF quotas have been increased periodically since 1944, but the Fund's resources have not kept pace with the growth of the world economy. Later, as capital mobility and pressures on the exchange rate system increased, the major industrial countries supplemented these limited facilities in the 1960s with the Gold Pool (1961), swap facilities (1962), the General Arrangements to Borrow (GAB) (1962), and SDR allocations (from 1969).[66] These new financing arrangements largely benefited the industrial countries. The shortage of IMF liquidity ensured that in practice most adjustment pressure remained on deficit countries, especially those in the developing world.

The Cold War had another effect on the balance between financing and adjustment. Although IFI lending and associated policy conditionality was meant to be based on politically neutral criteria, the rise of

---

[66] James, *International Monetary Cooperation*, chap. 6.

the Cold War seriously strained the credibility of this neutrality for both the IMF and the World Bank.[67] This was compounded by the fact that voting power in the Executive Boards of the Fund and Bank were weighted according to country contributions, with the United States possessing the largest (and wielding effective veto power over important decisions). After the withdrawal of the USSR and mainland China from the Bretton Woods institutions, the United States and its European allies dominated both IFIs. Other countries aligned with the dominant Western powers tended to get better financing deals and very weak enforcement of policy conditionality.[68]

FROM BRETTON WOODS TO GLOBAL FINANCIAL INTEGRATION

By the early 1960s, the Bretton Woods system had evolved in directions unforeseen in 1944 and was in serious difficulty. It limped on until the early 1970s only through US unilateral actions and America's ability to obtain the support of most of its political and military allies. The growing political demands for domestic stabilization policies contributed to the further marginalization of gold in the international monetary system and the emergence of a "dollar standard." Another major long-term development was the reemergence of private international financial markets in the 1960s. Together, these processes undermined the pegged exchange rate system and increasingly marginalized the institutions of public international finance established at Bretton Woods.

From Gold-Exchange Standard to Dollar Standard

It was already clear by the late 1950s that the gold-exchange standard was in difficulty. In the late 1950s, US gold losses accelerated as large

---

[67] The World Bank, intended to provide longer-term public finance to war-torn and developing countries, operated on a different model. With $10 billion in initial capital commitments from member states, the Bank would borrow at low rates in private international capital markets and lend the proceeds to member countries.

[68] Strom C. Thacker, "The High Politics of IMF Lending," *World Politics* 52:1, 1999, 38–75.

overall US payments deficits were financed by the accumulation of dollar reserves by central banks in Europe and elsewhere. At the same time, steady wartime and postwar inflation had eroded the real price of gold (given its fixed nominal price of $35 per ounce), making it less profitable to mine and encouraging excess private demand. The growing shortage of gold's supply relative to dollars led to growing speculation against the dollar.[69]

Triffin argued that these developments showed that the gold-exchange standard was "inherent unstable" and was bound to collapse.[70] The sustained expansion of international trade, he argued, increasingly depended on new liquidity provided by US payments deficits, but the growing relative shortage of gold compared to dollars would undermine the fixed-price relationship between the dollar and gold. If the United States tried to maintain the dollar price of gold by reducing its overall payments deficits, a global liquidity crisis and recession would result. Fearing the latter outcome, Triffin argued for replacing both gold and key currencies with a new international fiduciary money that could be created and managed by the IMF (reviving Keynes's "bancor" proposal of the early 1940s).

Triffin's diagnosis of the weaknesses of the Bretton Woods system was perceptive, but his political economy analysis was less strong. First, to expect the United States to reduce its external deficit was naive, given the growing domestic pressure for welfare spending and job creation in the United States and the large contribution of FDI, military, and aid outflows to America's external deficits. Second, Triffin's supranational solution was utopian and at odds with domestic political considerations in the United States and elsewhere. In reality, there were only three plausible solutions to the gold-dollar problem. One solution, eventually adopted, was to break the link with gold permanently and to move to a dollar standard.[71] A second solution was to maintain the gold-dollar

---

[69] This is an example of "Gresham's Law," the claim that "bad [depreciating] money drives out good" (i.e., appreciating money is hoarded rather than spent). It suggests that dual monetary standards are prone to instability.

[70] Triffin, *Gold and the Dollar Crisis*.

[71] Emile Despres, Charles P. Kindleberger, and Walter S. Salant, "The Dollar and World Liquidity—a Minority View," *The Economist*, February 5, 1966, 526–29; Ronald I. McKinnon, *Money in International Exchange: The Convertible Currency System* (New York: Oxford University Press, 1979).

standard by periodically revaluing gold against all currencies in the system, including the dollar.[72] A third, which was adopted after the collapse of the short-lived dollar standard, was to allow the major currencies to float against each other.

Politics initially strongly favored the dollar standard over the second and third solutions. The gold revaluation proposal was politically unappealing for a number of reasons. First, it overlooked that continuous postwar inflation in the major countries rendered an anchor role for gold increasingly untenable: periodic gold revaluations would have been tantamount to accommodating this inflation, undermining the core rationale for a commodity price anchor. Second, the United States was increasingly unwilling to accept the constraint on its own macroeconomic policy flexibility that gold convertibility implied.[73] Third, loyal allies of the United States like West Germany and Japan were willing to hold dollar reserves even if they were not convertible into gold. Only France under de Gaulle, chafing under American preponderance, felt sufficiently autonomous of Washington both to withdraw from NATO's military structure and to sell its dollar reserves. Vocal French demands for a return to a "politically neutral" gold standard also hardened US political opinion against gold revaluation, already resisted out of concern that it would favor the "gold bugs" (speculators) and unsavory gold-producing countries like the USSR and South Africa.

If a reinvigorated gold exchange standard was politically unappealing, the flexible exchange rate proposal also enjoyed very little support in the late 1960s except among a few maverick economists (we discuss this further in the next chapter). This left the dollar standard as the only alternative that was acceptable to the United States and its major allies. The "Two-Tier" agreement of 1968 ended official attempts to maintain the fixed price of gold in the private gold market, though the $35 per ounce price was retained for transactions between central banks. This was the first formal step toward the demonetization of gold in the international monetary system, though it did little to relieve the pressure on the dollar and continuing losses of US gold reserves. In August 1971,

[72] Milton Gilbert, *Quest for World Monetary Order*, ed. Peter Oppenheimer and Michael Dealtry (New York: Wiley, 1980).
[73] Gowa, *Closing the Gold Window*.

President Nixon unilaterally decided to close the gold window and in December that year obtained the agreement of other major countries to a formal dollar standard, in which other currencies were pegged to a gold-inconvertible US dollar. As we discuss in chapter 5, the dollar standard proved even more unstable than the gold-dollar standard, but the position of key currencies as reserve assets in the international monetary system has become ever more entrenched since then.

The Reemergence of Financial Integration

The second major change in the international monetary system over the course of the 1960s and 1970s was the reemergence of private international capital markets. There is a large literature describing the dramatic increase in short-term capital mobility and longer-term international financial flows since the 1960s that need not be repeated here.[74] One indication of the importance of international capital flows is the very high level of *daily* global turnover in foreign exchange markets, which reached $1,900 billion in April 2004, compared to $620 billion in 1989.[75] Another indication is the increase in the stock of financial assets owned by foreigners. According to McKinsey, by 2005, "foreigners [held] 12 percent of US equities, 25 percent of US corporate bonds, and 44 percent of Treasury securities, up from 4 percent, 1 percent and 20 percent, respectively, in 1975."[76] Although there is general agreement about the rapidity of the growth in financial integration, there is debate and some skepticism concerning its absolute level.[77] As figure 4.2 shows, although most regions have seen an increase in levels of capital account

[74] For a recent assessment of the scope and depth of global financial integration, see McKinsey Global Institute, *Mapping the Global Capital Market: Third Annual Report* (San Francisco: McKinsey & Co., January 2007). For political economy assessments, see Eric Helleiner, *States and the Re-emergence of Global Finance* (Ithaca, N.Y.: Cornell University Press, 1994); and Benjamin J. Cohen, "Phoenix Risen: The Resurrection of Global Finance," *World Politics* 48:2, 1996, 268–96.

[75] Bank for International Settlements data, available at http://www.bis.org/publ/rpfx05.htm, accessed December 9, 2005.

[76] McKinsey Global Institute, *118 Trillion and Counting: Taking Stock of the World's Capital Markets* (San Francisco: McKinsey & Co., February 2005), 19.

[77] Philip R. Lane and Gian Maria Milesi-Ferretti, "International Financial Integration," IMF Working Paper, WP/03/86, April 2003.

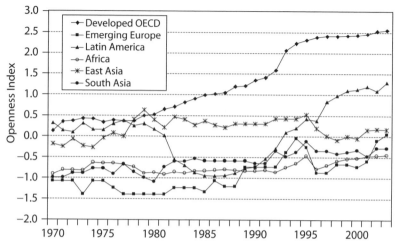

FIGURE 4.2. Capital Account Openness, Selected Country Groups, 1970–2003
Source: Menzie Chinn and Hiro Ito, KAOPEN database, capital openness indices for 163 countries over 1970–2003, http://web.pdx.edu/~ito/ (accessed December 9, 2005).

openness since 1970, financial openness is higher in developed countries and trends vary considerably by region.

Given the potentially transformative implications of greater financial openness, we must first ask what explains this broad trend and the varying cross-regional and cross-country patterns we observe. Here, we discuss international, domestic, and ideational explanations. We focus on the removal of barriers to short-term or portfolio capital mobility, especially capital controls, but keep in mind that financial liberalization more broadly also encompasses the liberalization of domestic financial markets, including the removal of controls on financial activities and on entry into financial businesses, including by foreign financial firms.

INTERNATIONAL EXPLANATIONS

The most general explanation is that international competition between states promotes financial liberalization over time.[78] As we saw in chapter 3, realist accounts of trade policy have claimed that interstate competition tends to promote either unilateral protection or cautious, reciproc-

---

[78] Philip G. Cerny, "Globalization and the Changing Logic of Collective Action," *International Organization* 49:4, 1995, 595–625; Helleiner, *States and Re-emergence*.

ity-based trade liberalization. What is different about finance, realists have argued, is that unilateral liberalization improves the competitive position of national financial sectors and can attract multinational financial firms.[79] Hence, relatively closed national financial systems such as generally prevailed in the 1950s and 1960s are seen politically unsustainable over time. Evidence for this claim is provided by the evident competition between global financial centers like London and New York, and within regions like Europe and East Asia, which do appear to have promoted unilateral removal of capital controls and of constraints on international financial business and entry by financial MNCs. The "Eurodollar" markets emerged in the 1960s because of the British authorities' willingness to allow London banks to provide wholesale dollar-based financial services to foreign residents, even though capital controls on *sterling* transactions remained in place until the late 1970s. The United States responded at the end of 1973 by removing the remaining capital controls that inhibited Wall Street's international financial role and encouraged American banks to conduct international business in London. A related argument is that such competition can spiral out of control, causing a race to the bottom in financial regulation, taxation, and financial transparency as ever more jurisdictions compete for international financial business. Concerns have focused particularly on "offshore financial centers" (OFCs), which offer low taxes, light financial regulation, and substantial anonymity for individuals, companies and financial institutions.[80]

However, not all governments choose to compete for international financial business. The removal of capital controls has also taken place very unevenly, both over time and across different countries.[81] At the least, we need to explain why the United States and a few other coun-

[79] This claim can be criticized for ignoring the potential for gains in economy-wide competitiveness that may stem from unilateral trade liberalization, as well as the growing practice of unilateral trade liberalization since the 1980s.

[80] E.g., Tax Justice Network, "Tax Us If You Can," Briefing Paper, September 2005. Definitions of OFCs vary, but the IMF identifies dozens, including many microstates (Ahmed Zoromé, "Concept of Offshore Financial Centers: In Search of an Operational Definition," IMF Working Paper, WP/07/87, April 2007; see also Ronan Palan, *The Offshore World: Sovereign Markets, Virtual Places, and Nomad Millionaires* [Ithaca, N.Y.: Cornell University Press, 2006]).

[81] IMF, *Country Experiences with the Use and Liberalization of Capital Controls* (Washington, D.C.: IMF, 2000).

tries (such as Switzerland, Canada, and West Germany) removed capital controls much earlier than others. Helleiner's argument is that the relative political influence of financial interests within these countries helps to explain their decisions, which takes us into domestic politics. Another, compatible explanation is that the IT revolution substantially reduced the costs of international financial transactions, providing increased incentives for governments to engage in competitive liberalization. The related dramatic fall in transactions costs has also unleashed successive waves of innovation in financial markets, which has spurred their growth and further raised the costs of financial protectionism. As we will see in chapter 6, such technological explanations have been applied to growing capital mobility in general.

Others retain an international explanatory focus by arguing that the major Western countries, above all the United States, have actively promoted financial liberalization abroad to enhance their structural power within the global system.[82] Although this argument also has realist origins, it interprets the general trend in more coercive terms. Potential benefits for the United States include greater business opportunities for highly competitive US financial firms, as well as the possible benefits that the United States as a whole may gain from the international use of its currency, and from financial inflows from other countries, including for the purpose of obtaining cheap finance for its fiscal and payments deficits.

There is evidence that the United States and the EU have promoted greater financial openness abroad in recent years through trade and investment negotiations (notably in the WTO financial services agreement of 1997, but increasingly through bilateral deals). Some also argue that the major countries have used the IMF to promote capital account liberalization abroad.[83] But this overlooks the other side of the argument, especially that financial liberalization might benefit indigenous firms and that growing US dependence on foreign finance might di-

---

[82] Michael Loriaux, "The End of Credit Activism in Interventionist States," in Loriaux, ed., *Capital Ungoverned: Liberalizing Finance in Interventionist States* (Ithaca, N.Y.: Cornell University Press, 1997), 1–16; Leonard Seabrooke, *US Power in International Finance: The Victory of Dividends* (London: Palgrave Macmillan, 2001).

[83] Robert Wade, "The Coming Fight over Capital Controls," *Foreign Policy* 113, Winter 1998–99, 41–54.

minish rather than enhance America's global leverage.[84] Moreover, international pressures to converge on open capital account policies were not always successful or especially strong. A recent independent review of IMF policy notes that although the IMF did try to persuade governments to liberalize, it lacks the legal authority to require capital account liberalization (a legacy of the Bretton Woods articles of agreement). Generally, it suggests that domestic factors were usually more important in governments' liberalization decisions.[85]

Simmons and Elkins show that capital account liberalization has clustered both temporally and spatially, suggesting that domestic factors alone are insufficient to explain this pattern.[86] One explanation for this is the competitive liberalization process discussed above. Another channel Simmons and Elkins identify is that countries may observe peer group policies for purposes of gaining information in a situation of uncertainty (i.e., a learning effect), an argument for which they find some support. The IFIs may have played a role in promoting this cross-border diffusion of policy trends.

A final international explanation of capital account liberalization is offered by Haggard and Maxfield, who argue that financial crises induce capital-poor developing countries to open their capital accounts to signal that the risk of future closure should not deter potential investors.[87] It is doubtful, however, that any such signals are very credible to investors, since the cost of reintroducing capital controls in the future during a crisis may not be high. Indeed, figure 4.2 suggests that East Asia on average tightened rather than liberalized capital controls after the regional crisis of 1997–98.

[84] For different views concerning the recent debate about the consequences of growing US external indebtedness, see Michael P. Dooley, David Folkerts-Landau and Peter Garber, "An Essay on the Revived Bretton Woods System," NBER Working Paper, 9971, September 2003; Barry J. Eichengreen, *Global Imbalances and the Lessons of Bretton Woods* (Cambridge: MIT Press, 2006); and Maurice Obstfeld and Kenneth Rogoff, "The Unsustainable US Current Account Position Revisited," NBER Working Paper, 10869, November 2004.

[85] IMF, Independent Evaluation Office, *Report on the Evaluation of the IMF's Approach to Capital Account Liberalization* (Washington, D.C.: Independent Evaluation Office, IMF, April 2005).

[86] Beth A. Simmons and Zachary Elkins, "The Globalization of Liberalization: Policy Diffusion in the International Political Economy," *American Political Science Review* 98:1, 2004, 171–89.

[87] Stephan Haggard and Sylvia Maxfield, "The Political Economy of Financial Internationalization in the Developing World," *International Organization*, 50:1, 1996, 35–68.

DOMESTIC EXPLANATIONS

The comparative political economy literature suggests a range of domestic interest group and institutional factors that help explain the complex pattern of liberalization. Interest-based approaches begin by specifying group preferences, typically using either the Stolper-Samuelson or specific factors models of trade theory. In the former case, in advanced economies capital as the abundant factor gains and labor loses from financial openness (since capital will be exported). In developing economies, labor gains from capital importation and domestic capital loses. Building on this model, Quinn and Inclán predict different labor preferences according to skill levels and test hypotheses about the circumstances under which left-of-center and right-of-center political parties will support or oppose financial openness.[88]

In contrast, Frieden uses the specific factors model to predict that financial industries will gain from financial openness and those with sector-specific assets lose because they will pay higher borrowing costs when capital flows abroad.[89] In developing countries, industries with sector-specific assets win because they will pay lower borrowing costs. MNCs with internationally diversified asset portfolios will gain because of their ability to borrow at low cost and from their ability to make intrafirm financial transfers. Owners of liquid financial assets in developed countries will gain while those in developing countries will lose as interest rates rise in the former and fall in the latter. These predictions are consistent with some aspects of conventional wisdom, such as the apparently broad support for financial openness among firms and workers engaged in the financial sector of major countries since the 1970s, and among the multinational corporate sector in general.

Some difficulties emerge in both of these approaches, though neither has been subject to decisive testing to date. First, some of the predictions are not obviously consistent with the evidence. For example, domestic firms in specific sectors in the advanced countries may not have lost from capital openness, since many firms now enjoy access to a much greater pool of capital than before because of widespread

---

[88] Dennis P. Quinn and Carla Inclán, "The Origins of Financial Openness: A Study of Current and Capital Account Liberalization," *American Journal of Political Science* 41:3, 1997, 771–813.

[89] Frieden, "Invested Interests."

liberalization across many countries. Indeed, both theories rely for their predictions on the standard neoclassical assumption that financial openness will promote capital exports from developed countries to capital-poor developing countries. It is not commonly recognized in the political economy literature that this crucial assumption is not supported by the evidence, with the United States acting as a net importer of capital from developing countries for many years.[90] Second, it is one thing to attempt to identify those groups who win and lose from financial openness, but this does not mean that such groups will mobilize to lobby policymakers. As for trade policy, institutions matter for financial policy outcomes, including the political parties that Quinn and Inclán consider. However, political parties may represent multiple interest groups who are differently affected by financial opening. More generally, it is not clear how strong and coherent the preferences of interest groups will be, since financial openness raises a range of complex issues. As Frieden notes, financial openness has important implications for the exchange rate, so much may depend on whether specific assets are employed in the traded or non-traded-goods sector (see chapter 5, the section "Financial Integration and Exchange Rate Policies"). Voters possess multiple identities in practice: as savers, as workers or employers, as consumers, and so on, which can result in ambiguous preferences. Banks may have global fund management and international lending divisions that favor financial openness, but their domestic lending departments with corporate clients in the traded goods sector may favor exchange rate stability over capital openness. The majority of the benefits of financial liberalization tend to accrue to particular, often politically influential, groups, including financial firms and MNCs.[91] The potential costs of such liberalization, such as greater exchange rate instability, lower macroeconomic policy autonomy, and financial crises tend to be delayed and more widely distributed among societal groups. Given this asymmetric distribution of costs and benefits and the obstacles to collective action among losers, liberalization is likely to win out in the long run.

[90] This is generally known as the "Lucas paradox" after Robert E. Lucas Jr., "Why Doesn't Capital Flow from Rich to Poor Countries?" *American Economic Review* 80:2, 1990, 92–96.

[91] John B. Goodman and Louis W. Pauly, "The Obsolescence of Capital Controls? Economic Management in an Age of Global Markets," *World Politics* 46:1, 1993, 50–82.

If policymakers have some autonomy from societal interests in this area, what determines their preferences? One possible answer, addressed below, is economic ideas. Another is that the state itself, often the largest debtor within countries, may favor financial openness if this expands its borrowing capacity and lowers its cost of debt (a generalization of Loriaux's argument from the previous section). Governments of countries with low domestic savings or underdeveloped capital markets might be particular beneficiaries. Governments facing highly independent central banks may enjoy little influence over monetary policy with or without capital controls, undermining the rationale for retaining them. Central banks themselves might favor capital mobility either because they are open to capture by the financial sector or because they believe it will constrain the government's propensity to run fiscal deficits.[92] These possibilities remain speculative at present.

Finally, what impact has democratization had on capital account policies? It is difficult to believe that there is a simple linear relationship between democracy and capital account policy. The restriction of the franchise in nineteenth-century Britain and the political dominance of the asset-owning elite may have favored the policy of financial openness under the gold standard until 1914. Ruggie's argument that the "reembedding" of economic liberalism within a social democratic framework made capital controls politically acceptable pushes in the same direction.[93] Others find that more recently, democracy has had a positive effect on financial liberalization in developing countries.[94] Countries in which voters support social democratic welfare policies have moved in recent years toward greater financial openness (notably most of developed western Europe in a relatively coordinated fashion as part of the 1992 Single Market Programme). This might demonstrate that as these voters have become richer over time they have also come to favor financial openness to maximize returns on savings, or it may simply be that they are relatively poorly informed or weakly mobilized. Evidently, this important area is ripe for further research.

---

[92] However, if the central bank is required to defend a currency peg, it may favor capital controls.

[93] Ruggie, "International Regimes."

[94] Nancy Brune, Geoffrey Garrett, Alexandra Guisinger, and Jason Sorens, "The Political Economy of Capital Account Liberalization," unpublished paper, December 2001, available at http://www.isop.ucla.edu/cms/files/capacct.pdf.

IDEATIONAL EXPLANATIONS

Capital account decisions may be influenced by particular ideas if policymakers have some autonomy from domestic and international interests. In the early post-1945 period, the orthodox (Keynesian) consensus among economists and technocrats was that capital controls were a necessary plank of national macroeconomic stabilization policy. By contrast, most contemporary economists argue that capital controls rarely work for long, create large inefficiencies in the global allocation of capital, and promote corruption.[95] This broad ideational shift is associated with the rise of an anti-Keynesian policy consensus since the 1970s that monetary policy should focus mainly (if not entirely) on inflation stabilization and in favor of floating exchange rates.

The question of how much this new orthodoxy influenced *policy* outcomes is a difficult one. Optimism concerning the net benefits of capital account liberalization probably played a role in a number of decisions by developing countries to liberalize in the early 1990s, though the impact of neoliberal ideas on financial policy varies considerably across countries.[96] Those Latin American governments adhering to the new "Washington consensus" concerning the benefits of neoliberal market reform were most prone to ideological conversion to the capital liberalization cause, Mexico's economist-dominated government being the most notable example.[97] But it is difficult to separate the role of ideas from that of pressure from powerful external actors. The US Treasury and the IMF proselytized in favor of financial liberalization in the 1990s, and the former was associated with proposals in the mid-1990s for an amendment to the IMF's articles of agreement to give the IMF authority to promote capital account liberalization. These proponents

[95] Alberto Alesina, Vittorio Grilli, and Gian Maria Milesi-Ferretti, "The Political Economy of Capital Controls," in Leonardo Leiderman and Assaf Razin, eds., *Capital Mobility: The Impact on Consumption, Investment, and Growth* (New York: Cambridge University Press, 1994), 289–321; Richard J. Sweeney, "The Information Costs of Capital Controls," in C. P. Rios and Richard J. Sweeney, eds., *Capital Controls in Emerging Economies* (Boulder, Colo.: Westview Press, 1996); Sebastian Edwards, "How Effective Are Capital Controls?" *Journal of Economic Perspectives* 13:4, 1999, 65–84.

[96] Jeffrey M. Chwieroth, "Neoliberal Economists and Capital Account Liberalization in Emerging Markets," *International Organization* 61:2, 2007, 443–63.

[97] Sarah Babb, *Managing Mexico: Economists from Nationalism to Neoliberalism* (Princeton, N.J.: Princeton University Press, 2001).

played down the costs of financial openness: though they recognized at the conceptual level that premature capital account liberalization could be risky, in practice little attention was given to these concerns before the Asian crises of the late 1990s.[98] Although key players in the US Treasury and IMF may have been convinced of the intellectual case in favor of financial openness, in both cases material interests arguably pushed in the same direction. Ideational and material factors also interrelate in the impact of the end of the Cold War, which led to a transition toward market democracies in many central and eastern European countries in the early 1990s.

An example of the role of ideas in influencing material outcomes is the effect of financial theory on the way in which financial markets operate. Finance theorists working within the neoclassical tradition on risk and portfolio optimization laid the foundation for modern financial techniques that revolutionized the financial sector. As Bernstein notes, some of these academic theorists went on to work in the financial markets, providing a direct link between academic ideas and financial practice.[99] The rapid growth of the financial sector that this helped to produce increased its political influence, including over the nature and content of financial regulation. This also has made it more difficult for countries with substantial financial sectors to contemplate the reintroduction of controls that inhibit financial innovation and globalization.

In short, it seems clear that both international and domestic factors matter in explaining the uneven patterns of financial liberalization over the past few decades. Ideational and material factors are difficult to separate, though the relative importance of ideas may be greater in some countries than in others, depending among other things on the coherence of policymaking teams.[100] Ideas also have been important in reshaping the financial sector in ways that have in turn influenced policy and the shape of financial regulation (see chapter 5).

[98] IMF, *Evaluation of the IMF's Approach.*

[99] Peter L. Bernstein, *Capital Ideas: The Improbable Origins of Modern Wall Street* (New York: Free Press, 1992). See also Donald MacKenzie, *An Engine Not a Camera: How Financial Models Shape Markets* (Cambridge: MIT Press, 2006); and Perry Mehrling, *Fischer Black and the Revolutionary Idea of Finance* (Hoboken, N.J.: Wiley, 2005).

[100] Chwieroth, "Neoliberal Economists."

CONCLUSION

We have argued in this chapter that the very uneven process of democratization in combination with Keynesian economic ideas promoted demands for national macroeconomic activism by governments and monetary authorities. Over the course of the past century, this process undermined the role of gold in international monetary organization and rendered pegged exchange rate systems increasingly unviable. In the 1970s, the principle of national macroeconomic activism came under challenge from monetarist and new classical economics, but most central banks have retained the Keynesian idea that discretionary monetary management remains a powerful policy tool. Domestic political pressure for monetary activism remains strong in most developed democracies.[101]

Although one of the components of national monetary activism was the often substantial use of capital controls to limit international financial interdependence, over time this proved unsustainable. The re-emergence of private international financial markets has been driven by a range of international and domestic forces, both material and ideational. Combined with the continuing importance of national macroeconomic policy activism, growing financial interdependence has had a powerful impact on the shape of the international monetary organization, in particular by increasing the vulnerability of pegged exchange rate regimes. We consider this and other implications in more detail in the next chapter.

FURTHER RESOURCES

Further Reading

Harold James. *International Monetary Cooperation since Bretton Woods.* Washington, D.C.: International Monetary Fund; New York: Oxford University Press, 1996. An excellent history of international monetary relations since World War II.

---

[101] We discuss the possible exception of Europe in the following chapter.

Ngaire Woods. *The Globalizers: The IMF, the World Bank, and Their Borrowers*. Ithaca, N.Y.: Cornell University Press, 2006. Provides a clear analysis of the two main international financial institutions, their governance, and their relationships with developing countries that borrow from them.

Benjamin J. Cohen. *Global Monetary Governance*. London: Routledge, 2008. A collection of important essays on the evolution of the international monetary and financial system since the 1960s.

Useful Websites

- http://web.pdx.edu/~ito/. Menzie Chinn and Hiro Ito's "KAOPEN" database, which currently provides capital account openness indices for 181 countries over 1970–2005 and is periodically updated.
- http://www.imf.org/external/data.htm. The IMF's data and statistics site, which includes a range of important databases including International Financial Statistics, World Economic Outlook, the Joint BIS-IMF-OECD–World Bank Statistics on External Debt, the Dissemination Standards Bulletin Board, and the *Annual Report on Exchange Arrangements and Exchange Restrictions*.
- www.imf.org/ieo. The IMF's Independent Evaluation Office site, which produces useful independent reports on the IMF's role in international money and finance.
- http://www.brettonwoodsproject.org. The Bretton Woods Project site, an independent organization that monitors the IMF and World Bank and offers reform proposals.

5 | The Consequences of International Financial Integration

In this chapter, we first elaborate on the argument made in the previous chapter in the context of the demise of the Bretton Woods system, that international financial integration has substantially raised the costs of maintaining pegged exchange rates. This has resulted in a noticeable trend toward greater exchange rate flexibility since the 1970s. Second, we discuss how the dramatic growth of private international capital markets has not only overshadowed, but also altered, the role of public international finance because of the growing incidence of severe financial crises. Third, we consider the extent to which financial integration constrains domestic economic policy autonomy, including macroeconomic, welfare, and developmental policies. On balance, the evidence suggests that the importance of these constraints is much greater for less developed countries but that there are important exceptions to this generalization.

FINANCIAL INTEGRATION AND EXCHANGE RATE POLICIES

In this section, we discuss how growing financial integration has raised the perceived costs for governments of maintaining pegged exchange rates. There are, however, some important exceptions to the general trend toward greater exchange rate flexibility since the early 1970s. Among developed countries, the most conspicuous of these exceptions is European monetary integration, pursued since the early 1970s and culminating in monetary union in 1999. Many developing countries also exhibit what has been termed a "fear of floating," reflected in a gap between announced and actual exchange rate policies for many and a continuing reluctance in some cases to adopt floating exchange rates (China being the most prominent contemporary example).

The Growing Costs of Pegged Exchange Rate Policies

As short-term capital mobility between the developed countries increased in the 1960s, the contradiction between governments' macroeconomic policy activism and pegged exchange rates became more apparent. It was especially clear in the central relationship in the dollar standard system from the late 1960s: that between the US dollar and the West German mark. Over the course of the 1960s, both countries used capital controls as the pegged exchange rate system came under growing speculative pressure, but these controls were not entirely effective. Speculation increased in response to a broader US-European dispute over who should bear responsibility for adjustment, which underlined the unwillingness of both sides to accept constraints on their policy autonomy.[1] The Europeans believed that America's growing payments deficits and high inflation necessitated US macroeconomic tightening, whereas the Americans believed European surpluses were the problem, requiring macroeconomic expansion or exchange rate revaluation by Germany and others.

The German Bundesbank's desire to keep inflation low and the German private sector's demand for a stable, competitive exchange rate led to an inflexible response from the German government.[2] Germany reluctantly accepted small upward revaluations of the mark against the dollar in 1961, 1969, and 1971, but they did little to resolve the underlying problem. Continued flows of short-term capital into the German economy eroded the Bundesbank's ability to control the growth of the domestic money supply and its support for the pegged exchange rate policy. Eventually, in March 1973, a massive speculative crisis led the German government to float the mark against the dollar, signaling the end of the dollar standard.

[1] Walter, *World Power*, chap. 6.
[2] Henning, *Currencies and Politics*, 182–83.

As we saw in chapter 4, the MF model implies that countries can choose pegged exchange rates if they are willing to sacrifice either monetary policy autonomy or financial openness. This model overstates the sustainability of pegged exchange rate regimes because capital controls diminish in ineffectiveness over time and because powerful political and technological forces have favored their removal. International macroeconomic policy coordination in principle provides a means of pegging exchange rates without capital controls, but the necessary coordination of policy has proven politically unattainable, despite periodic attempts by the G7 countries.[3] Thus, although national capital controls can provide some short-run relief, there appears to be a long-run trade-off between exchange rate fixity and monetary policy autonomy.

For countries that choose to peg, the costs of doing so have in many cases risen considerably in recent decades. Pegging to another country's currency at a competitive exchange rate benefits the traded sector. It can also provide a relatively transparent signal that monetary policy will not be relatively inflationary. But pegging also means that if monetary policy changes in the center country, followers must bear the costs of adjustment. If these costs are substantial for incumbent governments, the likely result is the declining credibility of the exchange rate commitment itself, since there will be strong incentives to renege on it.[4] Given the vast size of today's global foreign exchange market, the ability of any country to withstand a concerted speculative attack on a currency peg is now much lower than in the final years of the dollar standard. Indeed, the majority of exits from pegged to floating regimes in recent years have not been orderly but crisis-driven.[5] Over 1990–2001 the share of pegged exchange rate regimes in the total continued

[3] Michael C. Webb, *The Political Economy of Policy Coordination* (Ithaca, N.Y.: Cornell University Press, 1995). Wesley Widmaier ("The Social Construction of the 'Impossible Trinity': The Intersubjective Bases of Monetary Cooperation," *International Studies Quarterly* 48:2, 2004, 433–53) argues that another constraint was that the rise of neoclassical economic ideas helped to redefine state interests in ways that favored lower levels of international cooperation. Even without this ideological shift, however, it is doubtful that the requisite degree of policy coordination would have been attainable.

[4] Stanley Fischer, "Modern Central Banking," in Capie et al., *Future of Central Banking*, 288–89.

[5] Rupa Duttagupta, Gilda Fernandez, and Cem Karacadag, "From Fixed to Float: Operational Aspects of Moving towards Exchange Rate Flexibility," IMF Working Paper, 04/126, 2004.

to decline from 80% to 56%.[6] The result, according to a conventional view, is that "soft" pegs are especially vulnerable to speculative attack, producing a "hollowing out" of intermediate options between floating and "hard" pegs.[7]

Explaining the European Exception: EMS and EMU

Floating exchange rates are likely to be more costly for countries with large traded sectors than for less open economies such as the United States and Japan. Since the demise of the Bretton Woods exchange rate system, many of the relatively open European economies chose to float against the US dollar while attempting to maintain exchange rate stability within Europe. This initially took the form of the loose currency "snake" adopted in 1973, the more successful European Monetary System (EMS) from 1979, and monetary union (EMU) from 1999. Although there are a few other examples of regional monetary cooperation, it is doubtful that the European policy can be explained simply by reference to relatively high levels of regional trade integration and the related preference of the traded goods and services sectors for exchange rate stability.[8] Although the trade motive is strongest for the smaller open European countries, it does not explain the different attitudes toward monetary cooperation of the major European countries (notably, Britain's skepticism compared to France, Germany, and Italy). A different interest-based approach offers the more plausible explanation that close financial relationships between banks and industrial firms in continental European countries create a more unified private sector prefer-

---

[6] Andrea Bubula and Ynci Ötker-Robe, "The Evolution of Exchange Rate Regimes since 1990: Evidence from De Facto Policies," IMF Working Paper, WP/02/155, 2002. These figures are for de facto or actual exchange rate policies rather than official ones (see our subsequent discussion).

[7] Stanley Fischer, "Exchange Rate Regimes: Is the Bipolar View Correct?" Distinguished Lecture on Economics in Government, Meeting of the American Economic Association, New Orleans, January 6, 2001.

[8] For interest-based accounts, see Charles Wyplosz, "EMU: Why and How It Might Happen," *Journal of Economic Perspectives* 11:4, 1997, 3–22, and Jeffry A. Frieden, "Real Sources of European Currency Policy: Sectoral Interests and European Monetary Integration," *International Organization* 56:4, 2002, 831–60. For a discussion of the rather different African franc zone, East Caribbean, and other regional exceptions, see Cohen, *Geography of Money*, chap. 4.

ence for pegged exchange rates.[9] By contrast, in the United Kingdom, where capital markets are a more important source of corporate finance, banks and firms share fewer common interests. Indeed, banks may favor floating exchange rates if they increase banks' trading income.

The problem with this and other interest-based theories is that there is little evidence of either strongly held preferences or concerted lobbying on European monetary matters by the major interest groups they identify.[10] One possible reason for this is that large firms in the tradables sector can partially insulate themselves from the effects of exchange rate instability by purchasing financial derivative contracts. Another is that the very broad distributional effects of monetary policy create higher barriers to collective action than in the case of trade policy.[11]

Nor can the economic theory of "optimal currency areas" (OCA) resolve the puzzle of varying national attitudes toward European monetary cooperation. OCA literature suggests that exchange rate stability is best for countries with high levels of trade interdependence, a low likelihood of experiencing shocks that affect countries asymmetrically, and high interregional labor mobility.[12] Britain is not exceptional on these measures: its industrial structure is similar to that of the other major economies, its labor mobility is unexceptional, and UK oil exports are insufficiently important to explain the difference in policy. Nor can the OCA literature account for the pro-monetary integration attitudes of the other European countries, given Europe's relatively low labor mobility and lack of "federal" fiscal policy tools compared to the United States.

If societal interests are less important than some suggest, European governments have probably enjoyed considerable autonomy on the question of exchange rate policy. But if so, what has determined govern-

[9] Henning, *Currencies and Politics.* This is because banks will have a stronger interest in the competitiveness of firms in the traded sector if they lend to them or hold their shares.

[10] Kathleen R. McNamara, *The Currency of Ideas: Monetary Politics in the European Union* (Ithaca, N.Y.: Cornell University Press, 1998).

[11] Joanne S. Gowa, "Public Goods and Political Institutions: Trade and Monetary Policy Processes in the United States," *International Organization* 42:1, 1988, 15–32.

[12] Peter B. Kenen, "The Theory of Optimal Currency Areas," in Robert A. Mundell and Alexander K. Swoboda, eds., *Monetary Problems of the International Economy* (Chicago: University of Chicago Press, 1969), 41–60.

ment preferences? In the 1980s, it was often argued that major continental European governments (other than Germany's) saw exchange rate pegs as a transparent means of importing anti-inflationary credibility from Germany.[13] This argument cannot explain Germany's preference for close European monetary cooperation, or that of other low-inflation countries. Furthermore, this supposed "solution" for relatively inflation-prone countries like Italy only transferred the underlying credibility problem to the exchange rate peg: when market agents perceived the political costs of unemployment to be high, as in the 1992 EMS crisis, the credibility of the exchange rate commitment collapsed.[14] Disinflation took time and was imperfect, resulting in eroding competitiveness. In the end, only the willingness of the authorities in Italy or France to sustain high unemployment enabled inflation to fall. Frieden finds little empirical support for the anti-inflationary credibility argument, including for the related partisan version that left-of-center governments should have most incentive to import such credibility.[15]

Given the shortcomings of the aforementioned theories, it is difficult to avoid the conclusion that the strong commitment of France, Germany, and other European governments (left and right) to monetary union has much to do with the broader goal shared by political elites of promoting deeper political integration.[16] This shared goal helps to explain the importance political elites also attach to related goals of promoting European political cohesion by avoiding competitive devaluations and protecting the system of price supports of the Common Agricultural Policy (CAP). Above all, it helps to explain why, in the wake of German reunification, French and German political elites wished to replace the EMS with the more radical EMU. Although plausible economic arguments for EMU were formulated, they were largely uncompelling, not least for Germany, which had benefited considerably

---

[13] Francesco Giavazzi and Marco Pagano, "The Advantage of Tying One's Hands: EMS Discipline and Central Bank Credibility," *European Economic Review* 32:5, 1989, 1055–75.

[14] This particular crisis was made worse by destabilizing policies in the center country. German reunification strained to the limits the de facto policy coordination required under EMS, as German fiscal deficits led to higher interest rates throughout the EU.

[15] Frieden, "Real Sources."

[16] For an argument along these lines, see Jeffry A. Frieden and Barry Eichengreen, eds., *The Political Economy of European Monetary Integration* (Boulder, Colo.: Westview Press, 2000).

from EMS. British political elites, meanwhile, are notoriously skeptical about deeper European political integration and understand that their continental partners see EMU as a means to achieve this goal. An economically plausible alternative policy strategy was also available to Britain: the retention of a floating currency combined with an independent, inflation-targeting central bank. In France, Germany, and other pro-integration countries, such alternatives were barely discussed.[17]

Developing Countries and "Fear of Floating"

After 1973, most developing countries continued to peg their currencies by retaining capital controls, though there has been an apparent trend toward floating in recent years.[18] Exits from pegged exchange rates in recent years have often been followed by a floating exchange rate combined with CBI and domestic inflation targeting. Examples include Mexico after the 1994–95 crisis, much of East Asia after 1997–98, and Argentina after 2002. Broz argues that this preferred solution is only credible for established democratic countries with relatively transparent processes for setting policy. Less transparent, authoritarian governments can relatively easily interfere with monetary policymaking behind the scenes.[19] In addition, for many developing countries with a history of high inflation, hard currency pegs remained attractive. Argentina's (pre-2002) and Hong Kong's currency board arrangements and fixed pegs against the dollar were prominent examples of this strategy. Partial or complete "dollarization" (in which a country adopts the US dollar or another major currency as a medium of exchange) has been another option for some countries, since it effectively abolishes the exchange rate. In these hard peg cases, the complete loss of monetary policy autonomy is, at least in principle, the main cost, though this

[17] Kenneth Dyson and Kevin Featherstone, *The Road to Maastricht: Negotiating Economic and Monetary Union* (New York: Oxford University Press, 1999).

[18] William Bernhard, J. Lawrence Broz, and William Roberts Clark, "The Political Economy of Monetary Institutions," *International Organization* 56:4, 2002, 701; Carlo Cottarelli and Curzio Giannini, "Credibility without Rules? Monetary Frameworks in the Post–Bretton Woods Era," IMF Occasional Papers 154, December 1997, 10–13.

[19] J. Lawrence Broz, "Political System Transparency and Monetary Commitment Regimes," *International Organization* 56:4, 2002, 861–87.

loss is largely hypothetical for countries in which unofficial private sector dollarization is already well advanced.

Economists have noted that even though a rising number of developing countries have announced floating exchange rate policies, in practice many have retained relatively fixed exchange rates via a mix of capital controls, macroeconomic policy, and currency intervention. This difference between policy rhetoric and practice has been put down to "fear of floating."[20] Empirically, high levels of export dependence (particularly commodity exports) and large foreign currency indebtedness are related to developing countries' pegging. As noted above, Broz argues that undemocratic countries are more likely to adopt (announced) pegged exchange rates than CBI because they lack the political transparency that could make the latter choice credible, but this does not distinguish between announced and de facto exchange rate policies. Alesina and Wagner, who do make this distinction, find that developing countries with better institutions are more likely to combine announced floats with de facto exchange rate management (although institutional quality is not strongly correlated with democracy).[21] They hypothesize that these countries' choices may stem from a desire to signal that they have the ability to adopt "rigorous" policies, distinguishing themselves from governments lacking this ability.

A more straightforward explanation is that the increased threat of currency crises in recent years has encouraged governments to announce currency floats so as to avoid giving financial markets a visible exchange rate target. That is, there is also a growing fear of pegging. Meanwhile, China persists in using capital controls and closely manages its currency against the US dollar (in July 2005 it introduced a limited degree of flexibility by repegging to a currency basket, the components of which are not publicly disclosed). Given China's growing importance in global trade and its position as the most important destination for FDI in the developing world, its currency policy increases the incentive for other developing countries to manage their exchange rate against the dollar.

[20] Calvo and Reinhart, "Fear of Floating."
[21] Alberto Alesina and Alexander Wagner, "Choosing (and Reneging on) Exchange Rate Regimes," NBER Working Paper, 9809, June 2003.

THE CHANGING NATURE OF PUBLIC
INTERNATIONAL FINANCE

What has been the consequence of the revival of private international financial markets for public international finance? We suggest that although private finance increasingly dominates public international finance, the latter is unlikely to disappear because the IFIs remain useful to the major countries. Because many developing countries have experienced financial crises since the 1980s, the role of the IFIs as policy enforcers has increased over time even as their role as providers of finance has diminished.

The political limits to public international finance were obvious in the 1920s in the era of the League of Nations and again at the establishment of the Bretton Woods system in the 1940s. During the Bretton Woods negotiations, American financial interests and Congress argued strongly for limits on the provision of credit to deficit countries on the grounds that unlimited public international finance would ultimately require America to foot the bill for inflationary policies abroad. Since then, this position has become more entrenched. The major developed countries created "club" goods outside of the IMF, such as the G10's reserve swap network in the 1960s. More importantly, they have been able to borrow extensively from private international capital markets. In 1976, when the governments of Britain and Italy lost access to international capital markets, they were forced to accept IMF loans and policy conditionality at considerable domestic political cost. Since the late 1970s, the IFIs have only lent to developing and transition countries. As a result, developed countries increasingly came to see the IFIs less as institutions for collective management as envisaged at Bretton Woods and more as development finance institutions that are potential drains on their fiscal resources and sources of moral hazard. As figure 5.1 shows, there has been a broad trend for private international finance to increase at the same time that all forms of public international financial flows to developing countries have fallen. Official flows (including grant aid) were larger than private flows in the mid-1980s, but since then private capital flows have come to completely dominate external financing in developing countries.

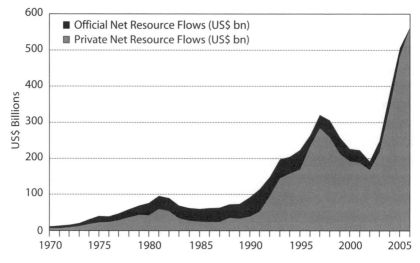

FIGURE 5.1. Total Official and Private Financial Flows to Developing Countries, 1970–2006. *Source*: World Bank, *Global Development Finance* database, 2007.

This development has had two main implications. First, despite periodic increases in the resources of the IMF and World Bank, their total resources have steadily diminished over time in relation to the size of the world economy and especially compared to global capital flows.[22] By the 1960s, creditor countries like West Germany and the Netherlands opposed substantial increases in public international finance. Although the United States was by then a major deficit country, its unequaled ability to borrow without recourse to the IMF has meant that it too has continued to resist substantial increases in IMF resources. This is not to say that the G7 countries have lost interest in the IFIs, as they remain useful tools for managing the consequences of crises in developing countries and, at times, as a source of leverage over them. For example, the Latin American debt crisis of the early 1980s shifted the Reagan administration's position from one of general ideological aversion to international institutions to seeing the IMF and World Bank as highly useful (and briefly helped to bring public international finance back to center stage in the 1980s). The threat posed by the crisis to the stability of US banks was one reason for this shift; concerns about the

[22] James, *International Monetary Cooperation*, 153–54.

broader political, strategic, and economic consequences of the Latin crisis were another.

Second, because the creditor countries themselves no longer conceive of borrowing themselves from the IMF and because they dominate its executive board, they have taken a stricter position on policy conditionality so as to reduce the potential for moral hazard (i.e., the concern that the availability of official finance will encourage risky behavior by the borrower or by private creditors).[23] Since the IMF lacks the resources to act as international LLR, the creditor countries have increasingly emphasized its role as an "agency of constraint," the idea that the Fund can act as a credible external institutional substitute for weak domestic political institutions in developing countries.[24] The growing emphasis on policy conditionality and technical advice, on IFI "stamps of approval" for private capital inflows, and on the IFIs' role in promoting domestic institutional reform all reflect this creditor viewpoint. Since private international capital markets now dominate as a source of international finance, the IFIs are increasingly seen as their handmaiden rather than an alternative. This has eroded the legitimacy of the IFIs, but at the same time their limited enforcement capacity renders illusory the idea that the IFIs can act as credible facilitators of private capital inflows into developing countries.[25]

IFI conditionality has nevertheless allowed the major creditor countries increased influence over developing countries' policies. The growing focus on "good governance" in borrowing countries has been one of the results. IFI conditionality can also work to the advantage of private sector trade, financial, and FDI interests in the developed countries that stand to benefit from the enhanced market access in developing countries that conditionality can bring. For example, the market open-

[23] On IMF conditionality, see Jacques J. Polak, "The Changing Nature of IMF Conditionality," *Princeton Essays in International Finance*, 184, 1991. More generally, moral hazard arises when an explicit or implicit insurance contract induces one or more of the parties to take greater risks.

[24] Michael Bordo, Ashoka Mody, and Nienke Oomes, "Keeping Capital Flowing: The Role of the IMF," IMF Working Paper, WP/04/197 October 2004; Carlo Cottarelli and Curzio Giannini, "Inflation, Credibility, and the Role of the International Monetary Fund," IMF Paper on Policy Analysis and Assessment, PP/AA/98/12, 1998.

[25] Graham Bird and Dale Rowlands, "Catalysis or Direct Borrowing: The Role of the IMF in Mobilising Private Capital," *World Economy* 24:1, 2001, 81–98.

ing achieved in Latin America in the 1980s and some East Asian countries in the late 1990s provided an important political justification for the IMF in the US Congress.[26] This has further reduced the legitimacy of the IFIs for developing countries and incentivized governments to avoid borrowing from them. In recent years, many borrowing countries used favorable economic and financial conditions to repay IMF loans early, producing concerns in some quarters that private international capital markets will after all render the IFIs irrelevant. It is too early to tell whether the growing dominance of private capital inflows in financing will be sustainable, or whether future financial crises will bring developing countries back into the waiting arms of the IMF.

FINANCIAL INTEGRATION AND NATIONAL POLICY AUTONOMY

The declining importance of IFI conditionality as a source of economic policy constraint for many developing countries raises a broader question. Does financial integration in itself constrain domestic economic policy and politics? We address this question initially by discussing the constraints identified by the Mundell-Fleming (MF) model. Although this model suggests that macroeconomic policy retains qualified power under conditions of capital mobility, it significantly underestimates other constraints on policy. Beyond the MF model, there are growing concerns that capital mobility also constrains the ability of governments to tax, borrow, and spend, forcing convergence on a dominant "neoliberal" model. Although such convergence arguments are often overdone, convergence pressures are on average greater for developing countries than for developed countries.

The Mundell-Fleming Model and Policy Constraints

As we saw in the previous chapter, standard macroeconomic theory suggests that capital mobility imposes powerful constraints on national

---

[26] On the relationship between the United States and the IFIs generally, see Ngaire Woods, *The Globalizers: The IMF, the World Bank, and Their Borrowers* (Ithaca, N.Y.: Cornell University Press, 2006).

monetary policy. Given rising capital mobility, this theory says that governments must choose between a fixed exchange rate and monetary policy autonomy. Nevertheless, even if monetary policy is ineffective under fixed exchange rates, fiscal policy remains powerful. Hence, the MF trade-off under conditions of capital mobility could also be described as one between fiscal policy and monetary policy autonomy.

The weaknesses of this model are considerable. First, the model and the related unholy trinity argument are not theories of political economy; that is, they do not explain which choices governments will make. Second, the MF model ignores the credibility problem of fixed exchange rates identified earlier, as well as the importance of the institutional relationship between the government and central bank. Third, the model assumes that in a closed economy, monetary and fiscal policy will both be very powerful. This assumption traces its origins to postwar macroeconomics, dominated by the famous "Phillips curve," which suggested that there was a stable negative relationship between rates of inflation and of unemployment.[27] Keynesian economists popularized the idea in the United Kingdom and United States, arguing that governments could, at least in the short run, choose a desired mix of inflation and unemployment through appropriate fiscal and monetary policy.[28]

An early attempt to explain a government's macroeconomic policies was the theory of "political business cycles" (PBCs), which emerged from Keynesian economics in the 1970s. This suggested that given an exploitable short-run Phillips curve, incumbent governments could use fiscal and monetary policy to maximize their vote prior to elections.[29] This theory predicted a pattern of preelection macroeconomic policy expansions (and hence the possible abandonment of exchange rate pegs) to maximize median voter income, followed by postelection contractions.

An alternative theory was the "partisan" business cycle theory, which assumed that political parties pursue policies of a "left" or "right" variety that catered to their core electoral constituencies. An early contribution was made by Kalecki, who criticized Keynes for assuming full em-

[27] A. W. Phillips, "The Relation between Unemployment and the Rate of Change of Money Wages in the United Kingdom, 1861–1957," *Economica* 25:4, 1958, 283–99.

[28] Fischer, "Modern Central Banking," 266–70.

[29] William D. Nordhaus, "The Political Business Cycle," *Review of Economic Studies* 42:2, 1975, 169–90.

ployment policies were politically sustainable, arguing that employers would see their bargaining power vis-à-vis labor collapse in such circumstances.[30] He suggested that right-of-center, business-oriented governments would contract the economy before full employment was reached to ensure business profitability. Left-of-center governments, more attached to full employment policies, would be in constant conflict with private business preferences. This theory has received modest empirical support, but the demise of the Keynesian economic ideas that underpinned it has reduced its appeal.

Other partisan theories exist. In the Phillips curve tradition, Hibbs argued that left-of-center parties prioritize fighting unemployment and right-of-center parties fight inflation.[31] When in government, such parties would use monetary and fiscal policy to achieve a partisan position on the short-run Phillips curve. This theory also implies that left-wing governments will be more willing to sacrifice exchange rate pegs in order to achieve economic expansions. In contrast to the PBC theory, policy shifts would occur immediately after rather than before elections when new incumbents were in place. The ability of this theory to explain macroeconomic shifts in particular countries is also limited. It is inconsistent, for example, with expansionary policies under British Conservative governments in the early 1970s and late 1980s and with the famous "U-turn" of the French socialists under President Mitterand from 1983. Even so, more recent studies have found that a general partisan effect continues to exist even given high levels of capital mobility.[32]

A third kind political economy theory that takes account of openness is Frieden's sectoral approach, which we have already encountered. Briefly, this theory suggests that interest groups that are mainly dependent on the domestic economy (the nontradables sector generally and import-competing sectors) will prefer the government prioritize monetary policy autonomy rather than stable exchange rates. In contrast, export-oriented sectors will prefer stable exchange rates, since expan-

---

[30] Michael Kalecki, "Political Aspects of Full Employment," *Political Quarterly* 14, October–December 1943, 322–31.

[31] Douglas A. Hibbs, "Political Parties and Macroeconomic Policy," *American Political Science Review* 71:4, 1977, 1467–87.

[32] Garrett, *Partisan Politics*; Thomas Oatley, "How Constraining Is Capital Mobility? The Partisan Hypothesis in an Open Economy," *American Journal of Political Science* 43:4, 1999, 1003–27.

sionary monetary policy will have little effect on the final demand for their output and it could undermine their price competitiveness if it raises input costs. Financial sector interests are less easily determined and are likely to depend on the structure of corporate financing and of financial sector activities. Frieden also argues that different sectors also have different preferences relating to the *level* of the exchange rate, with, for example, export-oriented and import-competing sectors favoring a relatively undervalued exchange rate. As with the partisan theory, there is some evidence of sectoral pressures on macroeconomic policymaking, but extensive lobbying by societal interests on macroeconomic policy appears to be unusual.[33]

All of the above political economy literature depends on the MF model and assumes that the macroeconomic policy tools available to governments are potentially powerful. However, a series of influential criticisms of the embedded Keynesian assumptions in postwar macroeconomics implies substantial limits to stabilization policy even within financially closed economies. The 1970s experience of stagflation (simultaneously rising unemployment and inflation) undermined the assumption of a stable Phillips curve and shifted the policy debate decisively in favor of monetarists. This school argued that attempts by the authorities to keep unemployment permanently below the "natural rate" would lead to accelerating inflation once the private sector adjusted its expectations.[34] This "natural rate of unemployment" was defined as the equilibrium level of unemployment to which the economy would return in the long run. In a boom or recession, the actual rate of unemployment would temporarily be lower or higher than the natural rate. The government might engineer such a temporary boom with expansionary policy, but eventually this would feed through into higher inflation, and employment would fall back to its natural level. Additional macroeconomic stimulus would only produce even higher inflation.

[33] See, for example, the US evidence in I. M. Destler and C. Randall Henning, *Dollar Politics: Exchange Rate Policymaking in the United States* (Washington, DC: Institute for International Economics, 1989).

[34] Milton Friedman, "The Role of Monetary Policy," *American Economic Review* 58:1, 1968, 1–17; Edmund S. Phelps, "Phillips Curves, Expectations of Inflation, and Optimal Unemployment over Time," *Economica* 34:3, 1967, 254–81.

The policy implications of monetarist analysis were revolutionary. Keynesian "fine-tuning" could not permanently affect the real economy, and macroeconomic policy activism would only exacerbate the business cycle in the long run, accelerating wage and price inflation. Money itself was "neutral" in the long run and effectively irrelevant to the workings of the economy.

The rational expectations (RE) revolution in macroeconomic theory, which followed on the heels of the monetarist school, was a further blow for Keynesian economics and for the political economy theories that emerged from it. Keynesians and monetarists assumed that private actors were myopic: they had backward-looking, "adaptive" expectations and could be fooled every few years by crafty governments. RE theorists such as Lucas rejected this assumption.[35] If people were rational and took the intentions of government into account, they would adjust their behavior rapidly in anticipation. Predictable monetary expansion could therefore have no real economic effects even in the short run. In this case, the Phillips curve was vertical; if attempted, expansionary policies would lead only to higher inflation. It should be emphasized that these conclusions applied to *closed* as much as to open economies: they only required domestic firms and unions to adjust their expectations to higher inflation in a rational manner.[36] The RE theory predicted that left-of-center governments would be particularly constrained by rational private sector behavior since they would be most tempted by macroeconomic expansion.[37]

The theory implied that governments might still surprise voters, unions, and firms with policies that could not easily be predicted from electoral incentives or ideological preferences. PBC and partisan theories were subsequently reformulated along rational expectations lines, reinstating the earlier claims of a politically induced real business

[35] Robert E. Lucas Jr., "Some International Evidence on Output-Inflation Tradeoffs," *American Economic Review* 63:3, 1973, 326–34.

[36] Even so, financial openness could raise further the costs of macroeconomic activism by introducing the possibility of an inflation-depreciation spiral, and currency crises for countries with fixed exchange rates (Paul R. Krugman, "A Model of Balance of Payments Crises," *Journal of Money, Credit and Banking* 11:3, 1979, 311–24).

[37] Fritz Scharpf, *Crisis and Choice in European Social Democracy* (Ithaca, N.Y.: Cornell University Press, 1991).

cycle.[38] One partisan model assumed that voters, being uncertain in election years about which government would be elected, cannot know future output growth and inflation until the election is over.[39] If wage contracts are set in the preelection period according to the expected election outcome and persist beyond it, unless the "left" is expected to gain office with 100% certainty, a left victory leads to overexpansion of the economy in the postelection period and a right victory leads to contraction. Only when wage bargainers eventually reset contracts will the economy return to its natural equilibrium.

Although the empirical evidence did not favor extreme versions of the Lucas argument, the emerging consensus was that active demand management was more difficult than Keynesians had assumed.[40] Prominent economists provided theoretical arguments for making central banks independent of government so as to rule out politically driven policy surprises.[41] The German and Swiss experiences in the 1970s seemed to support the claim that independent central banks that targeted low inflation produced better overall macroeconomic performance in the long run.[42] Others argue that the evidence for these claims is weak and that the associated policy recommendations reflect ideology rather than hard science.[43]

[38] See the papers collected in Torsten Persson and Guido Tabellini, *Political Economy: Explaining Economic Policy* (Cambridge: MIT Press, 2000).

[39] Alberto Alesina, "Macroeconomic Policy in a Two-Party System as a Repeated Game," *Quarterly Journal of Economics* 102:3, 1987, 651–78.

[40] Fischer, "Modern Central Banking"; Robert King and Mark Watson, "The Post-war U.S. Phillips Curve: A Revisionist Econometric History," *Carnegie-Rochester Conference Series on Public Policy* 41, 1994, 157–219.

[41] Robert J. Barro and David B. Gordon, "Rules, Discretion and Reputation in a Model of Monetary Policy," *Journal of Monetary Economics* 12:1, 1983, 101–21; Kenneth Rogoff, "The Optimal Degree of Commitment to an Intermediate Monetary Target," *Quarterly Journal of Economics* 100:4, 1985, 1169–90.

[42] Alberto Alesina and Lawrence H. Summers, "Central Bank Independence and Macroeconomic Performance: Some Comparative Evidence," *Journal of Money, Credit and Banking* 24:2, 1993, 151–62; Alex Cukierman, *Central Bank Strategy, Credibility, and Independence* (Cambridge: MIT Press, 1992); Robert J. Franzese Jr., "Institutional and Sectoral Interactions in Monetary Policy and Wage/Price-Bargaining," in Peter A. Hall and David Soskice, eds., *Varieties of Capitalism: The Institutional Foundations of Comparative Advantage* (Oxford: Oxford University Press, 2001), 104–44.

[43] Philip Keefer and David Stasavage, "The Limits of Delegation, Veto Players, Central Bank Independence, and the Credibility of Monetary Policy," *American Political Science Review* 47:3,

The MF model suggests that fiscal policy only has strong effects under fixed exchange rates. But this does not mean that fiscal expansion will be avoided under floating exchange rates or that it is without powerful distributional effects. The costs of exchange rate appreciation are borne largely by the tradables sector, whereas sheltered sectors may benefit from fiscal activism. In the United States during the first Reagan administration, the tradables sector was politically weak compared to the constituencies that benefited from tax cuts and increased defense spending. Much also depends on the interaction between fiscal and monetary policy. In the Reagan-era case, fiscal expansion led an independent and newly inflation-conscious Federal Reserve to tighten monetary policy, resulting in rising interest rates and an appreciating currency that offset the expansionary effects and eventually threatened a protectionist backlash. A more subordinate central bank might have accommodated the fiscal expansion, producing higher inflation and currency depreciation. This occurred under the French socialist government of the early 1980s, which chose fiscal expansion and monetary accommodation, producing rising inflation, large external deficits, and a series of currency devaluations in the EMS. The different outcomes of the French and US fiscal expansions in the early 1980s also support the view that fiscal policy is weaker (under both fixed and floating exchange rates) as trade openness rises.

Many argue that a more important constraint on fiscal activism than its interaction with the exchange rate is the threat posed by capital mobility to government spending and taxation.[44] Mosley, for example, argues that financial markets place strong pressure on countries to reduce inflation and the size of fiscal deficits.[45] First, government borrowing reduces the available supply of savings, raising

---

2003, 389–403; Suzanne Lohmann, "Federalism and Central Bank Independence: The Politics of German Monetary Policy, 1957–92," *World Politics* 50:3, 1998, 401–46; Adam Posen, "Central Bank Independence and Disinflationary Credibility: A Missing Link?" *Oxford Economic Papers* 50:3, 1998, 335–59; Grabel, "Ideology, Power"; McNamara, *Currency of Ideas*.

[44] Here we restrict our discussion to the effects of capital mobility on fiscal deficits, leaving discussion of broad trends in spending and taxation to the following section.

[45] Layna Mosley, *Global Capital and National Governments* (Cambridge: Cambridge University Press, 2003).

the cost of new debt. Second, financial markets fear default as indebtedness rises. Default can take two different forms: partial default via inflation, which reduces the value of debt held by investors, or outright default (repudiation). The former is more likely in developed countries, since they usually have developed government bond markets. Institutions like CBI, balanced budget rules, and political checks and balances on executive authority can reduce the risk of inflation and thereby lower the marginal cost of additional debt. Outright default is more likely in developing countries, Mosley suggests, because they often lack developed government bond markets and they often borrow in foreign currencies from international investors. The lack of developed domestic financial markets in many developing countries should therefore increase the impact of capital account opening relative to developed countries.

On average, fiscal deficits in the developed countries have decreased since 1980, consistent with Mosley's argument. But there are important exceptions to this trend, suggesting that the constraining effects of capital markets are rather weak for developed countries. In spite of Japan's record and persistent fiscal deficits since the early 1990s, the nominal interest rates on government bonds have been extraordinarily low. The United States, as we have seen, has an unparalleled ability to finance fiscal deficits because of the role of the dollar as a global reserve currency. Heavy purchases of US Treasury bonds by central banks and private investors allowed the United States to run large fiscal deficits after 2001 without increasing borrowing costs (indeed, US government bond yields fell steadily over 2000–2003). In the case of the United Kingdom since 1997, a shift to the political left eventually resulted in rising levels of government expenditure, consistent with the claim that partisan politics remains alive under financial openness. Capital and income taxes also rose somewhat, but not by enough to finance the higher levels of government expenditure. The result was a rising fiscal deficit starting in 2001, but the political independence of the central bank from 1997 and low global interest rates facilitated falling rather than rising government borrowing costs. These cases suggest that financial openness allows very creditworthy governments to tap world savings and run fiscal deficits at low cost. European evidence in the

1990s also shows that debt costs fell for all countries even though average debt levels rose.[46]

What of the evidence regarding fiscal policy constraints in developing countries? For the "emerging market" countries that enjoy access to international capital markets, the degree of constraint imposed tends to be dynamically unstable because of herd behavior: very weak during good times, very strong during bad.[47] For example, many Latin American governments in the 1970s sustained heavy borrowing from international banks, only to see their access suddenly cut off during the crisis of the early 1980s. The same phenomenon can be seen in the heavy international lending to Asia in the early 1990s and the rapid retrenchment beginning in mid-1997. The oscillations of the long cycle of net financial transfers to developing countries in the form of bonds and bank loans can be seen clearly in figure 5.2. During good times, implied real interest rates on borrowing by developing countries have been low and sometimes negative, encouraging rather than constraining overborrowing.[48] As Willett has argued, international financial constraint has therefore been "too much, too late" for many developing countries.[49]

There is no agreement on what level of borrowing is sustainable for developing countries. Argentina's total federal and provincial public sector debt was 62% at the end of 2001, much smaller than Italy's, Belgium's, and Japan's.[50] Its consolidated fiscal deficit was nearly 6% of

[46] Bank of Italy, *Public Finance Statistics in the European Union*, Supplements to the Statistical Bulletin, n.s., Year 9, 62, December 31, 1999 (Rome: Bank of Italy), 7. Evidence from before 1914 also shows that governments did not lose access to international capital markets for debt ratios in excess of 200% of GDP, and that the cost of borrowing did not increase prohibitively at high debt levels (Flandreau, Le Cacheux, and Zumer, "Stability without a Pact?" 140–45).

[47] On herd behavior in financial markets generally, see Robert J. Shiller, *Irrational Exuberance* (Princeton, N.J.: Princeton University Press, 2nd ed., 2005).

[48] Rimmer de Vries, "Adam Smith: Managing the Global Wealth of Nations," in Morgan Guaranty Trust Company of New York, *World Financial Markets* (New York: The Company, 1990), 2. Most recently, real interest rates in the international interbank market for US dollars were negative between 2002 and 2005 and again in 2008.

[49] Thomas D. Willett, "International Financial Markets as Sources of Crises or Discipline: The Too Much, Too Late Hypothesis," *Princeton Essays in International Finance*, May 2000.

[50] However, in contrast to these developed countries, fully 97% of Argentina's public debt was in foreign currency. See IMF, *Argentina: 2002 Article IV Consultation*, IMF Country Report 03/226 (Washington, D.C., July 2003), 46.

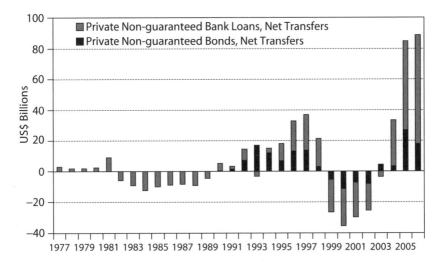

FIGURE 5.2. Net Transfers to Developing Countries, Bonds and Bank Loans, 1977–2006, US$ Billions. *Source:* World Bank, *Global Development Finance* database, 2007.

GDP, similar to that of the United States in recent years. The general tendency for developing countries to experience debt crises at levels of indebtedness that are generally easily manageable for developed countries is commonly referred to as "debt intolerance." In the Argentine case, when financial markets panicked in early 2002, what was formerly seen as a sustainable level of public debt suddenly became excessive. A deepening recession and dramatically increased interest rates prompted Argentina's government to default. Thus, although the degree of fiscal policy constraint imposed by global capital markets on developing countries is volatile, it is clear that the average level of constraint is much greater than for developed countries.[51]

This generalization is vulnerable to the criticism that the distinction between developed and developing countries is vague and overdrawn. The largest developed countries, the United States, Japan, and Germany, appear to be relatively privileged in their ability to borrow from global capital markets and may therefore be empowered rather than

[51] Carmen M. Reinhart, Kenneth S. Rogoff, and Miguel A. Savastano, "Debt Intolerance," *Brookings Papers on Economic Activity* 1, 2003, 1–74.

constrained by financial integration. China, among developing countries, also appears to be relatively privileged. The criticism also raises a number of interesting definitional and practical questions. Where should we (and where do global capital markets) draw the line between "developing" and "developed" countries? Is the line between them an absolute or a relative one? When do countries "graduate" to developed status? When they acquire "developed" domestic bond markets? There are no easy answers to these questions. As we have seen, Mosley argues that the presence of outright default risk is the characteristic that defines a developing country as such in the eyes of international investors. But as she notes, one of the reasons why such countries acquired default risk is because in the past they often borrowed in foreign currencies that they cannot print (original sin).[52] Yet it was investors who lent to developing countries in foreign currencies, thus creating default risk! This appears to be another area in which investor attitudes acquire self-fulfilling properties.

Convergence toward Neoliberalism?

We conclude this chapter by addressing arguments that financial openness increases pressure on states to converge on a neoliberal economic policy model. "Neoliberal" ideal types are as contentious as "social democratic" and "developmental state" models, and for reasons of space we avoid much of the debate concerning their nature.[53] Here, we restrict our attention to only two questions. First, has financial globalization undermined the welfare state in advanced countries? Second, has financial globalization undermined state-led development strategies?[54] Fi-

---

[52] Mosley, *Global Capital*, 114.

[53] On the first two, see Gøsta Esping-Andersen, *The Three Worlds of Welfare Capitalism* (Princeton, N.J.: Princeton University Press, 1990). On the developmental state, see Peter L. Berger and H. H. Michael Hsaio, eds., *In Search of an East Asian Developmental Model* (New Brunswick, N.J.: Transaction Books, 1987); Robert Wade, *Governing the Market: Economic Theory and the Role of Government in East Asian Industrialization* (Princeton, N.J.: Princeton University Press, 1990); and Meredith Woo-Cumings, ed., *The Developmental State* (Ithaca, N.Y.: Cornell University Press, 1999).

[54] For a succinct review of the domestic effects of globalization, see Suzanne Berger, "Globalization and Politics," *Annual Review of Political Science* 3, 2000, 43–62.

nally, we discuss briefly whether financial globalization is promoting the harmonization of financial regulatory policies across all countries.

THE END OF THE WELFARE STATE?

Those who argue that financial integration is undermining the European social democratic welfare model usually claim that capital mobility provides owners of capital with a powerful exit option, and a correspondingly enhanced political voice in policy outcomes. The result, they claim, is a process of convergence of policies on the preferences of market agents and an evisceration of the capabilities of the welfare state.[55] This process is also said to favor the political Right at the expense of the Left.[56]

Against this "efficiency hypothesis," the "compensation hypothesis" predicts instead a positive relationship between economic openness and welfare spending.[57] Economic openness increases the exposure of societal groups to international shocks, leading to increased demand for welfare policies that reduce the costs of adjustment to such shocks (including unemployment benefits, universal health-care provision, worker retraining, child-care provision, etc.).

Which of these two predictions is correct? The average trend in OECD countries' government spending has been upward for most years since the 1970s; the same is true for average levels of social welfare expenditure in particular.[58] This is taken by proponents of the compen-

---

[55] E.g., Philip G. Cerny, "International Finance and the Erosion of Capitalist Diversity," in Colin Crouch and Wolfgang Streeck, eds., *Political Economy of Modern Capitalism* (London: Sage, 1997), 173–81; Paulette Kurzer, *Business and Banking: Political Change and Economic Integration in Western Europe* (Ithaca, N.Y.: Cornell University Press, 1993).

[56] John Gray, *False Dawn: The Delusions of Global Capitalism* (New York: Simon and Schuster, 1998); William Greider, *One World Ready or Not: The Manic Logic of Global Capitalism* (New York: Simon and Schuster, 1998); Dani Rodrik, *Has Globalization Gone Too Far?* (Washington, D.C.: Institute for International Economics, 1997); Scharpf, *Crisis and Choice*.

[57] The efficiency hypothesis is sometimes given different names, such as the capital markets hypothesis, but these alternatives are less preferable because they do not always indicate the direction of the predicted effect. The original source of the compensation argument is David R. Cameron, "The Expansion of the Public Economy: A Comparative Analysis," *American Political Science Review* 72:4, 1978, 1243–61.

[58] Garrett, *Partisan Politics*; Vicente Navarro, John Schmitt, and Javier Astudillo, "Is Globalization Undermining the Welfare State?" *Cambridge Journal of Economics* 28:1, 2004, 133–52.

sation hypothesis as strong evidence in favor of their position that left-wing policies in the form of high levels of taxation and public welfare spending are sustainable in the face of globalization. Against this view is evidence of substantial reductions in social welfare expenditure as a proportion of GDP in some Scandinavian in the 1990s, notably Finland (table 5.1). Garrett argues that the retrenchment in Scandinavia was due to unrelated factors, such as the collapse of the USSR, domestic banking crises, and the pressures of EMU qualification. It is also evident from table 5.1 that average welfare expenditure across the OECD has continued to rise since 1980 and that it remains relatively high in Scandinavia. Some of the largest increases in welfare expenditure have occurred in outlier countries such as Mexico and Japan. Even if governments have been under pressure to reduce taxation and expenditure, which seems undeniable, voters and other organized interests such as unions have for the most part successfully resisted welfare cuts.[59] Consistent with this explanation, there is some evidence that financial openness reduces welfare spending in developing countries with relatively weak unions and authoritarian political regimes.[60]

As regards taxation, proponents of the efficiency hypothesis argue that capital mobility facilitates tax arbitrage, leading governments to reduce capital taxation in a race to the bottom. This may also force governments to shift the burden of taxation toward less mobile actors.[61] The evidence for this claim is mixed. Others argue that although taxes generally have risen over time to finance higher government expenditure, effective (as opposed to "headline") capital and corporation tax rates also show surprising stability over time—indeed, the average OECD effective capital tax rate has risen substantially since the 1960s.[62]

---

[59] Paul Pierson, "The New Politics of the Welfare State," *World Politics* 48:2, 1996, 143–79.

[60] Nita Rudra, "Globalization and the Decline of the Welfare State in Less-Developed Countries," *International Organization* 56:2, 2002, 411–45; Nita Rudra and Stephan Haggard, "Globalization, Democracy, and Effective Welfare Spending in the Developed World," *Comparative Political Studies* 38:9, 2005, 1015–49.

[61] Sven Steinmo, "The End of Redistributive Taxation: Tax Reform in a Global World Economy," *Challenge* 37:6, 1994, 9–17.

[62] Garrett, *Partisan Politics*; Andrew Glyn, "The Assessment: Economic Policy and Social Democracy," *Oxford Review of Economic Policy* 14:1, 1998, 1–18; Navarro, Schmitt, and Astudillo, "Is Globalization Undermining Welfare State?"; Duane C. Swank, *Global Capital, Political Institutions, and Policy Change in Developed Welfare States* (Cambridge: Cambridge University Press, 2002);

TABLE 5.1
Public Social Expenditure as a Percentage of GDP, Selected Countries and Years

	1980	1985	1990	1995	2000	2003
Finland	18.4	22.8	24.5	27.4	21.3	22.5
France	20.8	25.8	25.3	28.3	27.6	28.7
Germany	23.0	23.6	22.5	26.6	26.3	27.3
Japan	10.3	11.2	11.2	13.9	16.1	17.7
Mexico		1.9	3.6	4.7	5.8	6.8
Poland			15.1	23.1	21.2	22.9
Sweden	28.6	29.7	30.5	32.5	28.8	31.3
United Kingdom	16.6	19.6	17.2	20.4	19.1	20.6
United States	13.3	12.9	13.4	15.4	14.6	16.2
OECD average	17.4	18.5	17.9	19.9	19.6	20.9

Source: OECD, Social Expenditure Database, 2007.

The exceptions are a few "liberal" countries like the United States, Canada, and Japan where, contrary to popular perception, there is heavier reliance on capital taxes and where right-of-center parties have reduced effective capital taxation rates. In contrast, consensual and relatively labor-rich democracies, such as in Scandinavia, build in more checks against majority (labor) power, resulting in lower average capital taxation rates. Hays argues that this suggests that rising capital mobility has produced a convergence on *average* international levels rather than a race to the bottom.[63] In fact, the variance in effective capital taxation rates across the OECD has fallen over time, and capital taxation rates have also risen in countries with initially low rates. Furthermore, the average differential between labor and capital taxation has shifted steadily in favor of capital, consistent with the efficiency hypothesis.

In sum, globalization has not to date undermined social democratic welfare policies in Europe or elsewhere in the OECD, though there has been some retrenchment in some very high spending Scandinavian countries. In addition, in the United States and some other Anglo-Saxon countries, there has been a shift away from state welfare provi-

---

Duane C. Swank and Sven Steinmo, "The New Political Economy of Taxation in Advanced Capitalist Democracies," *American Journal of Political Science* 46:3, 2002, 642–55.

[63] Jude C. Hays, "Globalization and Capital Taxation in Consensus and Majoritarian Democracies," *World Politics* 56:1, 2003, 79–113.

sion toward a greater emphasis on the privatization of some services (such as health care) and the empowerment of individuals (notably through so-called workfare programs). Whether such microlevel changes in welfare policy are due to financial openness is not at all evident, however. Although there has been less change in continental Europe, all is not well with the European welfare state, as witnessed by the increasingly contentious national debates over welfare reform in many countries. Democratic politics and organized pro-welfare interests have often successfully resisted policies aimed at welfare cuts (in contrast to the situation in many developing countries). Again, it remains unclear how much this retrenchment pressure is due to financial openness and how much is due to other factors such as changing demographics. As regards the financing of government spending, it may be that the social democratic countries are less vulnerable to the erosion of the capital tax base than are the liberal majoritarian countries.

The End of State-Led Development Strategies?

Financial openness may impose constraints on policy in less developed countries in areas other than social welfare spending. During the Latin American debt crisis of the 1980s, a prolonged recession threatened the traditional strategy of "indebted industrialization."[64] Until the early 1980s, Latin American governments had used foreign borrowing to finance the large external deficits associated with an import substitution policy. Once the debt crisis broke in 1982, IFI conditionality led to greater openness to trade and capital flows. The crisis also favored the rise of new technocratic political elites in countries like Argentina, Brazil, and Mexico who favored a new policy of deeper integration into the world economy and who accepted the emerging Washington consensus on economic policy (see chapter 4). In short, the results of financial opening in Latin America have been periodic economic crises that, at least until recently, encouraged the rejection of past policies of development via import substitution industrialization (ISI). Ironically, however, although ISI was long associated with excessive external bor-

[64] Alice H. Amsden, *Asia's Next Giant* (New York: Oxford University Press, 1989); Jeffry A. Frieden, "Third World Indebted Industrialization: International Finance and State Capitalism in Mexico, Brazil, Algeria, and South Korea," *International Organization* 35:3, 1981, 407–31.

rowing, trade and financial opening did not reduce reliance on external borrowing. Indeed, neoliberal reforms were designed to keep the foreign money flowing in.

The financial crises suffered in Latin America resulted recently in a backlash against neoliberal policies in some countries, notably Argentina and Venezuela. This backlash has arguably been largely rhetorical, though the renationalization of private sector assets in Venezuela and Bolivia suggests it is more than talk. The strong desire of Argentina to escape IMF conditionality by rebuilding foreign exchange reserves and repaying its debts to the IMF early also reflect the disillusionment with neoliberalism and the perception that the international financial community has benefited at the expense of developing countries. Rising levels of economic inequality across the region have also fed disillusionment.[65] As yet, however, there has been no generalized return to ISI policies, even if region-wide free trade initiatives have stalled and governments have become more interventionist in some countries.

By contrast with ISI policies in Latin America, the East Asian developmental model in the mid-1990s seemed in robust health. Countries like Korea and Taiwan had very successfully focused on export promotion and avoided, in part because of their high domestic savings, heavy foreign indebtedness. Less discussed at the time was the very high indebtedness of firms in countries like Indonesia, Korea, Malaysia, and Thailand, a product of bank-financed expansion. After the Asian financial crisis of 1997, however, the conventional wisdom about the Asian model was turned on its head. Some argued that financial opening, said to be the result of IMF and US government pressure, had undermined these Asian economies by encouraging the substitution of domestic for cheaper foreign debt.[66] Others argued that the Asian model was itself fundamentally flawed: government-directed credit allocation and weak prudential regulation had created implicit guarantees of risky investments, excessive leverage, and high vulnerability to economic downturn.[67]

[65] Geoffrey Garrett, "Globalization's Missing Middle," *Foreign Affairs* 83:6, 2004, 72–83.

[66] Robert Wade and Frank Veneroso, "The Asian Crisis: The High Debt Model versus the Wall Street–Treasury–IMF Complex," *New Left Review* 288, March–April 1998, 3–23.

[67] Nicholas Crafts, "Implications of Financial Crisis for East Asian Trend Growth," *Oxford Review of Economic Policy* 15:3, 1999, 110–31; Paul R. Krugman, "What Happened to Asia?" unpublished paper, January 1998.

Both sides in this debate agreed that heavy external hard currency borrowing, mostly by the private sector, had proven disastrous in the crisis-hit countries. Growing financial openness combined with pegged or managed exchange rates facilitated this borrowing, much of which was short term. In countries like Thailand, capital increasingly flowed into speculation, notably in the real estate sector. In contrast, China, with an even weaker banking sector, was protected because the debt of state-owned enterprises was domestic (many would say because of the use of capital controls).

Although Wade and Veneroso are right that this growing reliance on external borrowing was problematic, it is not clear that capital account liberalization was a product of external pressure. In Thailand, domestic financial interests wished to promote Bangkok as a regional financial center, while in Korea, the chaebol (conglomerates) lobbied for greater access to cheaper foreign bank loans. In response, the Korean government liberalized short-term capital flows and offshore bank borrowing rather than FDI, which would have increased competition for the major chaebol. Although this partial version of capital account liberalization was especially risky, it was consistent with Korea's developmental model and domestic politics. This model was premised on the promotion of domestically controlled industrial groups, usually family owned, with foreign firms being substantially excluded from the domestic market.

The consequences of financial crisis for Indonesia, Korea, and Thailand have been great. When Asian currencies collapsed, the real external debt burden rose, and bankruptcies occurred throughout the economy. This required government bailouts of affected banks and firms, large international rescue packages, and IFI conditionality. The IMF programs placed pressure on these countries to reduce corporate debt levels and to end practices associated with old-style industrial policy, including extensive patronage networks in Indonesia. Across Asia and much of the rest of the developing world, governments were encouraged to adopt international "best practice" standards in areas ranging from banking regulation and supervision, corporate governance, and financial reporting (see below). As in Latin America, the IFIs found common cause with local technocratic reformers in the crisis-hit countries who favored a convergence on Western regulatory practices.

It is less clear how deep has been the change in financial governance in East Asia since the crisis. Compliance with international regulatory standards has often been superficial because the implied behavioral change is very costly for the private sector and governments and because the true quality of compliance is difficult for outsiders to monitor.[68] In Korea, the country besides Japan most associated with the East Asian developmental state, financial regulators still intervened to prop up faltering industrial giants some years after the crisis, including by encouraging banks to lend in contravention of new financial regulations.[69] A recent backlash against foreign ownership of banks and key industrial assets in Korea suggests that developmental state tendencies have not entirely disappeared. Meanwhile, in China, the government successfully combined partial integration with the global economy with extensive national economic management.

In short, financial integration has posed a substantial challenge to the East Asian developmental model. Financial regulation, which in the past was subordinated to growth and industrial policy objectives, has been upgraded and regulatory agencies have been newly created or improved. Average levels of corporate indebtedness in Korea have been dramatically reduced, and today average debt-to-equity ratios of Korean conglomerates are below that of Western countries. But some aspects of developmentalism persist, and it is doubtful that Korea and other Asian countries have converged on an Anglo-Saxon economic model, as some have claimed.[70] The impressive postcrisis growth of many East Asian countries has facilitated adaptation to financial openness rather than convergence.

INTERNATIONAL REGULATORY COORDINATION: TOWARD HARMONIZATION?

Finally, has financial globalization promoted international cooperation between financial regulators and regulatory policy convergence? The standard rationale for financial regulation is that financial markets are especially prone to market failure due to information asymmetries, be-

[68] Andrew Walter, *Governing Finance: East Asia's Adoption of International Standards* (Ithaca, N.Y.: Cornell University Press, 2008).

[69] Edward M. Graham, *Reforming Korea's Industrial Conglomerates* (Washington, D.C.: Institute for International Economics, 2003).

[70] See Walter, *Governing Finance*. For the alternative view that Asian capitalism is being fundamentally transformed, see Iain Pirie, "The New Korean State," *New Political Economy* 10:1, 2005, 25–42; and Kanishka Jayasuriya, "Beyond Institutional Fetishism: From the Developmental to the Regulatory State," *New Political Economy* 10:3, 2005, 381–87.

cause lenders possess less information than borrowers.[71] Market failure comes in three forms. First, moral hazard can arise because borrowers misrepresent their real position on the assumption that if they run into difficulties, creditors will be forced to agree to better terms, or because creditors assume that in the event of borrower difficulties, other creditors will intervene to provide support. Second, poor information can lead creditors to underestimate underlying risk and to overlend (or to underprice credit) in economic upswings. Strategic considerations can exacerbate this tendency, producing herding and asset price booms, because in such circumstances cautious lenders risk losing market share to more aggressive lenders.[72] The counterpart of this is the tendency of creditors to overestimate risk during downturns and to ration credit to all borrowers, on the assumption that any demand for borrowing reflects a weak financial position (so-called adverse selection).[73] Third, "contagion effects" can lead rational depositors to withdraw money from solvent banks in fractional reserve systems, precipitating a generalized banking crisis and macroeconomic contraction.[74] As the prices of financial assets depend on expectations about the future, informational asymmetries can produce self-fulfilling crises.[75]

Some or all of these forms of market failure have been in evidence in recent developing country financial crises, and in the financial turmoil that spread from the US sub-prime mortgage market in August

[71] Joseph E. Stiglitz and Andrew Weiss, "Credit Rationing in Markets with Imperfect Information," *American Economic Review* 71:3, 1981, 393–410; Charles Wyplosz, "International Financial Instability," in Inge Kaul, Isabelle Grunberg, and Marc A. Stern, eds., *Global Public Goods: International Cooperation in the 21st Century* (New York: Oxford University Press, 1999), 152–89.

[72] During asset price booms, a kind of inverse Gresham's Law may apply in which bad banks drive in good banks. As Chuck Prince, former head of Citigroup, the largest US bank, said in 2007, "So long as the music is playing, you've got to keep dancing." (John Kay, "Bankers, Like Gangs, Just Get Carried Away," *FT.com*, February 12, 2008).

[73] This effect was evident in the UK mortgage market in early 2008, when many banks withdrew riskier mortgage loans in response to similar actions by competitors (presumably on the assumption that if they did not do so, they risked gaining clients with an above-average credit risk). When most banks are trying to *reduce* their market share, a credit crunch ensues.

[74] D. W. Diamond and P. H. Dybvig, "Bank Runs, Deposit Insurance, and Liquidity," *Journal of Political Economy* 91:3, 1983, 401–19.

[75] Nor may market solutions to these problems be sufficient. Risk insurance (including through the provision of financial hedging techniques) and risk assessment/credit rating are prone to similar information problems.

2007. This latest episode has demonstrated the willingness of central banks to provide LLR assistance to commercial banks in crises (and, since early 2008, to extend such assistance to other financial institutions linked to banks).[76] Some countries have also adopted deposit insurance schemes to limit the potential for bank runs. These policies potentially exacerbate the moral hazard problem, creating a rationale for "prudential regulation" that imposes constraints on bank behavior, such as reserve requirements and interest rate controls. Since the costs of such financial regulation are highly concentrated (falling heavily on banks) and its benefits (greater financial stability) are widely spread, the former have stronger incentives to lobby governments to loosen prudential regulation than the latter have to lobby for tightening. Financial innovation can also allow banks and other financial firms to circumvent regulation. The result is that even strong prudential regulation can erode over time, particularly in countries where banks are closely connected to centers of political power and to national development objectives.

Financial globalization has exacerbated this dynamic tendency toward domestic regulatory failure. The informational asymmetries typical in financial markets are often greater at the international level, and information about borrowers in developing countries is often especially poor. In such circumstances, destabilizing herding phenomena are more likely, when international banks and other investors follow major investors into (and subsequently out of) developing countries' economies, leading to self-fulfilling boom-and-bust cycles in international financial flows. In addition, the globalization of the financial industry itself has threatened to undermine national regulatory frameworks. Foreign entry into domestic financial industries has disrupted domestic banking cartels, complicated the problem of who regulates whom, and raised concerns that mobile financial firms might gravitate toward lightly regulated jurisdictions.

In response, central banks and regulators in developed countries have focused on two main areas: (1) clarifying national responsibilities for regulating international banks, and (2) coordinating improvements in

[76] The US Federal Reserve's bailout of Bear Stearns, America's fifth-largest investment bank, in early 2008 indicates the way in which LLR responsibilities can be forced to expand in response to financial innovation.

regulatory standards and practices. In the first area, governments want to ensure that they do not bear large regulatory and LLR costs when they permit foreign-owned financial firms to operate within their domestic markets. This concern is strongest for countries with international financial centers, notably the United States and United Kingdom, which helps explain why cooperation in this area has been substantial. Financial failures in 1974 led to the formation of the Basle Committee for Banking Supervision (BCBS) of central bank governors at the Bank for International Settlements.[77] In this narrow forum, the United States and United Kingdom insisted that "home" country regulators should accept primary responsibility for the supervision and liquidity of foreign subsidiaries of national banks.[78] The Basle Concordat of 1975 was based on this principle.

Subsequent failures of regulatory oversight of global banking operations by some home country authorities led other committee members to demand that *host* authorities retain substantial discretionary power over the entry and the supervision of foreign affiliates. There was also a growing recognition of a need for information sharing between home and host supervisors. These concerns led to revisions of the Concordat in 1983; since then, further clarifications have been made.[79] The BCBS has also encouraged nonmember countries, including often lightly regulated OFCs, to coordinate and to adopt Basle principles.

As regards the second area of international cooperation, the BCBS has also agreed and disseminated minimum bank regulatory standards ("Basle I and II"), which historically differ greatly across countries. Other international bodies, less successfully, have also promoted minimum global prudential standards for other financial firms, including the International Organization of Securities Commissions and the In-

---

[77] This group currently consists of the central banks (and, if different, the banking regulators) of Belgium, Canada, France, Germany, Italy, Japan, Luxembourg, the Netherlands, Spain, Sweden, Switzerland, the United Kingdom, and the United States.

[78] Ethan B. Kapstein, *Governing the Global Economy* (Cambridge: Harvard University Press, 1994). "Home" country, as opposed to "host," is defined as the country where the parent bank has its legal and operational headquarters. Different responsibilities are allocated according to whether the affiliate in question is a branch of a foreign bank (not separately incorporated), a separately incorporated subsidiary, or a separately incorporated joint venture.

[79] See the Basle Committee website: http://www.bis.org/bcbs/index.htm, accessed December 21, 2005.

ternational Association of Insurance Supervisors. A "Joint Forum" that included these two and the BCBS was established in 1996. The immediate origins of Basle I lay in the Latin American debt crisis of the 1980s, which put US regulators under congressional pressure to raise the minimum "capital adequacy standards" for overextended American banks.[80] The banks claimed that doing so unilaterally would erode their competitiveness vis-à-vis Japanese and European banks and that only coordinated international minimum standards would resolve this problem. Similar British concerns facilitated a US-UK deal on minimum risk-weighted capital adequacy standards in 1987.

The explicit threat that London and New York might refuse entry to affiliates of banks from noncomplying countries facilitated the 1988 Basle Capital Adequacy Accord. Although the distributive implications and motivations of the accord are debated,[81] higher average international capital standards were generally seen as a step in the right direction. Since the mid-1990s, however, growing recognition of the crude and arbitrary risk-weighting system of Basle I has resulted in modifications to the accord, allowing more sophisticated international banks and credit-rating agencies to play a much greater role in assessing risks.[82] This culminated in the wholly revised Basle II framework in June 2004, which extended the principle that banks should ideally use "riskmetrics" models to allocate capital across their asset portfolio.[83] Until 2007, when the US financial crisis undermined confidence in these models, this trend was widely seen as a major improvement on the Basle I approach.

It is clear that regulation can have powerful distributional effects between countries and between financial firms. Partly for this reason, some argue that major Western financial firms have been highly privi-

---

[80] Minimum capital standards determine how much capital (the core or "Tier I" form of which is shareholders' equity and disclosed reserves) a bank should hold for any asset on its balance sheet (e.g., a loan). Different categories of assets are weighted by their perceived riskiness.

[81] Kapstein, *Governing the Global Economy*; Oatley and Nabors, "Market Failure."

[82] On the international significance of private credit rating agencies, see Timothy J. Sinclair, *The New Masters of Capital: American Bond Rating Agencies and the Politics of Creditworthiness* (Ithaca, N.Y.: Cornell University Press, 2005).

[83] Riskmetrics models are used by banks to measure their total portfolio risk and to assign risk weights to different assets (as an alternative to the risk weights formerly assigned by the BCBS).

leged in the international regulatory process.[84] The BCBS and other standard setters have also focused on promoting the adoption of their standards in developing countries. This is for two main reasons. First, relatively lax regulation and supervision in developing countries can be costly for the major developed countries and their major financial institutions if they increase financial instability or facilitate money laundering and tax evasion. Second, the growing domestic economic importance of global financial services in the major countries has meant that there has been little political support there for attacking the problem by restricting the global activities of their own financial firms. Since the standard-setting bodies are dominated by representatives from the major developed countries, these "international standards" are in practice largely Western regulatory standards.

In sum, international regulatory coordination has ostensibly aimed at reducing the major developed countries' growing vulnerability to global financial activities by ensuring that global banks and other financial firms are well regulated, adequately supervised, and sufficiently capitalized. In addition, there has been a growing concern to ensure that there is no regulatory-supervisory race to the bottom by adopting and promoting minimum global standards. International cooperation (and sometimes coercion in the case of "noncooperative jurisdictions") in this area has been much more extensive than in the area of macroeconomic policy. This can be explained in part by the fact that the major countries and their international financial centers and private firms are much more vulnerable to foreign regulatory failures than to failures of macroeconomic policy coordination. It is ironic, therefore, that the most recent threat to global financial stability originated in the United States and United Kingdom rather than in developing countries, and that it has cast considerable doubt upon the very regulatory practices that these two countries have done so much to propagate globally.

Nor should the extent of harmonization be exaggerated. First, although these standards have been adopted in many countries, they remain voluntary, and the strength of market and official compliance

[84] Geoffrey R. D. Underhill, "Keeping Governments Out of Politics: Transnational Securities Markets, Regulatory Co-operation, and Political Legitimacy," *Review of International Studies* 21:3, 1995, 251–78.

pressures is disputed.[85] Although the IFIs now assess country compliance through the joint Financial Sector Assessment Program, such assessments are voluntary and their impact is limited. Second, the standards often lack specificity and therefore allow flexibility in national implementation. Third, the degree of harmonization is much weaker in areas such as securities and insurance than in banking. Given the blurring of the boundaries between these different financial activities, this is a major weakness, but also a fruitful area of political economy research.[86]

CONCLUSION

Global financial integration has had powerful effects on national policies and on international monetary and financial relations. It has made it more difficult for most countries to maintain explicit exchange rate pegs. The rise of global capital markets has increasingly marginalized the IFIs who provide public international finance, except when these institutions have had to deal with the consequences of financial crises or uncreditworthy borrowers. There is also evidence that financial liberalization has constrained macroeconomic policy autonomy, either directly (such as by raising the costs of fiscal deficits) or indirectly (such as by encouraging the adoption of CBI). But these constraints are weakest for the major developed countries, especially the United States despite this country's growing net debtor position, and strongest for developing countries who are heavily dependent on capital inflows.

Although there is no convincing evidence so far that financial integration has undermined the viability of European social democratic welfare states, it has probably increased the already substantial strain on them. Growing capital mobility may also have promoted conver-

[85] Beth A. Simmons, "The International Politics of Harmonization: The Case of Capital Market Regulation," *International Organization* 55:3, 2001, 589–620; Susanne Soederberg, Georg Menz, and Philip G. Cerny, eds , *Internalizing Globalization: The Rise of Neoliberalism and the Decline of National Varieties of Capitalism* (London: Palgrave Macmillan, 2005); Walter, *Governing Finance.*

[86] On the politics of the standard-setting process, see David Andrew Singer, *Regulating Capital: Setting Standards for the International Financial System* (Ithaca, N.Y.: Cornell University Press, 2007).

gence in capital taxation and shifted the overall tax burden toward labor. Financial integration also increased the frequency of deep financial crises in the developing world, in the process revealing deep vulnerabilities in the financial systems of developing countries in Latin America and Asia. This has prompted varying degrees of adoption of Western-style financial practices, facilitated in part by the desire of the major developed countries to reduce their own vulnerability by promoting a minimum degree of international regulatory harmonization. In sum, global financial integration has largely reinforced rather than reduced the asymmetries of power in the international political economy.

One final point can be made. Financial market actors have often been among the most vocal supporters of welfare state retrenchment and privatization and have often opposed state intervention in the economy. But it is less often recognized that the financial sector is itself one of the most heavily protected even in the most "liberal" economies. Most governments are unwilling to allow large financial institutions to fail. The financial turmoil in the major developed countries over 2007–8 brought home once again the lesson that financial sector actors prefer rapid and deep state intervention during crises (though bankers remain, of course, utterly opposed to proposals that government regulate their compensation in the interest of shareholders). In late 2007, in spite of its stated desire to avoid moral hazard, the Bank of England eventually made emergency loans to a large regional mortgage lender, Northern Rock, so as to stave off a broader run on deposit institutions in the United Kingdom. On Wall Street, the City of London and elsewhere, many bankers demanded that the major central banks take unprecedented emergency measures to reduce the level of stress in financial markets, despite the fact that the turmoil originated in highly risky (and in some cases certainly fraudulent) lending practices in some of the world's supposedly most sophisticated and well-managed financial institutions. Most central banks, notably the US Federal Reserve, duly obliged with massive liquidity provision to financial markets and discount rate cuts. In early 2008, both Democrats and Republicans in the United States vied with one another to produce an expansionary fiscal package to stave off a recession, despite the large existing fiscal deficit. To demonstrate their even-handedness, politicians also floated proposals to provide fiscal support to distressed homeowners. Evidently, Keynesianism and welfarism (for some) remains alive and well in advanced countries, perhaps because of, rather than despite, the liberalization and growing importance of financial markets.

FURTHER RESOURCES

Further Reading

Layna Mosley. *Global Capital and National Governments.* Cambridge: Cambridge University Press, 2003. A detailed study that investigates the effects of private investor preferences on national policies in developed and developing countries.

Nita Rudra and Stephan Haggard. "Globalization, Democracy, and Effective Welfare Spending in the Developed World." *Comparative Political Studies* 38:9, 2005, 1015–49. One of a small but growing number of studies that consider the effects of financial openness on policies in developing countries.

David Andrew Singer. *Regulating Capital: Setting Standards for the International Financial System.* Ithaca, N.Y.: Cornell University Press, 2007. Argues that the variation in the quality of international financial standards is a product of the domestic pressures faced by regulators in the major countries.

Andrew Walter. *Governing Finance: East Asia's Adoption of International Standards.* Ithaca, N.Y.: Cornell University Press, 2008. Argues that the substantial variation in the quality of compliance with international financial standards is due to differences in domestic private sector compliance costs and the difficulty of external monitoring.

Useful Websites

- http://www.imf.org/external/pubs/ft/GFSR/index.htm: The IMF's *Global Financial Stability Report* is a twice yearly publication focusing on developments in the global financial system and with cross-country data.

- www.fsforum.org: The Financial Stability Forum provides a compendium of international financial standards and standard-setting bodies that have arisen in recent years.
- http://www.bis.org/bcbs: The Basle Committee for Banking Supervision has become the most important standard-setting body in global finance.

6 | The Political Economy of Foreign Direct Investment

Although globalization skeptics often argue that trade and financial interdependence between countries is nothing new,[1] few doubt that multinational corporations (MNCs) have unprecedented importance in the contemporary global economy.[2] Of course, MNCs themselves are not new and were known in the ancient world. Certainly, by the early modern period, private firms heavily involved in international trade had established trading outposts and sourcing operations in other countries. Perhaps the most famous, the East India Company, had obtained monopoly privileges from the English state at the beginning of the seventeenth century and came to wield considerable political and military power in India and elsewhere.[3] Under the umbrella of imperialism, European firms established operations in many countries over the next few centuries. Meanwhile, banks established foreign branches to meet the financing needs of corporate and sovereign clients (e.g., the Rothschilds). From about the mid-nineteenth century, large firms emerged by exploiting economies of scale and scope, particularly in the new industries of chemicals, electricals, and later automobiles.[4] In the

---

[1] Paul Hirst and Grahame Thompson, *Globalization in Question: The International Economy and the Possibilities of Governance* (Cambridge: Polity, 2nd ed., 2000).

[2] Bordo, Eichengreen, and Irwin, "Is Globalization Today Really Different."

[3] John Keay, *The Honourable Company: A History of the English East India Company* (London: HarperCollins, 1991).

[4] Alfred D. Chandler, *Scale and Scope: The Dynamics of Industrial Capitalism* (Cambridge: Harvard University Press, 1990). Economies of scale occur when an increase in output is associated with falling average per unit cost. Economies of scope occur when average cost falls as the firm produces a larger number of different but related products.

early twentieth century, some of these large manufacturing firms, notably Ford and General Motors, established prototype factories in foreign countries. However, wartime nationalizations and the rise of economic nationalism, especially in newly independent developing countries after the war, retarded this expansion of MNC activities.

MNC activities in the global economy have expanded rapidly in recent decades, much faster than global trade or income. Today, MNCs dominate international trade flows in an historically unprecedented manner. About two-thirds of international trade involves MNCs and about one-third is "intrafirm" (i.e., trade between a parent firm and its foreign affiliates, or between affiliates). Moreover, local affiliates sales are often much larger than trade flows. On average, sales by affiliates of US MNCs to EU-based customers were nearly four times as large as US exports to the EU in 2001; the picture is similar for US-based European affiliate sales compared to EU exports to the United States.[5] Multinational financial firms also dominate the intermediation of international financial flows. The size and market power of MNCs also means that they can be an important influence over government policy, both directly via lobbying and indirectly via their growing ability to locate important parts of the production supply chain in countries of their choosing. Governments compete for the jobs, capital, technology, innovation, export capacity, and managerial expertise that MNCs often bring. For this reason, some argue that MNCs now rival states as dominant, autonomous actors in the global political economy.[6]

In this chapter, we are concerned with the preliminary question of why the activities and importance of MNCs in the world economy have grown so rapidly in recent decades. Accordingly, we postpone the question about power in the global political economy to the following chapter, as well as the related question of the evolving international regulation of business activities. Here, we first provide a brief outline of the growing importance of MNCs and FDI in the global economy. Second, we discuss economic explanations of foreign direct investment (FDI), which focus on the particular advantages MNCs enjoy over local firms.

[5] Georgio Barba Navaretti and Anthony J. Venables, *Multinational Firms in the World Economy* (Princeton, N.J.: Princeton University Press, 2006), 4.

[6] John Stopford, Susan Strange, and John S. Henley, *Rival States, Rival Firms: Competition for World Market Shares* (Cambridge: Cambridge University Press, 1991).

Although these advantages account for some of the recent growth of FDI, we argue that economic explanations are insufficient. Third, we assess political economy explanations of MNC activity, focusing in particular on changing state attitudes toward such firms.

THE GROWING IMPORTANCE OF THE MULTINATIONAL CORPORATION IN THE WORLD ECONOMY

An MNC is a firm that owns and operates plants or other facilities in one or more "host" countries outside its "home" country base.[7] FDI is an international capital flow recorded in the balance of payments in which an MNC establishes control over and a lasting interest in corporate assets in a host country. For statistical purposes, this is generally deemed to be achieved when the parent firm owns at least 10% of the equity in the foreign affiliate.[8] FDI includes foreign affiliates' profits that are reinvested rather than repatriated to the parent company. Because FDI data is collected for balance-of-payments purposes, they tend to be more readily available than data on MNC operations, which are very dependent on the quality of national-level data.[9] Note that FDI data do not measure the real activities (e.g., capital investment) by

[7] An MNC's home base is (usually) the country in which the firm was first established and where a substantial proportion of its economic activity is still located, although there is no agreed-on precise definition in the literature. There is also a debate about whether or not MNCs (or "transnational" corporations) have or have not transcended their home base country and their actual degree of political autonomy (see Robert Reich, "Who Is US?" *Harvard Business Review,* February 1990, 53–64; Yao-Su Hu, "Global or Stateless Corporations Are National Firms with International Operations," *California Management Review* 34:2, 1992, 107–26). Our position is that this is always a matter of degree, but there is no agreed-on definition of how to measure either the degree of corporate transnationality or political autonomy (for one approach regarding transnationality, see UNCTAD, *World Investment Report 2006: FDI from Developing and Transition Economies, Implications for Development* (New York: UNCTAD, 2006), annex table A.I.11).

[8] Foreign affiliates come in two forms. The IMF and OECD define a *subsidiary* as a firm in which a foreign investor owns at least 50% of the voting shares, and an *associated enterprise* as one in which the foreign investor owns between 10% and 50% of the voting shares (see Navaretti and Venables, *Multinational Firms,* appendix).

[9] The best national data on MNC operations is from the United States: see http://www.bea.gov/bea/di/home/directinv.htm. For international data largely based on FDI statistics, the annual UNCTAD *World Investment Report* is the best source: see http://www.unctad.org/Templates/Page.asp?intItemID=1485&lang=1. In what follows, we use data from the 2005 report unless otherwise specified.

MNCs and can be misleading as a measure of the latter. For example, an acquisition in a host country financed by domestic (host) country borrowing is not counted as FDI. In addition, FDI stocks (assets) are measured at historical cost rather than at current market values. Over three-quarters of all FDI today is in the form of mergers and acquisitions (M&As) of existing firms rather than "greenfield" investments in which foreign firms build new plants in host countries. Most M&A activity occurs in developed countries; in developing countries, M&As account for only about one-third of all inward FDI.

By 2004, MNCs comprised 70,000 parent firms and approximately 690,000 foreign affiliates. Their contribution to global output and capital formation has increased dramatically since the nineteenth century, and especially since the 1970s. The foreign affiliates alone had total sales of over $18 trillion, assets of $36 trillion, gross product of nearly $4 trillion, and exports of $3 trillion. The 100 largest nonfinancial MNCs alone are a formidable economic and political presence in the world economy, accounting respectively for 12%, 18%, and 14% of the total assets, sales, and employment of all MNCs. The growing significance of international production is underlined not just by the absolute growth of FDI, but its increase relative to both global GDP and global exports. From 1985 to 1999, real-world GDP grew by 2.5% per year and world exports by 5.6%, whereas real inflows of FDI worldwide increased by 17.7%.[10] The sales of all foreign affiliates of MNCs are now 1.7 times as large as global exports, compared to 1.2 times exports in 1982. This implies that large firms increasingly obtain access to foreign-based customers via FDI rather than via exports from their home base. Such firms can also loom large relative to many national economies, though populist comparisons of MNC assets and sales to country GDPs wrongly imply that global firms are much larger than most.[11] Table 6.1 lists the world's major nonfinancial MNCs in 2004 (ranked by their total assets according to historic cost accounting methods). Although

---

[10] Navaretti and Venables, *Multinational Firms*, 3.

[11] GDP measures total value added in an economy in one year, whereas measures of corporate assets and sales are usually multiples of firms' actual value added. For an explanation of the dangers of comparing apples and oranges in this area, see Paul De Grauwe and Filip Camerman, "How Big Are the Big Multinationals?," unpublished paper, 2002. The authors also point out that individual MNCs often disappear, usually via mergers, whereas states very rarely do.

TABLE 6.1
The World's Top 40 Nonfinancial MNCs, Ranked by Foreign Assets, 2004 (billions of US$ and thousands of employees)

	Home	Industry Classification	Assets		Sales		Employment		Number of Affiliates	
			Foreign	Total	Foreign	Total	Foreign	Total	Foreign	Total
1 General Electric	US	Electrical & electronic equip't	449	751	57	153	142	307	787	1,157
2 Vodafone Group	UK	Telecommunications	248	259	53	62	46	57	70	198
3 Ford Motor	US	Motor vehicles	180	305	71	172	103	226	130	216
4 General Motors	US	Motor vehicles	174	480	59	194	115	324	166	290
5 British Petroleum	UK	Petroleum expl./ref./distr.	155	193	232	285	86	103	445	611
6 ExxonMobil	US	Petroleum expl./ref./distr.	135	195	203	291	53	105	237	314
7 Royal Dutch/Shell Group	UK/Netherlands	Petroleum expl./ref./distr.	130	193	170	265	96	114	328	814
8 Toyota Motor Corp.	Japan	Motor vehicles	123	234	103	171	95	266	129	341
9 Total	France	Petroleum expl./ref./distr.	99	115	123	152	62	111	410	576
10 France Télécom	France	Telecommunications	86	131	24	59	82	207	162	227
11 Volkswagen AG	Germany	Motor vehicles	84	173	80	110	165	343	147	228
12 Sanofi-Aventis	France	Pharmaceuticals	83	105	15	19	69	96	207	253
13 Deutsche Telekom AG	Germany	Telecommunications	80	147	47	72	74	245	266	390
14 RWE Group	Germany	Electricity, gas, and water	79	127	24	52	42	98	345	552
15 Suez	France	Electricity, gas, and water	74	86	39	51	100	161	546	846
16 E.on	Germany	Electricity, gas, and water	73	155	22	61	33	72	303	596
17 Hutchison Whampoa	Hong Kong	Diversified	68	84	17	23	151	180	94	103
18 Siemens AG	Germany	Electrical & electronic equip't	66	108	59	93	266	430	605	852
19 Nestlé SA	Switzerland	Food & beverages	65	77	69	70	240	247	460	487
20 Électricité de France	France	Electricity, gas and water	65	200	18	56	51	156	240	299

Source: UNCTAD, *World Investment Report 2006*, Annex table A.I.11.

TABLE 6.1 (cont'd)
The World's Top 40 Nonfinancial MNCs, Ranked by Foreign Assets, 2004 (billions of US$ and thousands of employees)

	Home	Industry Classification	Assets		Sales		Employment		Number of Affiliates	
			Foreign	Total	Foreign	Total	Foreign	Total	Foreign	Total
21 Honda Motor Co.	Japan	Motor vehicles	65	89	62	80	77	138	76	188
22 Vivendi Universal	France	Diversified	58	94	12	27	23	38	245	435
23 ChevronTexaco	US	Motor vehicles	57	93	80	151	31	56	121	250
24 BMW AG	Germany	Motor vehicles	56	92	40	55	71	106	124	153
25 DaimlerChrysler	US/Germany	Motor vehicles	55	249	69	176	101	385	324	641
26 Pfizer Inc	US	Pharmaceuticals	54	124	23	53	50	115	82	104
27 ENI	Italy	Petroleum expl./ref./distr.	50	99	48	90	30	71	162	222
28 Nissan Motor Co.	Japan	Motor vehicles	50	95	56	79	112	184	53	140
29 IBM	US	Computer and related activities	48	109	61	96	176	329	338	371
30 ConocoPhillips	US	Petroleum expl./ref./distr.	46	93	41	143	14	36	44	85
31 Hewlett-Packard	US	Computer and related activities	46	76	51	80	93	151	106	144
32 Mitsubishi Corporation	Japan	Wholesale trade	44	88	5	38	22	51	212	357
33 Telefonica SA	Spain	Telecommunications	43	86	15	38	78	174	62	279
34 Roche Group	Switzerland	Pharmaceuticals	43	51	25	25	36	65	137	158
35 Telecom Italia Spa	Italy	Telecommunications	42	104	8	39	16	91	75	111
36 Anglo American	UK	Mining & quarrying	40	53	17	26	163	209	173	502
37 Fiat Spa	Italy	Motor vehicles	40	78	31	58	88	161	362	456
38 Unilever	UK/Netherlands	Diversified	38	46	44	50	171	223	314	466
39 Carrefour	France	Retail	37	53	46	90	142	431	130	311
40 Procter & Gamble	US	Diversified	36	62	31	57	63	110	357	447

Source: UNCTAD, World Investment Report 2006, Annex table A.I.11.

the largest firms with strong brand names are most associated with FDI, many small and medium-sized firms have also engaged in FDI in recent years.

Since 1990, the United States, Luxembourg, the United Kingdom, France, and Germany have dominated FDI outflows (table 6.2). Given the historically dominant position of MNCs of American and British origin, MNCs from these two countries remain most important in aggregate and in key sectors such as oil, minerals, and finance. Developing countries such as Taiwan, Korea, Russia, India, and China are also responsible for a growing proportion of total global FDI outflows. The developing countries' share of world FDI outflows peaked at 15% in 2005 and will probably continue to rise over the longer term. FDI from developing countries primarily goes to other developing countries, though recently there have been some notable examples of acquisitions of firms in developed countries by firms from developing countries.

The sectoral distribution of inward FDI tends to vary with the level of economic development of the country. FDI inflows in the service sector, for example, have in recent years become more significant for advanced countries, while manufacturing FDI still dominates in middle-income industrializing ones, above all in China. FDI in services has also been growing in developing countries, especially India, while FDI in primary (extractive) industries has diminished in importance over time.

Although MNCs operate today in almost every country, the geographical distributions of FDI inflows and MNC activity are also highly skewed, being heavily concentrated in advanced countries and a handful of developing ones. The top ten recipient countries received over 70% of global FDI inflows in 2004. In the same year, the top five developing countries (China, Brazil, Mexico, Korea, and Chile) received half of all FDI flows to developing countries. Meanwhile, all of Africa received less than 8% of all FDI flows into developing countries in 2004, about the same amount as Brazil and less than 30% of China's total. Most developing countries receive modest absolute levels of FDI, though such inflows can constitute a relatively high proportion of their domestic capital formation. Although the proportion of developing countries in total FDI inflows has risen considerably since the 1970s, around 55%–65% of global flows still go to the developed countries

TABLE 6.2
FDI Flows, 20 Major Countries, 1990–2005 (ranked by inflows in 2005)

	Inflows, US$ Billions							Outflows, US$ Billions						
	1990–99 Avg.	2000	2001	2002	2003	2004	2005	1990–99 Avg.	2000	2001	2002	2003	2004	2005
United Kingdom	32.5	118.8	52.6	24.0	16.8	56.2	164.5	57.4	233.4	58.9	50.3	62.2	94.9	101.1
United States	89.1	314.0	159.5	74.5	53.1	122.4	99.4	86.9	142.6	124.9	134.9	129.4	222.4	-12.7
China	29.0	40.7	46.9	52.7	53.5	60.6	72.4	2.3	.9	6.9	2.5	-.2	1.8	11.3
France	20.5	43.3	50.5	49.0	42.5	31.4	63.6	34.7	177.4	86.8	50.4	53.1	57.0	115.7
Netherlands	15.4	63.9	51.9	25.0	21.7	.4	43.6	23.8	75.6	50.6	32.0	44.2	17.3	119.5
Hong Kong, China	9.0	61.9	23.8	9.7	13.6	34.0	35.9	16.5	59.4	11.3	17.5	5.5	45.7	32.6
Canada	10.6	66.8	27.7	22.2	7.6	1.5	33.8	12.9	44.7	36.0	26.8	21.5	43.3	34.1
Germany	12.5	198.3	26.4	53.5	29.2	-15.1	32.7	43.1	56.6	39.7	18.9	6.2	1.9	45.6
Belgium				16.3	33.4	42.0	23.7				12.3	38.9	33.5	22.9
Spain	11.8	39.6	28.3	39.2	25.9	24.8	23.0	10.8	58.2	33.1	32.7	27.5	60.5	38.8
Singapore	8.5	16.5	15.6	7.3	10.4	14.8	20.1	4.6	5.9	20.2	2.3	3.1	8.5	5.5
Italy	4.3	13.4	14.9	14.5	16.4	16.8	20.0	8.0	12.3	21.5	17.1	9.1	19.3	39.7
Mexico	8.5	17.6	27.2	18.3	14.2	18.7	18.1	.6	.4	4.4	.9	1.3	4.4	6.2
Brazil	9.9	32.8	22.5	16.6	10.1	18.1	15.1	.9	2.3	-2.3	2.5	.2	9.8	2.5
Russian Federation	2.3	2.7	2.7	3.5	8.0	15.4	14.6	1.4	3.2	2.5	3.5	9.7	13.8	13.1
Bermuda	3.4	12.2	10.9	1.5	2.3	14.8	13.6	3.1	10.3	-3.1	4.3	-4.2	-.5	-5.5
Sweden	13.0	23.4	10.9	12.2	5.0	12.6	13.4	10.5	41.0	7.3	10.6	21.1	21.0	25.9
United Arab Emirates	.1	-.5	1.2	1.3	4.3	8.4	12.0	.1	.4	.2	.4	1.0	1.0	6.7
Cayman Islands	1.6	6.9	4.4	-.2	-2.6	6.0	11.2	1.3	7.6	7.2	-5.8	4.9	4.7	2.2
Czech Republic	1.8	5.0	5.6	8.5	2.1	5.0	11.0	.1		.2	.2	.2	1.0	.9
World	404.0	1,409.6	832.2	617.7	557.9	710.8	916.3	417.4	1,244.5	764.2	539.5	561.1	813.1	778.7
Developed economies	277.3	1,133.7	599.3	441.2	358.5	396.1	542.3	368.3	1,097.5	684.8	485.1	514.8	686.3	646.2
Developing economies	121.5	266.8	221.4	163.6	175.1	275.	334.3	47.9	143.8	76.7	49.7	35.6	112.8	117.5

Source: UNCTAD, World Investment Report 2006, annexes. Note that there are discrepancies between estimates of world inflows and outflows.

(depending on the year), especially North America and Europe. China now consistently ranks behind the United States and United Kingdom as one of the largest recipients globally.

ECONOMIC EXPLANATIONS OF FOREIGN DIRECT INVESTMENT

Economists explain MNCs as a response to imperfect product and factor markets as well as government interventions such as taxation and trade barriers.[12] While the competitive firm of economic theory sells its products at marginal cost and earns zero excess profits, the MNC earns rents by virtue of its market power, which it exploits via FDI. There are two main forms of FDI: vertical and horizontal. Vertical FDI entails the production of intermediate inputs in more than one location for the manufacture of a final product and is associated primarily with the search for lower costs via global supply chain management (for this reason, it is sometimes called *cost-seeking* FDI). The choice for firms between outsourcing parts of the production process to unrelated suppliers,[13] foreign licensing, manufacturing in-house domestically, or through a foreign subsidiary depends among other things on the relative price of labor, the difficulty of contracting with potential suppliers, and other costs of geographic fragmentation.[14] These choices determine what is often called the "boundary" of the firm. Horizontal FDI involves the production of final output in different national locations and is motivated primarily by the desire for proximity to the end market (and for this reason is often called *market-seeking* FDI). Historically, horizontal FDI has dominated vertical FDI, and the fact that most inflows continue to go to high-income countries shows that this is still true. But vertical FDI has been growing rapidly in recent years as MNCs have

---

[12] Richard E. Caves, *Multinational Enterprise and Economic Analysis* (Cambridge: Cambridge University Press, 2nd ed., 1996); James R. Markusen, "Foreign Investment and Trade," Centre of International Economic Studies, Policy Discussion Paper, 19, April 2000.

[13] It is often easiest to think of physical components in a manufacturing process, but such inputs can also include services (such as in much recent offshoring of "back office" functions to Indian suppliers).

[14] Gene M. Grossman and Elhanan Helpman, "Outsourcing versus FDI in Industry Equilibrium," *Journal of the European Economic Association* 1:2–3, 2003, 320–21.

fragmented their production process geographically to reduce costs.[15] As this has happened, FDI has tended to become more trade-intensive, since horizontal FDI is in part a substitute for international trade.

What prompts a firm to engage in FDI? After all, both forms of FDI entail costs beyond initial setup costs and the difficulty that many firms face when operating abroad: they are not well embedded in the host country socially or politically. This can mean that MNCs face greater political and regulatory hurdles than local firms, though this disadvantage may be partly offset by superior financial and managerial resources. Horizontal FDI, which accesses a foreign market via local production, can also result in the dilution of plant-level economies of scale compared to the option of exporting from a large home base plant or foreign licensing. Vertical FDI may overcome the scale optimization problem if the firm locates large-scale specialist production units in different countries. On the other hand, vertically integrated MNCs tend to suffer costs of fragmenting production in different locations. These include the political and regulatory risks we have mentioned, as well as the managerial costs of managing integrated global supply and production networks.

Of course, FDI would not occur unless there were offsetting advantages, so FDI decisions involve trade-offs between the costs and benefits of international operations. Horizontal FDI may avoid costly trade barriers or obtain benefits from proximity to key customers. Vertical FDI can help the firm to minimize global production costs. More formally, Dunning, who synthesized a large amount of earlier work, famously classified these advantages under three headings, each of which emphasizes the role of market imperfections: ownership, location, and internalization (the so-called eclectic "OLI" framework).[16] This framework claimed that FDI derived from some combination of all three advantages vis-à-vis domestic firms. Ownership advantages arise from the possession of exclusive knowledge of a product or production processes that confer cost advantages. Location advantages arise from some imperative (e.g., tariff costs, transportation costs, or local resources) to produce abroad rather than at home. Internalization advantages derive

---

[15] Navaretti and Venables, *Multinational Firms,* 14–15.

[16] John Dunning, *Explaining International Production* (London: Unwin Hyman, 1988).

from the exploitation of a firm's proprietary technology and assets in-house through fully owned subsidiaries, rather than allow a third party to produce or sell it under license (i.e., via markets that are external to the boundary of the firm).

Dunning's emphasis on existing "advantages" can be somewhat misleading, because FDI may occur when a firm currently lacking such advantages acquires them via the purchase of a foreign firm (e.g., the Chinese firm Lenovo's acquisition of IBM's personal computer business in 2004). Thus, it is better to think of FDI as *a product of a strategic decision to internalize activities within the firm's boundary in ways that cross political boundaries.* The decision to internalize or to outsource is the crucial one.[17] In practice, many MNCs combine internalization and outsourcing and over time may move different activities across the firm's boundary (e.g., by outsourcing a data-processing function previously done in-house) as well as across countries (e.g., by relocating an internal R&D facility from the United Kingdom to India).

A related but more recent theory is the "knowledge capital" model, which emphasizes the central role of proprietary knowledge such as technology, brands, patents, and managerial expertise in a firm's decisions.[18] These intangible assets can create large firm-level economies of scale that offset the possible dilution of individual plant-level economies of scale entailed by foreign production in the case of horizontal FDI. Hence, foreign production is more likely when firm-level economies of scale are high relative to plant-level economies. MNCs may export knowledge-based services in the form of managerial know-how, engineering, finance, trademarks, copyrights, or reputation and combine them with foreign assembly operations or outsourcing. Decisions about the appropriate boundaries of the firm (e.g., foreign affiliate production vs. subcontracted outsourcing) may be substantially determined by management judgments about how best to exploit the firm's proprietary knowledge. Much may depend, for example, on the relative difficulty of writing contracts with foreign licensees or outsourcers that would allow the MNC to safeguard its core proprietary knowledge. The

---

[17] Navaretti and Venables, *Multinational Firms*, 99.

[18] James R. Markusen, *Multinational Firms and the Theory of International Trade* (Cambridge: MIT Press, 2002).

outsourcing of core activities may be especially risky if the firm believes potential suppliers will have incentives to compromise on quality. An example of the former possibility was provided in 2007, when the large, vertically integrated American multinational Mattel was forced to recall millions of toys made by contractors in China because of concerns about the products' safety. Outsourcing will also be risky if local firms are likely to steal proprietary knowledge. The loss of intellectual property is chronic in some countries. For this reason, FDI can be a response to a poor institutional environment in which the legal enforcement of contracts is difficult, even though foreign investors should generally benefit from good protection of property rights.[19]

Two other prominent examples illustrate the ways in which different firms have defined the boundaries between internalization and outsourcing. In the automobile sector, Toyota became famous for purchasing a much higher proportion of its components from other (domestic) parts suppliers than did its American rivals. Toyota's production networks were, like other Japanese "keiretsu" groupings, linked by cross-shareholdings, but depended heavily on Toyota's ability to coordinate network production with low levels of stock inventories, "just-in-time" delivery of components, and quality management throughout the network.[20] These close network relationships also meant that when Toyota began to establish foreign production facilities, often so as to avoid trade barriers, its related components suppliers followed, promoting further FDI. For this reason, some cast doubt on the size of the spillover benefits for firms in the host country.

On a different model, Apple's and Dell's more recent outsourcing of the assembly of their electronics products to China-based (Taiwanese) firms also demonstrate the advantages of an even higher degree of outsourcing. Intensifying competitive pressures may create a chain reaction in which more and more firms seek to exploit the opportunities of unbundled production. In many areas of manufacturing, from electronic products to textiles and footwear, the modern MNC essentially becomes a technology and brand manager, as emphasized in the knowledge capital model, outsourcing the production process to cheaper for-

---

[19] Navaretti and Venables, *Multinational Firms,* 16.

[20] James P. Womack, Daniel T. Jones, and Daniel Roos, *The Machine That Changed the World: The Story of Lean Production* (New York: Harper Perennial, 1991).

eign locations (with sales and customer service operations in many countries).[21]

If economists explain FDI as a product of market imperfections, what explains the recent dramatic expansion in the activities of MNCs in the global economy? The OLI and knowledge capital frameworks suggest that the rapid growth of FDI in recent decades might be explained by (1) a fall in the costs of foreign operations relative to the advantages that MNCs derive from their ability to exploit market imperfections, (2) an expansion of the market opportunities available to MNCs, and (3) a growing need for firms to defend market positions through international expansion. Each of these possibilities is considered in what follows.

Falling Foreign Operating Costs

A drop in the costs of operating abroad may promote FDI. Two main arguments along these lines are commonly given. First, the information technology (IT) revolution arguably reduces the managerial costs of unbundling different parts of the production process and locating them in countries so as to maximize productive efficiency. Of course, this need not always promote FDI: the greater ease of managing complex global supply chains may also encourage the outsourcing of parts of the production chain (including services) to independent foreign-based firms. This can be seen in areas such as software engineering, global call centers, and the back office processing operations of financial services firms, as well as in production outsourcing. As the importance of MNCs' in-house knowledge has risen, the importance of in-house production may have declined rather than increased, resulting in a growth of outsourcing relative to foreign affiliate production.[22] But the IT revolution also seems to promote FDI by enhancing the ability of MNCs to manage complex intrafirm global production and distribution networks via vertical FDI. Hence, the falling transactions costs of managing intra- and extrafirm relationships has probably promoted an

[21] Gary Gereffi, "The Global Apparel Value Chain: What Prospects for Upgrading by Developing Countries?" Sectoral Studies Series, United Nations Industrial Development Organization, 2003.

[22] Navaretti and Venables, *Multinational Firms*, 99.

increase in both vertically integrated international production and the use of subcontracting or outsourcing to lower cost jurisdictions. As we noted earlier, individual MNCs can do both at once.

The second cost factor that reduces operating costs for MNCs is the general fall in the cost of international trade. There are two main sources of this: falling trade protection since the 1980s and continuing reductions in transportation costs. This provides particular advantages to MNCs that can exploit intrafirm assets through high levels of intrafirm trade. Proprietary knowledge and information management capacity allows the MNC to break up the production process into its individual components and distribute these geographically in a vertically integrated, trade-intensive multinational production structure. In this way, the firm is better able to exploit the potential synergies between the (shifting) comparative advantages of different countries and its own specific knowledge capital.

As with the IT revolution, lower tariffs and nontariff barriers to trade might cut both ways, since they could also encourage the offshore outsourcing of production and a reliance on importing into core markets (the Mattel case is a classic example); it could also encourage more traditional exporting strategies from large-scale plants. The bulk of the value in a global network like Mattel's is attached to the brand itself rather than the production process, and since the MNC has a range of potential outsourcing options, it has substantial bargaining power vis-à-vis contractors. The same may be said of the effects of falling transportation costs. The rapid growth of vertical FDI in recent years suggests that MNCs have exploited the possibilities of intrafirm trade as well as outsourcing. At the same time, the incentive to undertake old-style tariff-avoiding FDI has diminished as firms seek to take advantage of the potential of global supply and production networks.

This explanation of FDI trends focuses on supply-side effects and the growing relative importance of vertical FDI. It is less obvious how it can explain the growth of horizontal FDI, which still dominates total FDI flows.[23] Since horizontal FDI entails replicating similar production

[23] Howard J. Shatz and Anthony Venables, "The Geography of International Investment," World Bank Policy Research Working Paper, 2338, 2000; Ewe-Ghee Lim, "Determinants of, and the Relation between, Foreign Direct Investment and Growth: A Summary of the Recent Literature," IMF Working Paper, WP/01/175, 2001.

facilities in different locations, it should emerge when firm-level fixed costs (including knowledge capital, transport costs, and trade barriers) are high compared to plant-level economies of scale. If technological change has allowed manufacturers to achieve plant economies of scale at lower levels of production, this can help explain why horizontal FDI has also been growing quickly in recent years.

Expanding Foreign Opportunities

A demand-side explanation is provided by the new market opportunities in the world economy in recent years. The rapid growth of some emerging market countries has provided new sources of potential demand for MNCs' products. Economic development has produced a larger segment of the population with substantial disposable income and tastes similar to consumers in advanced countries (e.g., in advanced consumer segments such as mobile telephones). As the knowledge capital model emphasizes, MNCs are often able to offer an important intangible factor to consumers in the form of trademarks and brands, which in recent years have become conspicuous in many rapidly developing countries. The demand for such branded products can be highly income elastic—that is, demand rises more rapidly as average incomes grow—making markets in developing countries increasingly attractive for such firms.

Even if optimal plant sizes have been falling relative to MNCs' fixed costs and new market opportunities for MNCs have emerged, we still need to explain why many firms choose horizontal FDI rather than exporting or licensing as the means of market entry. The knowledge capital model's emphasis on the MNC's ability to exploit and need to protect its proprietary knowledge helps to explain why licensing is often avoided in developing countries. Locational factors must also be important, as MNCs so often choose to set up foreign subsidiaries rather than export to new markets. One reason is that average tariffs in the large emerging market countries generally remain higher than those in advanced countries, even though they have often fallen rapidly in recent years. In addition, since incomes remain much lower in developing countries, MNCs may need to access these new markets by exploiting the lower production costs available to competitors in developing countries. The need for MNCs to be sensitive to local variations in tastes can also favor geographic proximity to customers. Local presence is often necessary in many service sector industries, where demand has been growing rapidly (e.g., for telecoms and financial services).

Growing Competition and Corporate Strategy

Industrial organization approaches to FDI developed from the glaring empirical anomaly confounding both neoclassical and Marxist expectations: FDI flows occurred largely between advanced economies rather than from them to developing countries. Originally associated with Stephen Hymer, this approach attributed FDI to the achievement of positions of market dominance by MNCs.[24] According to Hymer, firms first achieve market power (capturing a larger share of the domestic market) by increasing their own productive capacity or merging with other firms. As a result, their profits rise until domestic growth becomes difficult and competition prevails between a number of oligopolistic firms. The logical next step is collusion between oligopolistic firms to expand abroad at the expense of local firms in host economies. Certainly, the search for new sources of demand abroad is a logical strategy for large firms operating in mature markets. However, trade and investment liberalization since the 1980s has meant that market competition has probably intensified rather than fallen since that time in many developed economies in Europe and North America. The rapid growth of FDI since then therefore poses a difficulty for this approach.

Raymond Vernon's emphasis on increasing returns to scale and intraindustry trade provided a more plausible account of corporate internationalization. For Vernon, these factors make it necessary for MNCs to internationalize in order to survive. His product life-cycle theory explained horizontal FDI as driven by the incentive of established large firms to search for lower production costs once a product becomes

---

[24] Stephen Hymer, *The International Operations of National Firms: A Study of Direct Foreign Investment* (Cambridge: MIT Press, 1976).

standardized.[25] In this model, initial domestic production and the export of a new product by innovative firms is followed in a subsequent phase by foreign production in an affiliate. The decision to produce abroad is designed to preempt foreign rivals, who might also enjoy protective barriers against the imported product. In a later phase, the product becomes standardized and the MNC may cease its manufacture within the parent's facilities and produce it instead in a third market that has cost advantages, even importing the product back into its original home market.

Product life-cycles in a range of industries (notably those related to IT) have been falling dramatically in recent years as the pace of innovation has accelerated. Firms are under growing competitive pressure to act quickly to sustain existing product market shares and to maximize the potential of new products by expanding market access quickly. Rising import penetration in many developed countries may have promoted such defensive strategies by domestic producers. Outsourcing production to contractors in cheaper foreign locations is one means of maintaining or improving price competitiveness. FDI, particularly in the form of M&As, can also allow a firm to expand market opportunities rapidly and preempt competitors. By implication, M&As can reduce the level of competition faced by the firm and strengthen its competitive position against rivals. Compared to greenfield investments, M&As allow operational activity to be commenced quickly without creating more industry-wide capacity or without having to establish new distribution networks.[26] M&As also allow the firm to acquire strategic assets quickly that would otherwise both take time to develop and involve uncertainty of outcome in the effort to create them. There is, by definition, no ready-made market for proprietary assets like R&D, technical know-how, patents, brand names, supplier or distribution networks, or licenses. Even so, many M&As in practice fail to increase the value of the acquiring firm's assets.[27]

[25] Raymond Vernon, "International Investment." See also Raymond Vernon, ed., *Big Business and the State* (London: Macmillan, 1974).

[26] M&As have other advantages. For example, by increasing a firm's size, they may allow the MNC to raise capital more cheaply or to finance investment from internal revenues when information asymmetries exist between potential investors and corporate insiders.

[27] See UNCTAD, *World Investment Report 2000*, chap. 5.

POLITICAL ECONOMY EXPLANATIONS OF THE GROWTH OF FOREIGN DIRECT INVESTMENT

The economic explanations of FDI outlined above place particular emphasis on accelerating technological change and shifting patterns of demand as the primary causes of the rapid growth of international production since the 1960s. It is unlikely that these factors alone can explain the key trends in FDI. Political economy explanations, by contrast, focus on the changing policy environment within which firms operate. Such policies and conditions include the degree of openness to trade and financial flows, domestic content requirements and rules of origin,[28] export requirements,[29] tax incentives for foreign investors, intellectual property protection, and corruption, among other things. Such policies can significantly affect firms' operating and market entry costs as well as market size and the level of competition within the market.

In the first few decades after 1945, MNCs faced hostility in much of the developing world, and often (though to a lesser degree) in advanced countries as well. Countries often suspected MNCs of withholding key technologies, exploiting local labor, and depriving them of tax revenues via transfer pricing (by using intrafirm transactions to transfer profits to affiliates in locations with lower corporation taxes). Many governments also believed that MNCs threatened their political and economic autonomy because of these firms' extensive economic resources and their political connections with their home state (most often the United States). Most states also wanted to establish so-called national corporate champions and feared that MNCs would overwhelm them. When MNCs were allowed into the home market, restrictions were often placed on their operations to protect domestic firms and (it was hoped) to raise the net benefits for the local economy.[30] Relations between host

---

[28] Domestic content requirements typically require MNCs to source a specified proportion of their total inputs (often measured by value-added) from domestic factors of production (usually defined geographically rather than by ownership). They are frequently used in regional integration agreements as "rules of origin" (i.e., definitions of goods and services that qualify for duty-free access). So, for example, the rule for automobile MNCs based in NAFTA countries is that firms wishing to obtain duty-free access to NAFTA markets must source a minimum of 60% or 62.5% of final product value-added (depending on the product) from the NAFTA region.

[29] These usually require that a specific minimum proportion of total output be exported.

[30] In the early postwar decades, for example, the Japanese government required foreign firms to share technology with domestic firms as a condition of being allowed to operate in Japan. Joint

governments and MNCs were often especially fraught in extractive and infrastructure industries, where the sharing of rents between MNCs and the host state was a matter of controversy and because the latter had a strong incentive to renege once costly investment in fixed assets had taken place—the so-called obsolescing bargain.

In 1973, the UN General Assembly at the behest of the G77 group of developing countries passed Resolution 3171 regarding "Permanent Sovereignty Over National Resources," which held the principle of nationalization of foreign-owned assets to be an expression of sovereignty. The number of nationalizations of MNC assets by developing countries, often with derisory compensation, peaked in the mid-1970s.[31]

Since then, the policy environment for FDI and MNC operations has become much more favorable for global firms. Reflecting and reinforcing this trend, there has been a proliferation of bilateral, regional, and multilateral treaties between states that have provided for the liberalization and greater protection of foreign investments, including in those sectors in which restrictions have always been severe (chapter 7). By the UNCTAD's calculation, between 1991 and 2001 94% of aggregate policy changes made the conditions for FDI more liberal. Although many developed countries have also adopted more liberal policies toward inward FDI, in general there has been a convergence toward the already relatively liberal policies of the large capital-exporting countries. Since this policy shift appears to have promoted and facilitated increased FDI flows, what explains it? Below, we discuss four kinds of explanation: (1) changing societal interests, (2) changing state interests, (3) changing ideas, and (4) coercion by hegemonic actors.

Changing Societal Interests

The distributional effects of inward FDI have parallels to the effects of international trade liberalization, but distributional analysis is more complex than for trade because FDI is a bundle of different factors. One complicating factor is whether capital to finance the investment

---

ventures were intended to promote learning by domestic firms. These policies were widely copied in other countries, often with less success.

[31] Charles Lipson, *Standing Guard: Protecting Foreign Capital in the Nineteenth and Twentieth Centuries* (Berkeley and Los Angeles: University of California Press, 1985).

is imported or raised locally. According to the H-O-S framework, for example, the import of capital favors labor and reduces the returns to capital in the host economy, but the reverse occurs if capital is raised locally. Greenfield FDI can increase industry capacity, which could favor nonspecific labor (unless it dramatically increases capital intensity, leading to workforce downsizing) but hurt industry-specific labor and capital. Even for nonspecific labor, FDI inflows can be associated with reforms of labor law and practices that reduce the bargaining power and overall political influence of organized labor, which may prompt opposition. Any form of FDI can also bring new technology to the host economy. This is likely to be broadly beneficial for host economy factors, except for specific firms and labor disadvantaged by superior technology. Hence, the distributional effects of FDI are likely to vary depending on the particular bundle of factors involved in a given case.

The societal interest approach suggests that even if most FDI had net positive aggregate welfare benefits for recipient countries, governments might still restrict it if some powerful domestic groups oppose entry by MNCs. Much is likely to depend on the mode of entry of FDI (greenfield or M&A) and especially on whether the investment is intended to serve demand in the local market or in export markets. Competing domestic firms are most likely to oppose FDI intended to produce goods and services for the domestic market that are not already imported (as in the case of Korea before 1997, examined in chapter 4). Competing domestic firms often oppose greenfield FDI on the grounds that it will increase industry capacity, while M&As are opposed on grounds of retaining the control of existing (domestic) owners. Export-oriented FDI is often less threatening to domestic firms—indeed, domestic supplier firms may favor it along with labor. This helps us understand why governments in developing countries have often liberalized entry conditions for export-oriented FDI while continuing to restrict heavily domestic market-seeking FDI.

Although we can make some generalizations of this kind about the likely preferences of domestic societal interests regarding FDI, it is less clear how a societal interests approach can explain the general policy shift toward greater openness. In particular, it is not obvious why opposition to inward FDI has declined on various fronts. Economic crises can sometimes weaken such opposition. In Korea, the 1997–98 crisis weakened the chaebol politically, and this allowed the government greater room to liberalize FDI. But crises are unlikely to be the only factor behind this policy shift, as we discuss below. The greater ability of firms to manage international supply chains because of the IT revolution may also have weakened the bargaining power of organized labor, though labor is often not the main source of opposition to inward FDI.

MNCs may also have learned to avoid provoking domestic opposition by engaging in relatively "friendly" forms of FDI, such as M& As, thereby neutralizing domestic political opposition. They may have avoided political controversy in developing countries by focusing on export-oriented FDI, though the economic explanations discussed earlier seem better able to account for efficiency-seeking FDI of this form. Above all, a societal interests account does not easily explain why governments have been so keen in recent years to attract export-oriented FDI.

Changing State Interests

States can possess their own goals regarding FDI, but state interests regarding FDI are very difficult to define autonomously of economic theories. If the government wishes to promote national economic development and employment, for example, much depends on how it believes FDI affects these goals. Here, there has been much controversy among experts concerning the economic impact of FDI. Neoclassical economists generally assumed that inward investment in capital-poor developing countries promotes development by increasing efficiency, productivity, and exports. But the emphasis of the economic theorists of FDI on its source in market imperfections cast doubt on this assumption. Certainly, many governments of developing countries distrusted the liberal view. They saw MNCs as controlling access to capital and technology, hindering rather than promoting economic development and undermining national sovereignty.

Particular groups associated with the state may derive direct or indirect personal benefits from FDI that lead them to favor openness. Indirect benefits may come in the form of claiming credit for successful policies or electoral advantage for politicians caused by the positive economic benefits FDI may provide to particular groups (e.g., more employment for voters). Direct benefits may take the form of bribes paid by MNCs to senior government officials and related individuals who must approve FDI projects (such bribes can include cash and equity participation in joint ventures). This is fairly common in many countries with formal or informal inward investment approval regimes and with less transparent, less democratic political regimes.[32] It is unclear, however, how this helps to explain the recent liberalization of FDI policies, since reducing restrictions on FDI will imply less opportunity for official enrichment (unless this increases inflows while retaining approval powers).

The shift toward more liberal policies in host countries is more likely to be related to the changing nature of FDI. First, the sectoral pattern of global FDI flows has changed over time, with inflows in the more politicized extractive sector in developing countries declining in importance over time and inflows in manufacturing and services growing in significance. In manufacturing and services projects, rents are less visible and more related to the intrafirm advantages brought by the MNC than to their use of local resources. (It is interesting in this regard that rapid increases in commodity prices since 2002 have led to a reemergence of political conflict over FDI in extractive industries in Latin America, notably resulting in the renationalization of oil and gas projects in Bolivia in 2006). Second, as firms and investment have become more mobile and the importance of firms' knowledge capital has increased, hostile attitudes toward inward FDI in technology-intensive sectors may have become self-defeating. The strong version of this argument is that states are now forced to compete for mobile investments by unilaterally liberalizing their regulatory treatment of MNCs.[33] This argument is discussed further in chapter 7, but it has limited relevance for most FDI, which is market-seeking rather than cost-minimizing.

State interests have also arguably shifted in response to economic crises. Historically, restrictive FDI policies were often part of a broader

---

[32] Simeon Djankov, Rafael La Porta, Florencio Lopez-de-Silanes, and Andrei Shleifer, "The Regulation of Entry," *Quarterly Journal of Economics* 117:1, 2002, 1–37.

[33] Cerny, "Globalization and Changing Logic."

ISI strategy, which suffered a fatal blow in Latin America with the onset of the debt crisis of the 1980s (chapter 5). Indebted countries needed to achieve rapid improvements in their external position, and the promotion of FDI could help by importing capital and by increasing exports. FDI was increasingly seen as a form of capital inflow less risky than bank loans in hard currencies, insulating the balance of payments during economic downturns. The privatization of state-owned assets by heavily indebted governments also created new opportunities for FDI. Trade liberalization strategies increased levels of competition for domestic firms, reducing the salience of some previous arguments for restricting inward FDI. The liberalization of portfolio capital flows (discussed in chapter 4) has probably also promoted FDI, as MNCs prefer to be able to transfer internal funds within the firm without restriction (though causal relationships flow in both directions here).[34]

Crises cannot explain liberalization in general because it has occurred in countries that have not suffered major financial crises. It may be that liberalizations in crisis-hit developing countries increased the pressure on other developing countries to compete for mobile investments, at least in the case of efficiency-seeking FDI. It is also possible that crisis-driven liberalizations led to a diffusion of liberal policies as other countries learned from the positive experience of early liberalizers.[35] But such a sequence of effects remains to be demonstrated.

Liberalization as a Response to New Ideas

The potential for learning is one answer to the question of how policy norms diffuse through the global political economy. A related though distinct answer is the constructivist claim that expert groups define viable policies and spread them through international institutions and other mechanisms. As we have noted, attempts to explain rising FDI

[34] The removal of portfolio capital controls in the *advanced* countries may also have promoted FDI by increasing the volatility of exchange rates. To the extent that MNCs can source inputs from domestic (or same currency) suppliers, FDI is a hedge against exchange rate fluctuations.

[35] On policy diffusion generally, see Frank Dobbin, Beth Simmons, and Geoffrey Garrett, "The Global Diffusion of Public Policies: Social Construction, Coercion, Competition, or Learning?" *Annual Review of Sociology* 33, 2007, 449–72; Simmons and Elkins, "Globalization of Liberalization."

flows by reference to changing state interests are difficult to separate from arguments that new policy ideas have helped states to redefine their interests. In the case of FDI, political ideas were arguably as important as economic ones in shaping national policies in the mid-twentieth century. The initially hostile attitude toward FDI exhibited by many developing countries reflected in part a perceived linkage between MNCs and colonialism. The negative publicity that resulted from the foreign political activism pursued by companies like ITT in Chile and United Fruit in Guatemala during the Cold War encouraged most MNCs to take a more neutral political stance. This, the declining salience of the anticolonial movement, and the diminution and eventual end of the Cold War conflict contributed to the declining politicization of foreign investment in recent years.

The academic consensus among economists also shifted decisively in favor of FDI. The dependency school, in contrast to classical variants of Marxism, had generally seen MNCs as restricting development.[36] The original dependency position rejected, a priori, the possibility of economic development within the capitalist world economy.[37] In this view, the remittance of monopoly profits by MNCs from underdeveloped to advanced countries drained savings from the former and locked developing countries into a fixed hierarchy of global production relations (specializing in the export of raw materials). Dominant local classes were compromised by their dependence on foreign economic interests, supporting a form of neoimperialism. There were less deterministic variants of this argument,[38] but skepticism about the benefits from FDI was widespread.

Over time, evidence accumulated that some developing countries achieved rapid growth while relatively open to FDI.[39] Hong Kong, Indonesia, Malaysia, Singapore, and Thailand all encouraged FDI in manu-

---

[36] Although orthodox Marxists regarded FDI inflows as exploitative, they also saw the entry of foreign capital into developing countries as having a positive long-run impact on the development of national capitalism. See Bill Warren, *Imperialism, Pioneer of Capitalism* (London: Verso, 1980).

[37] See Dudley Seers, ed., *Dependency Theory: A Critical Reassessment* (London: Pinter, 1981).

[38] Fernando Henrique Cardoso and Enzo Faletto, *Dependency and Development* (Berkeley and Los Angeles: University of California Press, 1979).

[39] Sanjaya Lall, "FDI and Development: Policy and Research Issues in the Emerging Context," Queen Elizabeth House Working Paper Series, 43, 2000.

facturing and achieved rapid economic development; more recently, China has had an even more powerful positive demonstration effect. There were other Asian countries that achieved similarly rapid growth that were relatively closed toward inward FDI, including Japan, Korea, and Taiwan.[40] However, the positive role of economic openness in the Asian growth miracle tended to receive emphasis in official reports.[41]

The IFIs, along with most economists, now argued that countries in Latin America and elsewhere could increase exports and productivity and improve infrastructure by attracting globally competitive MNCs. The dynamic benefits of inward FDI deriving from the diffusion of technology and the enhancement of market competition received greater emphasis in the academic literature, though the findings of empirical studies were often strikingly mixed.[42] This mixed evidence should not have been surprising given that academic work in this area had argued that MNCs had their origin in market imperfections. Even so, the shifting policy consensus in favor of liberalization was epitomized by the UNCTAD's move from a skeptical to a positive position on the developmental benefits of inward FDI.[43]

New ideas concerning the benefits to be derived from the privatization of state-owned enterprises (SOEs) since the 1980s also had implications for FDI. The sale of SOEs certainly allowed many countries to improve their fiscal balance. Combined with new attitudes toward inward FDI, it also facilitated the growth in international M&As in utilities, finance, and infrastructure. The acquisition of privately owned domestic firms by MNCs often remains very difficult because of the dominance of controlling block shareholders (generally families or the state)

---

[40] Korea followed the Japanese strategy of importing technology rather than relying on FDI. Taiwan was more receptive to FDI, but state- and family-owned firms were often protected, and MNCs were subject to stringent export performance, local content, and technology transfer requirements. See Wade, *Governing the Market*, chap. 5.

[41] Expounded notably in the World Bank's *East Asian Miracle* report.

[42] E.g., Brian Aitken, Gordon H. Hanson, and Anne E. Harrison, "Spillovers, Foreign Investment, and Export Behavior," *Journal of International Economics* 43:1, 1997, 103–32; Eduardo Borensztein, Jose De Gregorio, and Jong Wha Lee, "How Does Foreign Direct Investment Affect Economic Growth?" *Journal of International Economics* 45:1, 1998, 115–35.

[43] UNCTAD, *World Investment Report 1992: Transnational Corporations as Engines of Growth* (New York: UNCTAD, 1992).

in most countries.[44] The sale of large public stakes in SOEs, however, has sometimes allowed MNCs to bid alongside domestic firms, notably in Latin America.

Although the influence of new ideas regarding the economic benefits of FDI seems important, we should not exaggerate their impact or the level of consensus. In a number of countries, governments retained national control (public or private) in key sectors, such as banking (Brazil, Malaysia) and telecommunications and energy (Mexico). In some countries that allowed foreign MNCs to acquire important stakes in large domestic firms in recent years, there has been a political backlash against foreign ownership and control. Such economic nationalism is not confined to a few countries in Latin America; it has also been evident in, for example, Korea, where MNCs made substantial inroads into the financial sector after 1997. FDI policy in many cases seems to be better described as pragmatic and ad hoc liberalization than as ideological liberalism. Another indication of the lack of international consensus on FDI is the thinness of multilateral rules in this area (chapter 7).

Liberalization as a Product of Hegemonic Coercion

Since the 1980s, the major developed countries have become more assertive about protecting the interests of their firms when investing abroad. This has not entailed a wholesale return to the era of extraterritorial protection of investor "rights" that characterized much of the nineteenth century,[45] but the United States in particular has pushed for greater protection of investors and for rights to enter new markets through a variety of mechanisms (see chapter 7). This has been especially true of US policy in the Americas, most notably toward Mexico (in the NAFTA treaty). The major developed countries have also supported the work of the IFIs in promoting the adoption of more liberal

---

[44] Rafael La Porta, Florencio Lopez-de-Silanes, and Andrei Shleifer, "Corporate Ownership around the World," *Journal of Finance* 54:2, 1999, 471–517. In the United States and United Kingdom, where (unusually) most firms are widely held by diverse shareholders, the market for corporate control is relatively open, except where it is blocked via direct government intervention.

[45] Lipson, *Standing Guard.*

trade and FDI policies in the developing world since the 1980s. Since many developing countries have exhibited a continuing reluctance to allow MNCs unrestricted access to their economies, does this suggest that hegemonic coercion rather than changing ideas or domestic interests best explains the changing pattern of FDI policies?

Although external pressure has certainly been important in particular cases, there are countervailing forces at work that limit the ability of advanced countries to enforce openness in developing countries. The first constraint is the absence of a multilateral regime that promotes and upholds principles of market access and investor protection. Although the advanced countries have negotiated bilateral and regional investment liberalization and protection deals, these have not been possible with some important emerging market countries (notably Brazil, China, India, and Russia—see chapter 7). A second constraint is the limited domestic political consensus within the advanced countries regarding unrestricted FDI flows. In principle, the H-O-S model suggests that a fall in the capital-labor ratio in the capital-exporting country should adversely affect wages (and in the short run, employment) and hence labor interests. Unions in advanced countries have often opposed unrestricted FDI inflows and outflows. There have also been concerns about the leakage of technology abroad, with implications for national autonomy, security, and prosperity.[46] Recent empirical research casts doubt on some of these concerns, in part because the importance of intrafirm trade for MNCs means that FDI can be positively correlated with exports and employment.[47] Yet such findings are unlikely to counter the growing popular perception that outsourcing and other forms of outward investment in particular are bad for jobs and wages. Such perceptions can work against the negotiation of international treaties that are seen to favor corporate as opposed to labor and local community interests.

Against this, there is the argument that ideas and interests in the advanced countries increasingly favor liberal FDI policies. In the United States, the general ideological aversion to government interference with

[46] Prestowitz, *Trading Places*.

[47] For US evidence, see Mihir A. Desai, C. Fritz Foley, and James R. Hines Jr., "Foreign Direct Investment and Domestic Economic Activity," NBER Working Paper, 11717, October 2005.

private investment activities may act as a barrier to interference in FDI, but FDI policies in Europe and Japan are in fact not very different from those in the United States. Is the broadly liberal trend of FDI policy in the advanced countries a product of a disproportionate political influence of large firms, making it difficult for governments to restrict capital outflows in spite of popular concerns that corporate and national interests often diverge?

Large business organizations in Europe and the United States have pushed hard, and often successfully, for FDI liberalization negotiations at the international level in recent years.[48] Governments are often sensitive to the argument made by large firms that in order to maintain their home market position in the face of growing international competition, they must succeed in global markets through both trade and FDI. Outward FDI can also eventually produce substantial future inflows of profits and dividends, bolstering a country's longer-term balance-of-payments position. For the United States, the net returns on the country's global asset and liability portfolio have made a significant positive contribution to the (deficit) US payments position despite growing capital inflows.[49] And yet the domestic corporate pro-FDI coalition has not prevented governments in advanced countries from restricting inward FDI in sensitive sectors. Nor has it succeeded in promoting a liberal international regime for FDI, as we discuss in the next chapter.

CONCLUSION

FDI has become a critical dimension of the contemporary global political economy. MNC-related trade and financial flows increasingly dominate international markets. The widespread postwar hostility toward FDI has significantly receded, but not disappeared. Hostility persists in some countries, and almost all governments still restrain the activities of MNCs in some sectors. As the role of FDI and MNCs in the global economy has grown, policy in this area remains highly politicized even

---

[48] Andrew Walter, "NGOs, Business, and International Investment Rules: MAI, Seattle, and Beyond," *Global Governance* 7:1, 2001, 51–73.

[49] Gourinchas and Rey, "World Banker."

if on average it is more liberal. This is inevitable not simply because MNCs are seen as foreign or as potentially disloyal, but perhaps primarily because MNCs are often so large.

Political borders and the national policies associated with them remain crucially important for FDI decisions. If anything, as many MNCs have developed global strategies, their investment decisions have become increasingly sensitive to policy choices and institutions in different political jurisdictions. Economic factors behind the growth of FDI, particularly rapid technological change and growth in parts of the developing world, have been important, but so too have decisions by governments to liberalize FDI flows. Material and ideational factors have both contributed to the liberalization trend in developing countries, but we have seen that the impact of these factors can be difficult to separate in practice. In the next chapter, we investigate in more detail the growth of new international rules relating to FDI, and the question of whether the rise of global firms produces national policy convergence.

FURTHER RESOURCES

Further Reading

Georgio Barba Navaretti and Anthony J. Venables. *Multinational Firms in the World Economy.* Princeton, N.J.: Princeton University Press, 2006. An up-to-date and accessible review of the theory and empirical data, concluding that, on balance, MNCs are a positive force in the global economy.

UNCTAD. *World Investment Report.* This annual report is the best source of information on FDI trends, MNCs, and related policy issues. Available for free download at www.unctad.org/wir.

Peter Dicken. *Global Shift: Mapping the Changing Contours of the World Economy.* London: Sage, 5th ed., 2007. A text on globalization by an economic geographer that emphasizes the growing importance of international production and provides useful case studies.

Useful Websites

- http://www.unctad.org/Templates/Page.asp?intItemID=1923& lang=1: The UNCTAD's Foreign Direct Investment Database provides aggregate FDI data for 196 countries as well as data on MNC operations in some countries.
- http://www.bea.gov/bea/di/home/directinv.htm: The Bureau of Economic Analysis at the US Department of Commerce provides unrivaled data on the operations of US MNCs abroad and foreign MNCs operating in the United States, as well as data on the significance of such firms in employment, GDP, trade, etc.
- http://www.doingbusiness.org: The World Bank's *Doing Business* website contains much useful information on the comparative costs, difficulties, and procedures in establishing and operating businesses in different countries.
- http://www.corporateeurope.org/ceolinks.html: The Corporate Europe Observatory website contains a list of the growing number of NGO sites dedicated to monitoring the activities of MNCs. See also the well-maintained US-based CorpWatch site: http://www.corpwatch.org/links.php.

7 | The Regulation and Policy Consequences of Foreign Direct Investment

In this chapter, we consider two related questions. The first concerns the relatively recent emergence of international rules on FDI. Although no comprehensive multilateral investment regime exists, there is an emerging web of bilateral and regional investment regimes that create an increasingly complex picture. Given that international regimes on trade and finance were created in the mid-twentieth century, the different pattern in the area of FDI rules requires further investigation. We argue that the general level of political support for a comprehensive international investment regime remains considerably lower than for international trade, even within the advanced countries. Second, we consider whether the activities of global firms are promoting the convergence of national economic policies. We argue that on this question the evidence is mixed, but strong claims of policy convergence are often unwarranted.

THE EMERGING INTERNATIONAL INVESTMENT REGIME

Before asking why the creation of an international investment regime has been relatively difficult compared to that for international trade, we must first briefly describe the increasingly complex patchwork of bilateral, regional, and multilateral agreements relating to FDI and MNCs. As we will see, bilateral and regional agreements have grown especially rapidly in recent years, whereas multilateral agreements have proven highly controversial and more difficult to achieve.

Bilateral Investment Treaties

Bilateral regimes have dominated the international investment scene since the 1960s and 1970s. Early bilateral investment treaties (BITs) were negotiated in the late 1950s and 1960s and reflected the cautious and often hostile attitudes toward FDI and MNCs that prevailed during this period. The heavy protectionism and restrictive regulation of MNCs led large Western MNCs to lobby their home governments to negotiate international agreements that could improve protection for existing foreign investments.[1] Few BITs were negotiated between the developed economies of the OECD, where standards of protection were generally higher than those in developing countries.[2] The first BIT was signed in 1959 between West Germany and Pakistan, though treaties of "Friendship, Commerce and Navigation" and "Amity and Commerce," which included some elements of modern BITs, are at least two centuries old. The historic outward investors with large stocks of FDI in developing countries led the way in negotiating BITs, including West Germany, the United Kingdom, the Netherlands, and Switzerland (tables 7.1, 7.2). The glaring exceptions were the United States and Japan, who began negotiating BITs at a relatively late stage. Many developed countries also adopted political risk insurance programs for outward FDI, with associated investment guarantee agreements with developing countries, which were intended to reduce the risks for domestic firms of investing and operating in host countries.

The number of BITs has grown very rapidly since the late 1980s. At the end of the 1980s, there were 385 BITs. The number grew dramatically in the 1990s, to 1,513 by the end of 1997 and 2,495 by the end of 2005, involving most countries and territories (table 7.2 lists the most active countries). In addition to these, the UNCTAD listed 2,758 double taxation treaties with significant implications for MNCs and 232 other agreements with investment aspects by the end of 2005.[3] Notably, fol-

---

[1] Lipson, *Standing Guard*, 97.

[2] The central importance of taxation issues to governments did, however, facilitate agreement on bilateral double-taxation treaties (DTTs), which were driven in part by the specific concern to negotiate the taxation of MNCs.

[3] UNCTAD, *World Investment Report 2006*, 26. Note that nearly 25% of the BITs negotiated by the end of 2005 had not yet entered into force.

TABLE 7.1
Outward FDI Stock, 10 Major Countries, 1980–2005 (US$ billions, ranked by
FDI stock in 2005)

	1980	1985	1990	1995	2000	2005
United States	215	238	431	699	1,316	2,051
United Kingdom	80	100	229	305	898	1,238
Germany	43	60	152	268	542	967
France	24	38	110	204	445	853
Netherlands	42	48	107	173	305	641
Hong Kong, China	0	2	12	79	388	470
Canada	24	43	85	118	238	399
Switzerland	21	25	66	142	230	395
Japan	20	44	201	238	278	387
Belgium				(5)	(8)	386

Source: UNCTAD, *World Investment Report 2006.*

lowing the NAFTA model, FTAs are becoming more ambitious in scope.
A number of recent bilateral FTAs have substantial investment promo-
tion and protection aspects as well as new investor market access
clauses.[4] Although North-South BITs remain the largest category,
South-South treaties are also growing rapidly, following the trend in
South-South FDI.

Various related factors are behind this trend. First, as FDI outflows
from the large outward investing countries have grown very rapidly
since the 1970s, they have increased the demand from MNCs for investment protection and promotion treaties. BITs, DTTs, and FTAs are a
lagging indicator of the growing economic importance of MNCs. The
failure to agree to a multilateral investment treaty in the 1990s has also
spurred a number of outward investing countries to improve investor
protection and market access through bilateral mechanisms.[5] Second,
the increasingly close link between trade and FDI (including of the

[4] Mark Manger, "Competition and Bilateralism in Trade Policy: The Case of Japan's Free Trade
Agreements," *Review of International Political Economy* 12:5, 2005, 804–28.
[5] Gilbert Gagné and Jean-Frédéric Morin, "The Evolving American Policy on Investment Protection: Evidence from Recent FTAs and the 2004 Model BIT," *Journal of International Economic
Law* 9:2, 2006, 357–82.

TABLE 7.2
Top 30 Signatories of BITs, End of 2005

Country	Number of BITs
Germany	133
China	117
Switzerland	110
United Kingdom	102
Egypt	98
France	98
Italy	96
Netherlands	91
Belgium-Luxembourg	84
Romania	83
Korea	80
Czech Rep.	79
Turkey	74
Malaysia	66
Sweden	66
Bulgaria	65
Finland	63
Austria	61
Poland	61
Spain	61
Ukraine	61
Indonesia	59
Argentina	58
Hungary	58
Croatia	57
Cuba	56
India	56
Denmark	53
Iran	53
Morocco	53

Source: UNCTAD, *World Investment Report 2006*, Annex A.I.10.

market-seeking variety) has meant that parties to trade liberalization agreements have increasingly accepted MNC demands to include complementary investment provisions. For services, market access often requires a local presence and hence investor access rights. Third, the shift toward more positive attitudes toward inward FDI and trade in developing countries has made them more willing to sign such treaties as a means of attracting FDI and increasing exports. Linking trade and investment also offers significant bargaining advantages to the larger countries in a bilateral context. Finally, increasing numbers of countries, including many developing countries, have become significant outward investors as their firms internationalize and governments have become more aware of the need to protect their firms' interests abroad.

Earlier BITs focused mainly on the protection of existing investments, whereas BITs since 1980 have also emphasized the promotion of new investment. More recent BITs also tend to offer greater quality of protection and promotion for foreign investors, often including investor-state DSMs (discussed below). Strong market access clauses are especially characteristic of US BITs, which have all been negotiated since the early 1980s.[6] European states and have instead favored more BITs at the expense of weaker treaties. This is a clear indication that the most powerful state, the United States, has used its bargaining power in recent years to obtain advantages for its firms. Yet there are limits to this negotiating power. Conspicuous by their absence from the US list of BITs are any major developing countries in East Asia and Latin America, with the exception of Argentina. Recent US FTAs with Malaysia, Singapore, South Korea, and Thailand indicate that strong investment agreements (e.g., in the Korean FTA) are likely to be more achievable if linked to trade.

Regional Investment Regimes

Regional investment agreements (RIAs) were rare until recently. Over the past two decades they have also grown very rapidly, and they too are closely linked to trade liberalization agreements. Regional agreements among developing countries have increasingly addressed the issue of investment liberalization (e.g., ASEAN and Mercosur), but none have approached the strength of the European and North American regimes. The most important regional investment agreement is the European single market. The Treaty of Rome (1957) and the Single European Act (1986) provide registered corporations with the right of establishment in other member states and for national treatment of foreign investments by those states. This principle was often poorly observed after

---

[6] The United States had some earlier Friendship, Commerce, and Navigation treaties with developing countries with some investment aspects.

1957 and the Single European Act aimed to strengthen its application. Whereas other RIAs typically include, as do most BITs, some form of DSM, the provisions of the European treaty are directly applicable in national courts of member states. Community law prevails over national provisions.[7] In addition, the European Court of Justice provides a supra-national legal forum in which companies or individuals can also bring investment disputes related to the treaty provisions to be adjudicated.

Like the United States and Japan, the EU has also entered into regional free trade area agreements with third countries and regions. There has been resistance to extending the full investment provisions of the single market to these agreements, since some member states fear that this would compromise their existing extensive BITs networks and hand too much power to the European Commission. In addition, some member states have been concerned that RIAs with developing countries will undermine European labor and environmental standards. The result is that most EU agreements with third parties focus on trade liberalization and have only general language in the area of investment.

NAFTA's chapter 11 is perhaps the best-known RIA, not least because of the controversy surrounding recent disputes between MNCs and NAFTA member states. The US government saw NAFTA as "state of the art" when agreed in 1993, with its strong provisions regarding investor preestablishment rights, investor protection, and an investor-state DSM. Even so, the Canadian and Mexican governments insisted on retaining the right to screen inward investment rather than to allow automatic approval, and the Canadians also successfully retained an exception to the nondiscrimination principle for investors in "cultural" industries. There are also substantial reservations tabled by Mexico that limit the sectoral coverage of NAFTA's investment provisions. In addition, contrary to the wishes of US MNCs, the Clinton administration bowed to domestic political pressures by attaching clauses establishing environmental and labor standards to the treaty. The United States has also been unable to negotiate a Free Trade Area of the Americas (FTAA) with an investment chapter.

---

[7] See European Commission, *Guide to the Case Law of the European Court of Justice on Articles 52 et seq. EC Treaty: Freedom of Establishment* (Brussels: European Commission, January 1, 1999).

Plurilateral and Multilateral Investment Regimes

Efforts to establish multilateral rules on FDI date back to the failed Havana Charter of the ITO in the late 1940s. One section of the Havana Charter dealt with the regulation of international business, but it appealed neither to the business lobbies who favored the protection and liberalization of international investments nor to those governments who wished to severely restrict MNC activities (during the war, MNC factories and other assets had sometimes been nationalized and converted to munitions production). The strength of nationalist economic thinking in the early postwar decades also encouraged widespread hostility toward MNCs. The memory of imperial powers protecting the foreign assets of their citizens also contributed to a strong desire in many developing countries to avoid the reestablishment of international legal rights for international investors. This combination of international investor lobbies, who believed that their historic international legal and economic rights had been eroded, and increasingly assertive economic nationalism created a stalemate that prevented further negotiations on an international investment regime until the 1990s.

As we have seen, attitudes changed considerably, though not completely, by the late 1980s. Although the WTO membership has so far been unable to agree to negotiate a substantive investment framework, some limited international agreements have been possible. The GATS agreement of 1993 on trade in services was in part an investment agreement as it provided in principle for market access via both trade and local MNC affiliates. Despite this achievement, the actual sectoral commitments of many countries under the GATS has been disappointing from the US and European perspective. The financial services and telecoms agreements under the GATS are the strongest of these commitments, but offer levels of investor protection and market access that are well below that of many BITs or the NAFTA. In addition to GATS, the URA included the agreement on Trade Related Investment Measures (TRIMS), which prohibited certain performance requirements in a few areas such as local content and trade balancing that had been heavily used in developing countries. The Government Procurement Agreement, which came into effect on January 1, 1996, also made some progress toward prohibiting "offsets" such as local content and investment requirements as a precondition of procurement awards to MNC affiliates. But this plurilateral agreement is of limited value in disciplining most developing countries, and signatories have often excluded key sectors such as telecommunications.

The OECD has also agreed on a mixture of binding and nonbinding codes on investment. These include the 1961 Code of Liberalization of Capital Movements, modified in 1984 to provide rights of establishment for greenfield FDI, and the Code of Liberalization of Current Invisible Operations, which allows the free transfer of capital and access to finance. OECD governments have agreed to avoid conflicting requirements on MNCs and to make their investment incentives as transparent as possible. There is also a nonbinding National Treatment Instrument applicable to foreign affiliates. Although many of these codes are binding, there are exceptions (including large sectoral exceptions on rights of establishment), and enforcement is provided by peer pressure only.

More ambitiously, and ultimately unsuccessfully, the OECD embarked in 1995 on negotiations for a Multilateral Agreement on Investment (MAI). MNCs' disappointment over the results of the GATT Uruguay Round led business organizations to lobby the US government to push for a stand-alone, binding multilateral investment agreement establishing national treatment (nondiscrimination), right of establishment (i.e., market entry), investment protection, and a NAFTA-style DSM that provided for investor-state dispute settlement. Given continuing opposition on the part of developing countries to investment rules within the WTO, the United States judged the OECD to be a more promising forum. Once MAI was achieved within the OECD, US firms and negotiators hoped that pressure could then be brought to bear on individual developing countries to adhere. Although many European firms and governments supported this idea in principle, there was more support in Europe for a WTO agreement on investment that would obtain broader coverage of developing countries from the start and which would provide only a state-state DSM.

In the negotiations, the US government sought full freedom of transfers and the prompt payment of fair and effective compensation in the event of expropriation. Controversially, this is an absolute standard of "general protection" (in contrast to the relative standards of National Treatment and MFN) for investors/investments that would apply to existing and future investment. Even more controversial was the US insistence, on the NAFTA model, on a so-called takings clause whereby investors would also be protected against "near expropriation." In principle, this could mean that any government policy that had the effect of severely impairing the value of a foreign investor's assets could be challenged by the investor in an international court.[8] Such panels would have the power, as in NAFTA, to require the signatory government to change the relevant policy or to pay monetary damages and restitution in kind.

The first draft of the agreement reached in January 1997 reflected opposition elsewhere in the OECD to these US objectives. The ultimate collapse of the negotiations was the result of opposition from many quarters.[9] Finance ministries in most countries demanded that taxation of all kinds be carved out of the agreement, out of fear that MAI could make tax treatment of MNCs subject to legal challenge and undermine the system of bilateral DTTs. France and Canada insisted on a broad carve-out of cultural industries, including audiovisual and publishing industries. Some developing and transition countries saw MAI as a threat to their policy autonomy in this area. In federal political systems, including in the United States, states and local governments feared that binding nondiscrimination clauses would provide foreign investors with the means to challenge local policies aimed at promoting minorities or generally fostering social cohesion. NGOs were also generally able to focus political attention on the way in which the combination of a broad takings clause and strong investor-state dispute settlement provisions might result in corporate challenges to all kinds of social, labor, developmental, and environmental legislation. The central objection was that MAI provided an absolute standard of investment protec-

---

[8] As in many BITs, there were provisions for the use of ICSID (the International Centre for the Settlement of Investment Disputes based at the World Bank), or as alternatives UNCITRAL (United Nations Commission on International Trade Law) or ICC (International Chamber of Commerce) arbitration.

[9] Edward M. Graham, *Fighting the Wrong Enemy: Antiglobal Activists and Multinational Enterprises* (Washington, D.C.: Institute for International Economics, 2000); David Henderson, *The MAI Affair: A Story and Its Lessons* (London: Royal Institute of International Affairs, 2000).

tion and investor rights that was not enjoyed by domestic citizens (in most countries, the government has the right of eminent domain). Opponents thus successfully linked MAI with the broader concern that globalization was producing a race to the bottom in regulatory standards, a concern increased by the experience of investor-state dispute settlement in NAFTA. When it became clear that at best only weak rules could emerge from the MAI negotiations, business support for the negotiations collapsed, and governments, led by France, promptly withdrew.

The claim by MAI opponents that the initiative reflected a general tendency among major country governments to insist on investor rights rather than responsibilities led to a few initiatives that targeted the latter issue. The Declaration on International Investment and Multinational Enterprises (1976), open to nonmembers to subscribe, and Declarations on the Guidelines for Multinational Enterprises (voluntary rules of conduct, updated in 2000), elaborated general rules for MNC good conduct. In addition, OECD countries agreed in 1997 to a binding Convention on Combating Bribery of Foreign Public Officials in International Business Transactions. This convention requires signatories to criminalize and otherwise discourage the direct or indirect bribery of foreign public officials by citizens, including firms. In this case, a peer review process has been established that monitors national implementation and allows for naming and shaming. The somewhat more robust approach in this area primarily reflects US concern that its firms have been disadvantaged in global business since Congress passed the Foreign Corrupt Practices Act in 1977 (bribery of foreign officials has been both commonplace and even tax deductible in some other major OECD countries).[10] The rising prominence of issues of corporate social responsibility in recent years is also reflected in the UN's voluntary Global Compact (2000), which is aimed at business, and the United Nations Convention against Corruption (2005), which includes provi-

[10] The Anti-Bribery Convention has led a number of OECD countries to modify their legislation to criminalize foreign bribery and to remove tax deductibility. Enforcement, however, continues to vary widely (see Fritz Heimann and Gillian Dell, "Progress Report 07: Enforcement of the OECD Convention on Combating Bribery of Foreign Public Officials," Transparency Interna-

sions aimed at constraining the acceptance as well as the supply of bribes to public officials. It is an open question how effective such conventions are in constraining the activities of global firms, especially when they operate in developing countries.

Given that the US government and MNC lobbies overestimated the level of political support for a strong multilateral investment regime, the question that follows is why there are any strong international investment agreements at all. There is evidence of general public concern in the advanced countries that big business already has excessive power, including in the United States.[11] This has made the ratification of broad investor rights regimes politically difficult. This also helps to explain why measures to promote good conduct by MNCs, such as the anti-bribery conventions, have been more successful.

Nevertheless, the political influence of MNCs remains substantial, and they have collectively been able to veto international agreements that would have given greater recognition to state interests. Corporate power is also reflected in the weaknesses of the global corporate conduct regimes and the continuing expansion of investor rights in regional and bilateral investment regimes. The latter in particular have allowed the major outward investing countries and their associated MNCs a bargaining advantage but also, crucially, a lower domestic political visibility than was possible in the MAI negotiations. Bilateral deals also have the domestic political advantage that (individually) they are less prone to the objection that investment liberalization and protection agreements will undermine national regulatory standards and facilitate the export of jobs to low-wage countries. Even if, as we discuss below, the evidence for such effects is not especially strong, the fear that extensive multilateral liberalization threatens national standards and jobs is likely to remain a major obstacle to a broader multilateral investment regime in the foreseeable future.

---

tional, July 18, 2007, available at http://www.transparency.org/news_room/in_focus/2007/oecd, accessed April 4, 2008).

[11] See the cross-country public opinion surveys by World Public Opinion.Org, such as http://www.worldpublicopinion.org/pipa/articles/btglobalizationtradera/154.php?nid=&id=&pnt=154&lb=btgl, accessed April 5, 2007.

DOES GROWING FDI PROMOTE POLICY CONVERGENCE?

What is the evidence for the claim that the globalization of firms puts downward pressure on regulatory standards, corporate taxation, employment, and wages? This race to the bottom hypothesis is one form of a general argument that globalization produces policy convergence, which we investigate in this section for the particular case of FDI. An alternative formulation is that governments increasingly adopt policies that minimize production costs for mobile firms, though this version does not necessarily imply convergence on a single set of policies.

Particular attention has often been accorded to FDI as a driver of policy convergence because of the supposed mobility of MNCs, their economic size and technological capacity, and their visibility as political actors within countries. In contrast to portfolio capital, it is often argued, MNCs possess political "voice" as well as the "exit" capacity or mobility that gives capital the ability to arbitrage policy regimes across different countries.[12] Different authors place different emphases on the relative importance of voice and exit capacity, though in combination they are often said to provide MNCs with structural power over immobile states, as well as citizens and workers.[13] As Charles Lindblom once claimed: "Either [MNC] demands are met, or the corporation goes elsewhere."[14]

Before we examine the empirical evidence for this claim, it is worth noting that both political lobbying and exit or nonentry involves costs for most firms. Exercising political influence via lobbying may not be easy if political networks and institutions are dominated by relatively

[12] On the classic exit/voice distinction, see Albert O. Hirschman, *Exit, Voice, and Loyalty: Responses to Decline in Firms, Organizations, and States* (Cambridge: Harvard University Press, 1970). For the view that this gives MNCs unrivaled power in the global political economy, see David Korten, *When Corporations Rule the World* (West Hartford, Conn.: Berrett-Koehler, 1995); and for an earlier example, Richard J. Barnet and Ronald E. Müller, *Global Reach: The Power of the Multinational Corporations* (New York: Simon and Schuster, 1974).

[13] Jan Art Scholte, "Global Capitalism and the State," *International Affairs* 73:3, 1997, 443; Stephen Gill and David Law, *The Global Political Economy* (Hemel Hempstead: Harvester-Wheatsheaf, 1988), 87; Leslie Sklair, "Transnational Corporations as Political Actors," *New Political Economy* 3:2, 1998, 284–87.

[14] Charles E. Lindblom, *Politics and Markets: The World's Political and Economic Systems* (New York: Basic Books, 1977), 180.

immobile domestic businesses or labor unions. If the threat of exit or nonentry is credible, firms may not need to exercise political voice. The credibility of the exit threat itself is likely to vary by sector and by company, depending among other things on the amount of sunk costs, the specificity and mobility of key assets, and the costs of renegotiating contracts. Firms are also likely face reputational costs associated with exiting a country or other political jurisdiction. If exit is simply too costly, Hirschman argued, actors are more likely to exercise their political voice (although voiced exit threats will lack credibility). In short, in contrast to claims in some of the literature, mobility and political voice will often be alternatives rather than mutually reinforcing.

Early dependency literature often made claims similar to the convergence school in arguing that MNCs held the major bargaining chips against vulnerable developing countries. The "bargaining" school opposed this view, arguing that the balance of bargaining power varied case by case, and providing supporting evidence from case studies on state-firm interaction.[15] A second generation of dependency theorists adopted the bargaining framework of the critics while arguing that MNCs had additional resources that the "liberal" bargaining approach ignored.[16] These resources included economic and political linkages in the host economy that would grow over time, as well as various aspects of in-house knowledge capital.[17] MNCs may also be able to call on their home governments to bring to bear diplomatic pressure on the host government to alter its policies. The formation of alliances with local partner firms, political elites, or other MNCs may also enhance an MNC's bargaining power vis-à-vis the host government. Even so, it

[15] Charles P. Kindleberger, *American Business Abroad* (New Haven: Yale University Press, 1969); Theodore H. Moran, ed., *Multinational Corporations: The Political Economy of Foreign Direct Investment* (Lexington, Mass.: D. C. Heath, 1985); Alfred C. Stepan, *The State and Society: Peru in Comparative Perspective* (Princeton, N.J.: Princeton University Press, 1978); Raymond Vernon, "Sovereignty at Bay: 10 Years After," *International Organization* 35:3, 1981, 517–39.

[16] Peter B. Evans, *Dependent Development: The Alliance of Multinational, State, and Local Capital in Brazil* (Princeton, N.J.: University Press, 1978). Richard Newfarmer, ed., *Profits, Poverty, and Progress: Case Studies of International Industries in Latin America* (South Bend, Ind.: Notre Dame University Press, 1985).

[17] For a critical discussion and analysis, see Stephen J. Kobrin, "Testing the Bargaining Hypothesis in the Manufacturing Sector in Developing Countries," *International Organization* 41:4, 1987, 609–38.

remained the case that dependency arguments were difficult to recon-
cile with the apparent successes of some East Asian countries in utiliz-
ing FDI as part of their export-oriented growth strategy.

The scope of the more recent convergence hypothesis can also be
extremely broad, making it difficult to assess. It is often applied to a
range of policies, from FDI policies themselves, to trade, financial,
labor, environmental, and spending and taxation policies. In principle,
all kinds of macro- and microeconomic policies that affect production
costs might be arbitraged by mobile firms. In practice, the impact of
different policies on firms' costs is likely to vary considerably by sector
and by firm. For example, a tightening of environmental standards in
one country may impose substantial costs on heavily polluting industries (chemicals, oil processing, transport, etc.), but the costs in many
other sectors could be much lower. Almost all government policies can
affect private production costs, but often these effects are indirect and
marginal. Some, such as corporate taxes, are more direct and apply
across different industries. Production costs may also be reduced by
state provision of public goods, including transparent and enforceable
rules of contract, public education and health care, and infrastructure
investment. Subsidies to specific industries, tax holidays, and the like
can also reduce firms' costs. Although MNCs may not necessarily be
willing themselves to finance such public expenditure via corporate
taxes, it does create some ambiguity about the predictions of the convergence hypothesis.

Hence, at a minimum, for policy arbitrage to produce policy convergence, (1) government policies must vary across political jurisdictions
and impose substantial costs on some firms, (2) these differential costs
must exceed by some margin the transactions costs firms would incur
in exercising their exit or nonentry option vis-à-vis high-cost jurisdictions (so that the threat of exit or nonentry is credible to the latter),
and (3) governments must be sensitive to MNCs' preferences and not
overly constrained by other domestic interests, and must compete strategically for investment.[18] This also assumes that states will not cooper-

---

[18] Miles Kahler, "Modeling Races to the Bottom," Graduate School of International Relations
and Pacific Studies, University of California, San Diego, undated.

ate to prevent such policy arbitrage, presumably because political competition or problems of collective action prevents them from doing so.[19]

An immediate difficulty with this argument is that in emphasizing the collective action problems faced by states, it underplays the collective action problems facing MNCs competing in oligopolistic global industries. If many firms desire access to a particular political jurisdiction (perhaps because of a large domestic market), they may compete for entry rather than engage in policy arbitrage. In addition, the costs of exit may be greater than the costs of nonentry, as emphasized in the obsolescing bargain literature.[20] The costs of nonentry into a particular market (in terms of loss of market opportunity, strategic disadvantage, etc.) may still be considerable, especially in the case of FDI oriented toward large local markets or access to raw materials. Exit costs, however, include the costs of nonentry and additional costs, depending on the nature of the assets involved. Exit may be more costly from a given MNC's home base country for reputational reasons and because a firm's competitiveness is often embedded in local formal and informal institutional linkages with the home base.[21]

These considerations suggest that the mobility of MNCs across jurisdictions may be lower than is sometimes argued, especially after investment has already taken place and for domestic-market-oriented or resource-oriented FDI in general. Exit threats may not always be credible, and at least in the short run it may be less costly for firms to engage in the exercise of political voice. But in doing so, MNCs will often compete for political influence with other societal groups, such as unions, broader business associations, NGOs, and voters. Lobbying of host as opposed to home governments will often be more difficult because MNCs may not enjoy high political legitimacy or knowledge in the former case.

Even if the convergence hypothesis has some theoretical shortcomings and ambiguities, what is the empirical evidence for its predictions? In what follows, we investigate the impact of corporate globalization in

[19] Gill and Law, Global Political Economy, 92; Stopford, Strange, and Henley, Rival States, Rival Firms, 215.

[20] Vernon, "Sovereignty at Bay"; Kindleberger, American Business Abroad, 150–55.

[21] Hu, "Global or Stateless Corporations"; Razeen Sally, States and Firms: Multinational Enterprises in Institutional Competition (London: Routledge, 1995).

four areas where it is generally thought to be high: FDI rules, tax and incentive policies, labor markets, and environmental standards.[22]

FDI Rules

Does the recent trend toward the liberalization of investment rules and increased incentives to attract inward FDI support the convergence hypothesis? There is an initial problem of causality in assessing this argument, since the liberalization of inward investment rules can also induce more FDI. The liberalization process also masks important anomalies. First, there can be a big difference between formal investment rules and the actual treatment of foreign investors. Second, many countries have liberalized entry restrictions but retain operating restrictions on MNCs, from performance requirements for manufacturers to domestic branching rights for global banks. Many developing countries and some developed countries retain nontransparent screening procedures for entry, widespread use of limits on foreign ownership, and outright prohibitions in designated strategic sectors.[23]

Interestingly, in some prominent cases, most notably China, illiberal FDI policy regimes have been associated with large inward FDI flows. By contrast, some developing countries with very liberal FDI regimes have often received little FDI, including most countries that have strong BITs with the United States.[24] Clearly, factors other than the relative liberality of the investment regime in developing countries often matter more for MNC location decisions, including market size and domestic and regional growth prospects. Governments in countries such as Malaysia, Indonesia, China, and Thailand appear to have been able to re-

[22] For other useful assessments, see Theodore H. Moran, *Harnessing Foreign Direct Investment for Development: Policies for Developed and Developing Countries* (Washington, D.C.: Center for Global Development, 2006); and Deborah L. Spar and David B. Yoffie, "Multinational Enterprises and the Prospects for Justice," *Journal of International Affairs* 52:2, 1999, 557–81.

[23] For annual compilations on a country-by-country basis of such restrictions from a US perspective, see the investment sections of US Department of State, *Country Commercial Guides*, and US Trade Representative, *National Trade Estimates*. Moran, *Harnessing Foreign Direct Investment*, argues that many of these policies fail to achieve their ostensible developmental objectives.

[24] Andrew Walter, "Globalization and Policy Convergence: The Case of Direct Investment Rules," in Richard A. Higgott, Geoffrey R. D. Underhill, and Andreas Beiler, eds., *Non-state Actors and Authority in the Global System* (London: Routledge, 2000), 51–74.

tain some onerous operating restrictions on MNCs because of intense competition among MNCs for access to their economies.

Meanwhile, relatively mobile, export-oriented FDI is often exempted from such restrictions in export processing zones (EPZs). Governments use such EPZs in part to insulate their general FDI policies from the effects of concessions to relatively mobile FDI. Even in EPZs, however, other attractions such as geographic position, regional trade liberalization, physical infrastructure, and human capital are often more important in MNCs' decisions on location.[25] In particular, a country's bargaining power relative to export-oriented MNCs will be increased by preferential access to large export markets. This is exemplified by the case of Mexico, whose attractiveness as a location for US-oriented exporters increased considerably as a result of NAFTA. Thus, although relatively high mobility does appear to induce more favorable treatment for many MNCs, other factors often predominate in corporate location decisions, even for export-oriented FDI. Furthermore, even in sectors in which a firm's technology is crucial and mobility is relatively high, severe competition between US, Japanese, and European multinational firms has often reduced the arbitrage pressure on host countries' policy regimes.[26]

Tax and Incentive Policies

Many empirical studies suggest that FDI is sensitive to taxation policies, perhaps increasingly so, providing potential for tax competition effects. Again, however, since taxation policies are not the only determinant of most decisions on where to invest, the reality of tax arbitrage may be more limited than some claim, especially for market-seeking FDI.[27] The bulk of FDI flows, even to lower-cost developing countries, is domestic market-oriented, not cost-minimizing, even if there has been an in-

[25] John H. Dunning, *Multinational Enterprises and the Global Economy* (Reading, Mass.: Addison-Wesley 1993) 144

[26] Lipson, *Standing Guard*, 161–82; Moran, *Multinational Corporations*, 8–9; Charles P. Oman, Douglas H. Brooks, and Colm Foy, eds., *Investing in Asia* (Paris: OECD Development Centre, 1997), 210–12.

[27] Kobrin, "Testing the Bargaining Hypothesis."

crease in the latter form in recent years.[28] In addition, variations in the level of host country taxation often lead to automatic compensatory adjustments because taxes paid in other countries are generally deducted from tax liabilities on profits repatriated home. Hence, low-tax policies and fiscal incentives in the host country may only succeed in increasing an MNC's profits and global tax liabilities in its home country.[29] Even so, MNCs at the margin might still prefer to invest in countries where tax rates are no higher than in their home base, thereby promoting convergence.

For relatively mobile FDI projects, many governments appear to be competing for FDI by offering costly financial inducements. Even in these cases, such incentives are often not decisive in decisions on where to invest and may therefore be wasted. Both survey and statistical research of such decisions has shown that market size, growth prospects, geographical location, access to large regional markets, local infrastructure, human capital, and political stability are more important in attracting investment than tax and other financial incentives. Many of these factors are beyond the control of governments, which may focus the attention of both MNCs and political authorities on tax and incentives.[30] MNCs have a clear interest in suggesting that financial incentives are decisive, and it may be very difficult for governments to know whether they are bluffing unless there is competition from other potential inward investors.

Even for market-seeking FDI, tax and incentives may be an important factor in the choice of a specific location within a wider integrated region. Indeed, market integration can unleash tax competition between political authorities at the subnational or subregional level. For example, US state and local government subsidies to greenfield automobile projects continued to escalate in the 1980s and 1990s

[28] OECD, *Foreign Direct Investment and Economic Development: Lessons from Six Emerging Economies* (Paris: OECD, 1998), 21–22.

[29] Jacques Morisset and Neda Pirnia, "How Tax Policy and Incentives Affect Foreign Direct Investment: A Review," World Bank Working Paper, 2509, 2000; OECD, *Corporate Tax Incentives for Foreign Direct Investment, No. 4* (Paris: OECD, 2001).

[30] Dunning, *Multinational Enterprises*, 139–48; McKinsey Global Institute, *New Horizons: Multinational Company Investment in Developing Economies* (San Francisco: McKinsey & Co., 2003), 25–27.

to well over $200,000 per job. In such large markets, the collective action dilemma shifts mainly to subfederal states and local authorities. Even if an MNC has no choice but to locate within the US market, the potentially large number of possible sites may allow the firm to play off one subfederal jurisdiction against another in the final choice of location. Thus, while the US federal government generally offers no specific incentives for MNCs to enter the US market, state and local competitors may believe they have no choice but to engage in an escalating war of incentives.

This implies that members of regional trade integration agreements risk becoming "subfederal" competitors vis-à-vis MNCs who wish to access the regional market. If a semiconductor manufacturer is relatively indifferent between Ireland, Scotland, and Hungary as a production site from which it can export to the whole European market, a low corporate tax rate for manufacturing FDI might be a useful incentive.[31] The EU and OECD have become increasingly concerned about such mutually destructive tax competition. In principle, such regions can overcome these dilemmas by harmonizing their policies on corporate taxation, but doing so has proven very difficult in practice. Interestingly, the EU has constrained such competition more than the United States, where federal political arrangements have largely prevented harmonization, helping to explain the escalation in within-US tax and incentive competition between subfederal authorities.[32]

Even if much FDI is sensitive to tax rates, this does not mean that market forces will systematically force corporate taxes down to a common level, let alone to zero. Since different investment locations offer a bundle of attributes, tax rates can differ in theory even with perfectly mobile capital. In practice, the evidence suggests no clear trend toward a generalized decline or convergence in effective (as opposed to headline) corporate tax rates.[33] The evidence for US MNC affiliates, for ex-

[31] Joeri Gorter and Ashok Parikh, "How Sensitive Is FDI to Differences in Corporate Income Taxation within the EU?" De Economist, 151:2, 2003, 193–204.

[32] Andrew Walter, "Do Corporations Really Rule the World?" New Political Economy 3:2, 1998, 292–95.

[33] Kenneth G. Stewart and Michael C. Webb, "Capital Taxation, Globalization, and International Tax Competition," Econometrics Working Papers, 301, Department of Economics, University of Victoria, 2003. For OECD Revenue Statistics, see http://stats.oecd.org/wbos/Index.aspx.

ample, shows that taxes paid by majority-owned nonbank affiliates of nonbank US parents vary considerably by country. Total average taxes paid by these affiliates were 5.3% of total sales in 1994 and 7% in 1999.[34] These figures also vary considerably by industry. Furthermore, these effective tax rates were considerably higher than the average paid by all US-based corporations, which was only 1.0% of total corporate sales in 1994.

Labor Wages and Standards

Similar considerations apply to the issue of wage costs. Many economists argue that the picture of MNCs progressively relocating jobs to economies with low wages and low labor standards, producing a race to the bottom in wage levels, is highly misleading, not least because most FDI still goes to high-income countries.[35] Proponents of the convergence hypothesis, on the other hand, point to the apparently rising share of developing countries in global FDI inflows (15% in 2005, compared to an average of 11% over 1989–2000). From this perspective, the rise of corporate service outsourcing to India and of assembly operations to China demonstrates the potential for downward pressure on wages and on labor, environmental, and other standards in advanced countries. The standard H-O-S model does indeed imply that North-to-South FDI will reduce wages in the advanced countries and increase them in developing countries. One could argue that this would be a positive development in terms of global equity, though the predicted deterioration of the income distribution within advanced countries might qualify this claim (since relatively low-skilled workers would be the main expected losers). From a political perspective, however, it could imply growing opposition to outward FDI and outsourcing in the advanced countries.

Consistent with the H-O-S theory and the convergence hypothesis, MNCs in low-wage economies on average pay wages considerably above the local economy average. This does not necessarily mean that FDI

---

[34] US Department of Commerce, Bureau of Economic Analysis, 1994 and 1999 benchmark studies.

[35] Graham, *Fighting the Wrong Enemy*, 106–7.

favors the poorest in developing countries. Since FDI often introduces new technology into host economies, it can increase growth and raise average wages but still favor the relatively high skilled. The wages of skilled Indian software engineers based in India, for example, have been rising at double-digit rates for the past decade and are now comparable to those in advanced countries (especially once productivity differences are taken into account).[36] This is not to say that MNCs do not exploit the cost opportunities provided by relatively low wages in developing countries, whether via FDI, outsourcing, or a combination of both. The search for lower cost in global supply chains may have beneficial employment and wage effects in poor countries, but most of the value in the supply chain is captured by the MNCs that own the brands, rather than by the workers involved in assembly in developing countries.[37]

As for effects in advanced countries, the evidence is mixed. Some evidence suggests that FDI, or the threat of relocation, has weakened the bargaining position of labor relative to management.[38] Such companies may also have other options, including offshore outsourcing. There are certainly cases in which the outsourcing of the production of branded goods from high- to lower-wage economies has destroyed jobs in advanced economies. Many Italian branded luxury goods companies in recent years have cut local jobs and outsourced production to China, for example, as they have come under growing price competition. Similarly, manufacturing and service MNCs such as ABB and IBM have reduced their total employment in advanced countries while creating many new jobs in India, China, and elsewhere.[39]

Other aggregate-level studies suggest that outward FDI, through its effects on trade, shifts home country employment from lower- to higher-paying jobs.[40] At the anecdotal level, there are also cases that

[36] Author interview with CEO of India- and US-based IT company, New York, January 2008.

[37] For one analysis, see the analysis of the global value chain in laptop computers by Jason Dean and Pui-Wing Tam, "The Laptop Trail: The Modern PC Is a Model of Hyperefficient Production and Geopolitical Sensitivities," *Wall Street Journal Online*, June 9, 2005.

[38] Graham, *Fighting the Wrong Enemy*, chap. 4

[39] Kynge, *China Shakes the World*, chap. 4.

[40] Magnus Blomstrom, Gunnar Fors, and Robert E. Lipsey, "Foreign Direct Investment and Employment: Home Country Experience in the United States and Sweden," *Economic Journal* 107:445, 1997, 1787–97.

provide a story different from the ones mentioned above. The tendency toward geographical agglomeration in a range of industries is related to the common need for large firms to obtain access to pools of skilled labor.[41] This phenomenon is evident in high-cost, high-technology areas (e.g., Silicon Valley in the United States, or Bangalore in India) as well as service industries such as financial services (e.g., Manhattan and the City of London), where MNCs have been highly active. In such circumstances, MNCs can find themselves competing for limited pools of highly skilled (and sometimes unusually mobile) labor, pushing compensation rates for key workers to very high levels. This can have positive spillover effects on compensation for less skilled workers in the same geographical area, though it can also increase their costs substantially (house prices, for example).

Consistent with this "winner takes all" phenomenon, income and wealth inequality in many countries has deteriorated in recent years, not just in advanced countries (only the latter is consistent with the H-O-S model). Most empirical studies find that this is more due to technological change than to trade and capital flows, though recent empirical work suggests that FDI does contribute to income inequality in both rich and poor countries.[42] Since FDI often facilitates the transfer of technology throughout the world economy, it can be very difficult to separate these two effects. Consumers who purchase cheap electronic goods, DVDs, clothing, and shoes also certainly benefit from cheaper goods, along with the large—and increasingly globalized—retail stores that sell these goods (Wal-Mart being the most prominent but far from the only example). But cheap goods in out-of-town hypermarkets may be small consolation to local communities that have suffered the loss of factory jobs. As factories relocate to lower-cost countries, MNCs may benefit, but smaller local firms that were formerly suppliers to larger factories can also lose, further disrupting local economic and social life. The net effects of these complex distributional and social effects are likely to vary considerably from case to case.

---

[41] Paul R. Krugman, "Increasing Returns and Economic Geography," *Journal of Political Economy* 99:3, 1991, 483–99.

[42] IMF, *World Economic Outlook, September 1997*, chap. 4.

On a more positive note, there is also evidence that FDI and the observance of core labor standards are on average positively related.[43] One explanation is that it can be less costly for global firms to adopt common policies worldwide rather than adhere to multiple national standards. In addition, voters and NGOs in all countries may not only resist efforts to lower minimum environmental and other standards, but actively pressure governments to raise them. Since most MNCs come from developed countries with relatively high labor (and other) standards, this can result in the export of high standards to developing countries. David Vogel has called this the "California effect," given this state's leading role in adopting and promoting high labor and environmental standards within the United States.[44] Similar "race to the top" possibilities arise for investment in public infrastructure, expenditure on education, and robust financial regulation.

Against this optimistic view, the offshore outsourcing of production to low-wage countries and to independent contractors may have less beneficial results on the treatment of labor in developing countries. Companies like Nike have been criticized for the way that their complex global supply chains, in which some subcontractors have paid very low wages and failed to observe minimum ILO standards, may have exploited differences in labor standards rather than promoted convergence. NGO pressure on such highly visible branded goods companies to pay greater attention to the treatment of labor throughout their global supply chain, including by their subcontractors, may have forced change in some cases. But this underlines the fact that market forces by themselves will not always promote international convergence.

Environmental Standards

The relationship between FDI and environmental standards may be similar to that between FDI and labor standards. Since most MNCs operate

---

[43] Sebastian Braun, "Core Labour Standards and FDI: Friend or Foe? The Case of Child Labour," SFB 649 Discussion Paper, 14, 2006, David Kucera, "Core Labor Standards and Foreign Direct Investment," *International Labour Review* 141:1–2, 2002, 31–69.

[44] David Vogel, *Trading Up: Consumer and Environmental Regulation in a Global Economy* (Cambridge: Harvard University Press, 1995).

in countries with relatively high environmental—and enforcement—standards (both are highly correlated with average income levels), the California effect may dominate over race-to-the-bottom effects. Also, most FDI flows from developed countries are in the services sector, where the environmental impact is often relatively small. A long line of econometric studies has found little evidence for the so-called pollution haven hypothesis that MNCs systematically relocate to countries with weaker environmental standards.[45] Either the advantages for MNCs of adopting a single global environmental policy outweigh those to be gained from adapting to multiple host country standards, or the effect of environmental policy on costs is too small to affect most decisions on location. The former interpretation is supported by the consideration that environmental standards, like labor standards, are embodied in production and product technologies, so that it can be difficult or impossible for global firms to adopt different standards in low-income countries.[46] This provides MNCs with an incentive to lobby for the international harmonization of these same high standards to entrench their competitive advantage. Locations may also try to attract FDI by enhancing the local environment and advertising high environmental standards, since this can enable firms to attract high-quality staff.

Although this argument may apply to most medium- to high-technology manufacturing and services, it does not for some industries, mainly in the natural resources sector. Nor does it apply to MNCs from low-cost, low-standard developing countries. Here, low environmental standards or weak enforcement may significantly reduce production costs—for example, low-cost access of timber companies to old-growth forests. MNCs that take advantage of such low standards may suffer reputational costs, which could include equity investor or consumer boycotts. MNCs from developing countries are less likely to face consumer boycotts in their home markets, and consumer boycotts are often impossible when companies produce no retail branded goods or services.

[45] See the review and discussion in Beata Smarzynska Javorcik and Shang-Jin Wei, "Pollution Havens and Foreign Direct Investment: Dirty Secret or Popular Myth?" *Contributions to Economic Analysis and Policy* 3:2, 2004, 1–32.

[46] Aseem Prakash and Matthew Potoski, "Investing Up: FDI and the Cross-Country Diffusion of ISO 14001 Management Systems," *International Studies Quarterly* 51:3, 2007, 723–44.

Thus, on average there is little evidence for strong race-to-the-bottom effects on environmental standards, and some evidence for convergence toward the relatively high standards that prevail in advanced countries. However, some firms and industries will undoubtedly be able to exploit opportunities that arise from the large differences in national environmental standards (as in other policy areas).

CONCLUSION

FDI is much less controversial today than it was in the 1970s, and many host countries adopt policies designed explicitly to attract it. But this is a relative trend: FDI is still one of the most politically controversial forms of global economic integration. Because of the market and political power that can be wielded by MNCs, governments continue to try to influence how such firms operate in their economies. Even in the advanced countries, both outward and inward FDI is often politically controversial. Public opinion often remains hostile to large firms, and MNCs in particular, suggesting scope for influence by NGO critics of MNCs. Perceptions that MNCs export jobs and tax revenues and produce downward pressure on labor, environmental, and other regulatory standards are widespread, and there is considerable anecdotal evidence—but less statistical evidence—to support such claims.

In such circumstances, it is perhaps unsurprising that agreement on terms for liberalizing investment (except for some services) has been impossible to date within international forums such as the WTO and OECD. Despite this continued political resistance, there has been a proliferation in recent years of bilateral and regional treaties that promote the further liberalization and protection of international investment. It seems reasonable to conclude that governments and international business lobbies have opted for such treaties because of their lower political visibility and the scope they offer for exerting greater bargaining power.

It is also striking that the general public mistrust of the motivations and effects of MNC activities in the global economy is not always well supported by aggregate empirical evidence. We have seen that the convergence hypothesis is problematic on a priori grounds, and that the empirical evidence for it is quite mixed. Even as regards taxation, which has direct effects on companies' operating costs, there appear to be no clear race to the bottom or convergence in effective taxation rates. Kahler argues that the persistence of rhetoric about a race to the bottom in the face of limited evidence is caused by an unholy alliance between NGO activists and corporate interests, both of which (for different purposes) wish to convince governments of the reality of pressures on high regulatory standards.[47] A less conspiratorial explanation is that the empirical evidence against race-to-the-bottom and convergence hypotheses is largely about *averages*, whereas it is always possible for opponents to find specific examples where global firms have outsourced jobs, cut wages, or exploited the opportunities provided by lower taxes or environmental standards. One of the major obstacles to resolving these issues is the poor quality of data in this area, notably the need for researchers to rely on FDI (i.e., balance of payments) data in the absence of good cross-country data on MNC activity. In the meantime, the willingness of the general public to believe the worst of global firms suggests that these issues are unlikely to become significantly less controversial over time.

FURTHER RESOURCES

Further Reading

David L. Levy and Aseem Prakash. "Bargains Old and New: Multinational Corporations in Global Governance." *Business and Politics* 5:2, 2003, 131–50. Examines the preferences and impact of MNCs on international regime formation and policy convergence.
Thomas Waelde and Abba Kolo. "Environmental Regulation, Investment Protection, and 'Regulatory Taking' in International Law." *International and Comparative Law Quarterly* 50:4, 2001, 811–48. Discusses the legal and political impact of investor-state dispute settlement procedures and investor protection clauses

[47] Kahler, "Modeling Races to the Bottom," 26.

on the ability of governments to pursue autonomous environmental policies.

John Braithwaite and Peter Drahos. *Global Business Regulation.* Cambridge: Cambridge University Press, 2000. Examines the changing regulation of global business across a wide range of policy areas.

Useful Websites

- http://www.iisd.org/investment: The International Institute for Sustainable Development website contains a range of information on FDI, dispute settlement, and related policy issues from a sustainable development perspective.
- http://www.unctadxi.org/templates/DocSearch____780.aspx: UNCTAD's Investment Instrument Compendium provides a comprehensive list of bilateral, regional, and multilateral agreements relating to FDI.
- www.icsid.org: The International Centre for the Settlement of Investment Disputes, based at the World Bank, provides information on the growing number of dispute settlement cases relating to FDI that have been brought to ICSID.

8 | Conclusion
| Looking Forward

Having assessed how political scientists and economists have analyzed the political economy of trade, money and finance, and foreign direct investment in the preceding chapters, in this concluding chapter we briefly address some broader questions. First, given the turn toward economics witnessed in international and comparative political economy in recent years, how much progress has been achieved in our field? Second, although we examined trade, money, and FDI separately in the preceding chapters, how should we analyze their interaction in the global political economy? Third and finally, what light does our survey throw on the question of how much the global political economy has changed? In particular, how should we understand the process of globalization?

HOW MUCH PROGRESS HAS BEEN ACHIEVED IN POLITICAL ECONOMY?

As we noted at the beginning of this book, the turn toward economics in political economy has been polarizing for many in the field. For some it creates a new hope for scientific advance; for others it is a retrograde step. Our own position is that the greater analytical clarity produced by the turn to economics has produced analytical and empirical progress. We also argued that there have been some costs in this reorientation of the field. Whether one is a critic or a supporter of the new economic approach, it is important to be aware of its strengths and its weaknesses.

We have seen that the main benefit of the new economic approach is the greater analytical clarity one finds in the field today compared to the 1970s and 1980s. The development of competing, testable theories of outcomes in different policy areas has facilitated an empirical research program that is producing cumulative progress in some important areas.

In the analysis of trade policy, the H-O-S model as deployed by Rogowski shed light on the class politics of trade over the past two centuries. Subsequent work by Frieden, who used the specific factors model, showed that trade policy interests vary by sector in theory and in practice. More recently, Hiscox showed that these two earlier approaches took extreme positions on the question of intersectoral factor mobility and that they therefore represented particular cases of a more general phenomenon.[1] Thanks to this research program, we better understand why, as a result of the greater specialization of human and physical capital over time, trade politics in the more advanced countries has changed over the course of the last century.

One weakness of this literature is that it has not explained why the level of demand for government policy interventions to limit or compensate for the redistributive effects of international trade has been much greater than for the disruptions produced by technological change. Technological innovation has, most economists believe, been a more powerful force for economic dislocation and the redistribution of wealth than have changes in levels of economic openness, as Schumpeter's famous concept of technology-induced "creative destruction" implies. And yet, the example of the Luddites aside, societal groups have been much less likely to mobilize to restrict technological change than they have to restrict international trade.[2] One possible answer to this paradox is that attitudes to trade and trade protection reflect widespread economic illiteracy, as many liberal economists are inclined to assume. As Rodrik has argued, the asymmetry in social mobilization may instead result from the important role that norms of procedural justice play in political debate and group mobilization. Redistribution

---

[1] Rogowski, *Commerce and Coalitions*; Frieden, "Sectoral Conflict"; Hiscox, *International Trade*.
[2] On the Luddite movement and the history of opposition to technological change, see Steven E. Jones, *Against Technology: From the Luddites to Neo-Luddism* (London: Routledge, 2006).

that results from innovation, and perhaps by implication from hard work and the desire for social improvement, may be more normatively acceptable than redistribution that results from "unfair" trade with countries whose cost advantages are perceived as arising from relatively low standards of various kinds. Economists in particular, but also those political scientists who have used economic models, have tended to ignore or to downplay the behavioral importance of fairness norms. As Davidson, Matusz, and Nelson have argued, "We are only at the very beginning of a systematic understanding of the public politics of trade policy, but it seems likely that an understanding of the politics of fairness will be central to any advance in this area."[3] Greater attention by political economists to the broader phenomenon at work (group mobilization), and to the normative motivations of human behavior, are likely to have beneficial results in this area and in many others.[4]

In monetary politics, the deployment of the Mundell-Fleming model also has produced greater analytical leverage in our field. It has been used to elucidate the conditions under which governments' macroeconomic policies were constrained, and how capital mobility has asymmetric effects on the power of monetary and fiscal policies. In conjunction with the specific factors model, it has been used to derive the monetary, exchange rate, and capital account preferences of sectoral interests.[5] Although the empirical results of this research program have been less fruitful than for trade politics, it illustrates that even inconsistencies between core theories and evidence can lead to progress in the explanation of monetary policies.[6]

As regards the analysis of international production and FDI more generally, economic theory has provided less analytical leverage for political economists than in the area of trade and money. This has much to do with the complex nature of FDI itself, which is a bundle of tech-

[3] Carl Davidson, Steve Matusz, and Douglas Nelson, "Fairness and the Political Economy of Trade," *World Economy* 29:8, 2006, 1001.

[4] On the normative motivations of human behavior more generally, see Richard Wright, *The Moral Animal: Why We Are the Way We Are* (London: Abacus, 1994).

[5] Jeffry A. Frieden, "Exchange Rate Politics," in Jeffry A. Frieden and David A. Lake, eds., *International Political Economy* (London: Routledge, 2000), 257–69.

[6] E.g. Mark Duckenfield, *Business and the Euro* (London: Palgrave-Macmillan, 2006); McNamara, *Currency of Ideas.*

nology, finance, networks, managerial expertise, and human capital that differs from case to case. This makes it difficult for standard interest-based theories to gain leverage in explaining the recent trend toward the liberalization of FDI inflows or in assessing its consequences. Much depends on the sector involved, whether FDI is primarily domestic market-seeking or export-oriented, and the technology deployed. The ambiguity of economic theories in this area suggests that changing ideas and related pressure from international institutions and major countries may have been important factors behind recent trends in policy. These analytical difficulties also make it difficult to assess the consequences of FDI, although it seems fairly clear that there is often a significant gap between public concerns about the possible negative effects of FDI and the empirical evidence. Why this is so is uncertain, and there is scope for more research in this area.

Although the new economic approach to political economy has produced progress in the field since the 1980s, we also noted some costs. In the light of the preceding chapters, one is that progress in the field has been driven by a few popular and tractable economic theories, while political and institutional variables have sometimes been relegated to the background. The interest-based approach to explaining trade policy and the common resort by political scientists to unholy trinity arguments in the field of monetary policy are examples. Meanwhile, areas where economic theory has proven less tractable for political scientists, notably FDI, have been relatively underresearched despite their great empirical importance. Although most scholars now accept the useful distinction between interest-based, institutional, and ideational explanations in political economy, the growing dependence on economic theory has meant that scholars have given much greater attention to material interests than to institutions and ideas. This gap is being narrowed to some extent by institutionalists and constructivists, as indicated by the competing theories that mainstream scholars now feel obliged to test.[7] But what the field continues to lack are metatheories that predict when one kind of factor material interests, institutions, or ideas—will be likely to have more powerful effects than the others.

---

[7] Dobbin, Simmons, and Garrett, "Global Diffusion."

232 | CHAPTER 8

The new economic approach has also de-emphasized international variables such as security as scholars have focused on delineating domestic economic cleavages. In the early 1990s it seemed as though the neorealist school had succeeded in (re)focusing disciplinary attention on security-related factors, but this proved fairly short-lived. This reflected the limitations of neorealism and the relative gains debate, but perhaps also the end of the Cold War, which temporarily deflected attention from security factors. Although we now have a much better understanding than two decades ago of the domestic determinants of economic policies, we have made less progress as regards the relative influence of international institutional and political factors. In an era when international factors have become more salient than ever for national economic policies, this is unfortunate. It may also indicate the biasing effects of an excessive reliance by IPE scholars on standard economic theories; on the relationship of economics and security, it has been often been economists rather than political scientists who have pushed the debate forward.[8]

THE INTERACTION OF TRADE, MONEY, AND INTERNATIONAL PRODUCTION

Most IPE, including this book, is driven by the search for tractable questions and theories in a very complex global political economy. This scholarly tendency avoids without eliminating the problem of empirical complexity. At the same time, complexity has probably grown in recent years, possibly raising the incentives for simplified treatments as well as the likelihood of predictive failures. The drawbacks to analyzing trade, money, finance, and FDI in isolation are epitomized by the rise of MNCs, including global financial institutions, as key players in the global political economy since the mid-twentieth century. As we have seen, FDI bundles finance, technology, trade, networks, and human

---

[8] See especially Ronald Finlay and Kevin H. O'Rourke, *Power and Plenty: Trade, War, and the World Economy in the Second Millennium* (Princeton, N.J.: Princeton University Press, 2008). An exception to this trend on the political science side is Jonathan Kirshner, *Appeasing Bankers: Financial Caution on the Road to War* (Princeton, N.J.: Princeton University Press, 2007).

capital differently in different times and places. It impinges on many debates in contemporary politics, from development, labor, and environmental issues to international regulation, money laundering, and terrorist finance. And yet, as we have seen, FDI remains relatively underresearched by political economists compared to the traditional bread-and-butter issues of trade and monetary politics.

The difficulty for social scientists is that the world is unmanageably complex, necessitating simplifying assumptions and artificial divisions of subject areas. The best approach, in our view, is to avoid the extremes of throwing up our hands in despair or trying to model the world in all its complexity. Rather, we should investigate on a piecemeal basis interactions between subject areas. For example, a few political economists have fruitfully explored the implications of the increasing inseparability of trade and FDI.[9] The implications of FDI for exchange rate policies remain largely unexplored, however. It seems likely, for example, that exchange rate as well as trade politics between the United States and East Asia have been modified by the growing importance of FDI. US pressure on Japan in the 1970s and 1980s to increase the dollar value of the yen, strongly backed by most large American firms, eventually proved irresistible. More recently, however, the West has found it more difficult to manage trade and exchange rate issues with China, in part because Western MNCs based in China account for about 50% of China's total exports (and 90% of its high-technology exports). The rise of China as the world's final assembly location and key manufacturing exporter, and the undervaluation of its currency, is from one perspective a consequence of a strategic alliance between the Chinese political leadership and global firms.

Financial innovation is also partly a response to the needs of MNCs. Many developing countries, including China, have believed it necessary to give local MNC affiliates relief from national capital controls, increasing the porosity and eroding the value of these controls. Sometimes FDI itself and the development of firms' regional supply networks are strategic responses to growing exchange rate volatility. Nevertheless,

[9] E.g. Hiscox, "International Capital Mobility"; Manger, "Competition and Bilateralism in Trade Policy"; Milner, *Resisting Protectionism.*

MNCs often remain relatively vulnerable to exchange rate movements, as in the case of the offshore outsourcing of production inputs or the location of production and assembly facilities in low-cost countries. MNCs have thus been prime clients for global banks offering derivatives instruments that reduce their exchange rate exposure. This has strengthened the coalition favoring financial innovation. It may also reduce the power of political economy theories that focus on domestic industry coalitions in exchange rate politics.

How much the growing interrelatedness between trade, money, finance, and FDI has altered the politics of economic policy is an empirical question—and there is much work to do in this area. Some effects are already apparent. The rise of private international capital markets and of FDI as a means by which developing countries can import technology and gain access to key export markets has thrown into question the roles of the IMF and the World Bank. These institutions, cornerstones of the international economic system in the middle of last century, are increasingly displaced by market-based capital flows and technology transfers. At the same time, multilateral rules for private capital markets and FDI are rudimentary and often possess limited effectiveness. Although some of these issues are discussed at the WTO, there is a danger that this institution could collapse under the weight of contradictory forces. There has also been some resort to public-private international regimes in areas such as corporate social responsibility (including, for example, issues such as trade in conflict diamonds, which has involved some NGOs). But the effectiveness of such initiatives has yet to be conclusively demonstrated.

How should students of political economy respond to the growing complexity of the global economy? As we have argued, it would be wrong to jettison the competing theoretical frameworks that have been built in the field since the 1970s, since we do not yet understand the full implications of these economic changes. Yet the need is pressing for the development of more theories that take into account the interactions outlined above, and more empirical testing of their impact and importance. It underlines the general theme of this book that economic literacy has become more important for political scientists than ever.

HOW SHOULD WE UNDERSTAND GLOBALIZATION?

Finally, in light of the discussion in this book, how should we understand the phenomenon of globalization? Although there are still some who see the world in extreme terms, either as one dominated by states or one in which states are increasingly irrelevant, we adopt the (mainstream) position that globalization is a process with no determined end point. We do not live in a completely globalized world; nor is steady progression toward such a world an inevitability. In fact, we live in a very imperfectly or weakly globalized world, in which national economies are variably interdependent but where states, geography, and distance still matter enormously.

One way to illustrate this is to consider the example of Canada, a country often ignored by authors but which on various measures is the most globalized of the G7 economies. In trade terms, Canada is the most open G7 economy and since 1988 has had close to completely free trade with the world's most important economy and country, the United States. It is the world's second largest country by geographical area, but 70% of Canadians share a common language with the United States, and 90% of its population lives within about 200 kilometers of the US border.[10] This unusually high level of access to the enormous US market and the horizontal distribution of the Canadian population should in theory have produced a growing preponderance of US-Canadian trade, as opposed to intra-Canadian commercial linkages. Certainly, Canada's trade with the United States has been growing faster than its national output. But Canada's domestic trade still dominates its international trade by large margins. To illustrate, Ontario's total exports to British Columbia, which has a GDP only 6% as large as California's, were 71% as large as its total exports to California in 2002. Since both British Columbia and California are at a similar distance from Ontario, this strong bias toward trade with another Canadian province cannot be explained by distance (though note that distance is well known to continue to have powerful negative effects on trade). Although a deeper analysis of this bias toward intra-Canadian trade

[10] BBC, Country Profile: Canada, accessed on http://news.bbc.co.uk, October 25, 2007.

would require a closer analysis of other possible contributing factors such as differences in demand patterns and economic structure, it strongly suggests that national borders continue to matter enormously even in a part of the world where they ought to matter least. National regulatory policies, cultural differences, and currency risks may all contribute to this bias. Similar points could be made about individual European countries, many of which are also among the most globalized in the world. Hence, even in a world in which trade and capital flows were essentially free, intranational economic transactions would likely remain much more important than international ones.

Notwithstanding the growing importance of FDI in the global economy and the globalization of some firms' strategies and operations, the world's major MNCs also demonstrate the limits of the process of globalization. The world's largest MNCs have a varying degree of transnationality, but most retain disproportionately important R&D operations, strategic management, and psychological attachments in their home base countries.[11] This varies by country and by firm, but more international affiliates and increasing international-to-domestic sales ratios can exaggerate the degree of globalization that has occurred to date. Increasingly, the production process itself may be a relatively secondary part of the MNC's home base activities. From the perspective of labor, this looks like extreme globalization; from the perspective of the firm, and especially its upper management, it may be just another means of strengthening or maintaining its market position, including in its home base.

The example of Canada implies that we are likely to remain in a weakly and variably globalized world for the foreseeable future. Relatively few countries are likely to achieve the degree of international integration we now see in North America and western Europe any time soon. Domestic political resistance to globalization, natural barriers to integration, the potential for reversals in the globalization process, and continuing international political and security conflicts all create barriers to deeper economic integration in most parts of the world. Recent work in the behavioral sciences suggests that the tendency to cooperate with insiders and to distrust outsiders has been strongly ingrained in

[11] UNCTAD, *World Investment Report 2006*, annex table A.I.11.

humans by the ancient environment in which our ancestors evolved.[12] This suggests that political economists should not be too quick to abandon theories that assume the importance of state and other group-level norms, politics, and institutions.

This point can be illustrated by considering an issue we have addressed only indirectly in this book, that of labor. It would be wrong to think that labor has relevance to the global political economy only to the extent that immigration becomes important. The enormous pool of relatively unskilled labor in the developing world, especially in India and China, has had important effects on the global political economy through the growth of their exports (including via FDI from advanced countries) and of their role in offshore outsourcing. The estimated fourfold increase in the global pool of labor since 1980 has gradually reduced the global capital-to-labor ratio and increased the share of corporate profits in national income (at the expense of the total labor share). It has also contributed to the relative stagnation of the wages of the less skilled in advanced countries, though on average these groups have been compensated by the positive consumption effects of cheaper imports.[13]

The continuing importance of welfare and security policies in national politics means that trade and FDI will remain the main mechanisms by which the global pool of relatively cheap labor affects advanced countries. Immigration as a percentage of the total labor force in advanced countries increased from 6% in 1990 to about 8% in 2006, but there are major domestic political limits to increased immigration in many countries. The exception is the United States, where immigration is relatively high (15% of the total labor force) and imports relatively low (15% of GDP).[14] Where there has been liberalization of immigration in advanced countries, most governments have targeted high-skilled immigrants rather than those with low skills in response to continued (and often increasing) voter resistance.

[12] For accessible introductions to this literature and its implications for the social sciences, see Paul Seabright, *The Company of Strangers: A Natural History of Economic Life* (Princeton, N.J.: Princeton University Press, 2004); Wilson, *Consilience*; and Wright, *The Moral Animal.*

[13] IMF, *World Economic Outlook, April 2007*, chap. 4.

[14] IMF, *World Economic Outlook, April 2007*, 163.

Issues such as labor migration and FDI constitute the changing subject matter of the political economy of globalization. As we have seen, however, they do not mean that either human nature or the world in which we live has changed out of all recognition. Economic literacy is essential for students of political economy who wish to understand better how the world has changed. Equally, however, an understanding of what we often inadequately simplify as "domestic" and "international" politics is crucial, as is, we suggest, a better understanding of the motivational roots of human behavior. These motivations and the political processes they create will continue to shape, block, or deflect economic forces. Understanding how they do so remains a vital ingredient of progress in our field.

FURTHER RESOURCES

Further Reading

Douglass C. North. *Understanding the Process of Economic Change*. Princeton, N.J.: Princeton University Press, 2005. North, whose previous work on the role of institutions in economic development has helped to bridge the gap between economics and other social sciences, now argues that institutions derive from social beliefs.

Edward E. Leamer. "A Flat World, a Level Playing Field, a Small World after All, or None of the Above? A Review of Thomas L. Friedman's *The World Is Flat*." *Journal of Economic Literature* 55:1, 2007, 83–126. An entertaining and enlightening review of one prominent popular book about globalization, the confusingly titled *The World Is Flat: A Brief History of the Twenty-first Century* by Thomas Friedman (New York: Farrar, Strauss and Giroux, 2005).

Useful Websites

- http://rodrik.typepad.com/dani_rodriks_weblog/: Dani Rodrik's web blog is one of the best among a growing number of political

economy blogs, covering a wide range of contemporary theoretical and practical international policy issues.
- http://www.rgemonitor.com/index.php: RGE Monitor is another excellent compilation of information, data, and opinion on contemporary issues in the global political economy (it requires a subscription, although blogs from some of its main authors are freely available).

Useful Economics Glossaries

- *The Economist* economics glossary: http://www.economist.com/research/Economics/
- Alan Deardorff's Glossary of International Economics: http://www-personal.umich.edu/~alandear/glossary/
- Biz/Ed economics glossary: http://www.bized.co.uk/glossary/econglos.htm.
- The *New Palgrave Dictionary of Economics* (2nd ed., 2008), is also available online at http://www.dictionaryofeconomics.com/dictionary.

Useful Political Science and Political Economy Glossaries

- Paul Johnson's glossary of political economy: http://www.auburn.edu/~johnspm/gloss/index
- Nelson publisher's political science glossary: http://polisci.nelson.com/glossary.html
- Webref's political science glossary: http://www.webref.org/political-science/political-science.htm
- Joan Spero and Jeffrey Hart's IPE glossary: http://www.indiana.edu/~ipe/glossary.html

Bibliography

Aitken, Brian, Gordon H. Hanson, and Anne E. Harrison. "Spillovers, Foreign Investment, and Export Behavior." *Journal of International Economics* 43:1, 1997, 103–32.

Alesina, Alberto. "Macroeconomic Policy in a Two-Party System as a Repeated Game." *Quarterly Journal of Economics* 102:3, 1987, 651–78.

Alesina, Alberto, Vittorio Grilli, and Gian Maria Milesi-Ferretti. "The Political Economy of Capital Controls." In Leonardo Leiderman and Assaf Razin, eds., *Capital Mobility: The Impact on Consumption, Investment and Growth.* New York: Cambridge University Press, 1994, 289–321.

Alesina, Alberto, and Lawrence H. Summers. "Central Bank Independence and Macroeconomic Performance: Some Comparative Evidence." *Journal of Money, Credit and Banking* 24:2, 1993, 151–62.

Alesina, Alberto, and Alexander Wagner. "Choosing (and Reneging on) Exchange Rate Regimes." NBER Working Paper, 9809, June 2003.

Alt, James E., and K. Alec Chrystal. *Political Economics.* Berkeley and Los Angeles: University of California Press, 1983.

Alt, James E., Jeffry Frieden, Michael J. Gilligan, Dani Rodrik, and Ronald Rogowski. "The Political Economy of International Trade: Enduring Puzzles and an Agenda for Enquiry." *Comparative Political Studies* 29:6, 1996, 689–717.

Alt, James E., and Michael Gilligan. "The Political Economy of Trading States: Factor Specificity, Collective Action Problems, and Domestic Political Institutions." *Journal of Political Philosophy* 2:2, 1994, 165–92.

Alt, James E., Margaret Levi, and Elenor Ostrom. *Competition and Cooperation: Conversations with Nobelists about Economics and Political Science.* New York: Russell Sage Foundation, 1999.

Alt, James E., and Kenneth A. Shepsle, eds. *Perspectives on Positive Political Economy.* Cambridge: Cambridge University Press, 1990.

Amin, Samir, Giovanni Arrighi, Andre Gunder Frank, and Immanuel Wallerstein. *Dynamics of Global Crisis.* London: Macmillan, 1982.

Amsden, Alice H. *Asia's Next Giant.* New York: Oxford University Press, 1989.

Axelrod, Robert. *The Evolution of Cooperation.* New York: Basic Books, 1984.

Babb, Sarah. *Managing Mexico: Economists from Nationalism to Neoliberalism.* Princeton, N.J.: Princeton University Press, 2001.

Bach, Christopher. "U.S. International Transactions, Revised Estimates for 1982–98." *Survey of Current Business.* US Department of Commerce, Bureau of Economic Analysis, 79, July 1999, 60–74.

Bailey, Michael A., Judith Goldstein, and Barry R. Weingast. "The Institutional Roots of American Trade Policy: Politics, Coalitions and International Trade." *World Politics* 49:3, 1997, 309–38.

Baldwin, David, ed. *Neorealism and Neoliberalism: The Contemporary Debate.* New York: Columbia University Press, 1993.

Bank of Italy. *Public Finance Statistics in the European Union.* Supplements to the Statistical Bulletin, n.s., Year IX, 62, December 31, 1999. Rome: Bank of Italy.

Barnet, Richard J., and Ronald E. Müller. *Global Reach: The Power of the Multinational Corporations.* New York: Simon and Schuster, 1974.

Barro, Robert J., and David B. Gordon. "Rules, Discretion and Reputation in a Model of Monetary Policy." *Journal of Monetary Economics* 12:1, 101–21, 1983.

Becker, Gary S. "A Theory of Competition among Pressure Groups for Political Influence." *Quarterly Journal of Economics* 98:3, 1983, 371–400.

Beinhocker, Eric D. *The Origin of Wealth.* Cambridge: Harvard Business School Press, 2006.

Berger, Peter L., and H. H. Michael Hsaio, eds. *In Search of an East Asian Developmental Model.* New Brunswick, N.J.: Transaction Books, 1987.

Berger, Suzanne. "Globalization and Politics." *Annual Review of Political Science* 3, 2000, 43–62.

Bernhard, William, J. Lawrence Broz, and William Roberts Clark. "The Political Economy of Monetary Institutions." *International Organization* 56:4, 2002, 693–723.

Bernstein, Peter L. *Capital Ideas: The Improbable Origins of Modern Wall Street.* New York: Free Press, 1992.

Best, Jacqueline. *The Limits of Transparency: Ambiguity and the History of International Finance.* Ithaca, N.Y.: Cornell University Press, 2005.

Bhagwati, Jagdish. *Trade, Tariffs, and Growth.* Cambridge: MIT Press, 1969.

———. *Writings on International Economics.* Ed. V. N. Balasubramanyam. New Delhi: Oxford University Press, 1998.

———, ed. *International Trade: Selected Readings.* Cambridge: MIT Press, 2nd ed., 1987.

Bird, Graham, and Dale Rowlands. "Catalysis or Direct Borrowing: The Role of the IMF in Mobilising Private Capital." *World Economy* 24:1, 2001, 81–98.

Block, Fred H. *The Origins of the International Economic Disorder.* Berkeley and Los Angeles: University of California Press, 1977.

Blomstrom, Magnus, Gunnar Fors, and Robert E. Lipsey. "Foreign Direct Investment and Employment: Home Country Experience in the United States and Sweden." *Economic Journal* 107:445, 1997, 1787–97.

Bloomfield, Arthur I. *Monetary Policy under the Gold Standard, 1880–1914.* New York: Federal Reserve Bank of New York, 1959.

Blyth, Mark. *Great Transformations: Economic Ideas and Institutional Change in the Twentieth Century.* Cambridge: Cambridge University Press, 2002.

Bordo, Michael D., Barry J. Eichengreen, and Douglas Irwin. "Is Globalization Today Really Different Than Globalization a Hundred Years Ago?" NBER Working Paper, 7195, June 1999.

Bordo, Michael D., Ashoka Mody, and Nienke Oomes. "Keeping Capital Flowing: The Role of the IMF." IMF Working Paper, WP/04/197, October 2004.

Borensztein, Eduardo, Jose De Gregorio, and Jong-Wha Lee. "How Does Foreign Direct Investment Affect Economic Growth?" *Journal of International Economics* 45:1, 1998, 115–35.

Bown, Chad P., and Bernard M. Hoekman. "WTO Dispute Settlement and the Missing Developing Country Cases: Engaging the Private Sector." *Journal of International Economic Law* 8:4, 2005, 861–90.

Brady, H. E., and David Collier, eds. *Rethinking Social Enquiry: Diverse Tools, Shared Standards.* Lanham, Md.: Rowman and Littlefield, 2004.

Braithwaite, John, and Peter Drahos. *Global Business Regulation.* Cambridge: Cambridge University Press, 2000.

Braun, Sebastian. "Core Labour Standards and FDI: Friend or Foe? The Case of Child Labour." SFB 649 Discussion Paper, 14, 2006.

Brenner, Robert. "The Origins of Capitalist Development: A Critique of Neo-Smithian Marxism." *New Left Review* 104, July–August 1977, 25–92.

Broz, J. Lawrence. "The Domestic Politics of International Monetary Order: The Gold Standard." In David Skidmore, ed., *Contested Social Orders and International Politics.* Nashville, Tenn.: Vanderbilt University Press, 1997, 53–91.

———. "Political System Transparency and Monetary Commitment Regimes." *International Organization* 56:4, 2002, 861–87.

Brune, Nancy, Geoffrey Garrett, Alexandra Guisinger, and Jason Sorens. "The Political Economy of Capital Account Liberalization." December 2001. Available at http://www.isop.ucla.edu/cms/files/capacct.pdf, accessed April 4, 2008.

Bubula, Andrea, and Ynci Ötker-Robe. "The Evolution of Exchange Rate Regimes since 1990: Evidence from De Facto Policies." IMF Working Paper, WP/02/155, 2002.

Buchanan, James M. "The Constitution of Economic Policy." *American Economic Review* 77:3, 1987, 243–50.

Buchanan, James M., and Gordon Tullock. *The Calculus of Consent: Logical Foundations of Constitutional Democracy.* Ann Arbor: University of Michigan Press, 1962.

Calvo, Guillermo A., and Carmen M. Reinhart. "Fear of Floating." *Quarterly Journal of Economics* 117:2, 2002, 379–408.

Cameron, David R. "The Expansion of the Public Economy: A Comparative Analysis." *American Political Science Review* 72:4, 1978, 1243–61.

Capie, Forrest, Charles Goodhart, and Norbert Schnadt. "The Development of Central Banking." In Forrest Capie et al., *The Future of Central Banking: The Tercentenary*

Symposium of the Bank of England. Cambridge: Cambridge University Press, 1994, 1–231.

Cardoso, Fernando Henrique, and Enzo Faletto. *Dependency and Development.* Berkeley and Los Angeles: University of California Press, 1979.

Carlin, Wendy, and David Soskice. *Macroeconomics and the Wage Bargain.* Oxford: Oxford University Press, 1990.

Caves, Richard E. *Multinational Enterprise and Economic Analysis.* Cambridge: Cambridge University Press, 2nd ed., 1996.

Cerny, Philip G. "Globalization and the Changing Logic of Collective Action." *International Organization* 49:4, 1995, 595–625.

———. "International Finance and the Erosion of Capitalist Diversity." In Colin Crouch and Wolfgang Streeck, eds., *Political Economy of Modern Capitalism.* London: Sage, 1997, 173–81.

Chandler, Alfred D. *Scale and Scope: The Dynamics of Industrial Capitalism.* Cambridge: Harvard University Press, 1990.

Chinn, Menzie, and Hiro Ito. KAOPEN Database. Capital openness indices for 163 countries over 1970–2003. Available at http://web.pdx.edu/~ito/, accessed December 9, 2005.

Chwieroth, Jeffrey M. "Neoliberal Economists and Capital Account Liberalization in Emerging Markets." *International Organization* 61:2, 2007, 443–63.

———. "Testing and Measuring the Role of Ideas: The Case of Neoliberalism in the International Monetary Fund." *International Studies Quarterly* 51:1, 2007, 5–30.

Cohen, Benjamin J. *The Geography of Money.* Ithaca, N.Y.: Cornell University Press, 1998.

———. "The Multiple Traditions of American IPE." 2007. Available at http://www.polsci.ucsb.edu/faculty/cohen/working/pdfs/Handbook_text.pdf, accessed April 4, 2008.

———. *Organizing the World's Money.* New York: Basic Books, 1977.

———. "Phoenix Risen: The Resurrection of Global Finance." *World Politics* 48:2, 1996, 268–96.

———. "The Transatlantic Divide: Why Are American and British IPE So Different?" *Review of International Political Economy* 14:2, 2007, 197–219.

———. "The Triad and the Unholy Trinity: Problems of International Monetary Cooperation." In Richard Higgott, Richard Leaver, and John Ravenhill, eds., *Pacific Economic Relations in the 1990s: Cooperation or Conflict?* London: Allen and Unwin, 1993, 133–58.

Cohen, Stephen S., and John Zysman. *Manufacturing Matters: The Myth of the Postindustrial Economy.* New York: Basic Books, 1987.

Conybeare, John A. C. *Trade Wars: The Theory and Practice of International Commercial Rivalry.* New York: Columbia University Press, 1987.

Cooper, Richard N. *The Economics of Interdependence: Economic Policy in the Atlantic Community.* New York: Published for the Council on Foreign Relations by McGraw-Hill, 1968.

Cottarelli, Carlo, and Curzio Giannini. "Credibility without Rules? Monetary Frameworks in the Post–Bretton Woods Era." IMF Occasional Papers, 154, December 1997.

———. "Inflation, Credibility, and the Role of the International Monetary Fund." IMF Paper on Policy Analysis and Assessment, PP/AA/98/12, 1998.

Cox, Gary W. *Making Votes Count: Strategic Coordination in the World's Electoral Systems.* Cambridge: Cambridge University Press, 1997.

Cox, Robert W. *Power, Production, and World Order: Social Forces in the Making of History.* New York: Columbia University Press, 1987.

Crafts, Nicholas. "Implications of Financial Crisis for East Asian Trend Growth." *Oxford Review of Economic Policy* 15:3, 1999, 110–31.

Cukierman, Alex. *Central Bank Strategy, Credibility, and Independence.* Cambridge: MIT Press, 1992.

Davidson, Carl, Steve Matusz, and Douglas Nelson. "Fairness and the Political Economy of Trade." *World Economy* 29:8, 2006, 989–1004.

Dean, Jason, and Pui-Wing Tam. "The Laptop Trail: The Modern PC Is a Model of Hyperefficient Production and Geopolitical Sensitivities." *Wall Street Journal Online,* June 9, 2005.

De Grauwe, Paul. *International Money.* Oxford: Oxford University Press, 2nd ed., 1996.

De Grauwe, Paul, and Filip Camerman. "How Big Are the Big Multinationals?" Unpublished paper, 2002.

Denison, Edward F. *Accounting for United States Economic Growth, 1929–1969.* Washington, D.C.: Brookings Institution, 1974.

Desai, Mihir, C. Fritz Foley, and James R. Hines Jr. "Foreign Direct Investment and Domestic Economic Activity." NBER Working Paper, 11717, October 2005.

Despres, Emile, Charles P. Kindleberger, and Walter S. Salant. "The Dollar and World Liquidity—A Minority View." *The Economist,* February 5, 1966, 526–29.

Destler, I. M. *American Trade Politics.* Washington, D.C.: Institute for International Economics, 3rd ed., 1995.

Destler, I. M., and C. Randall Henning. *Dollar Politics: Exchange Rate Policymaking in the United States.* Washington, D.C.: Institute for International Economics, 1989.

de Vries, Rimmer. "Adam Smith: Managing the Global Wealth of Nations." In Morgan Guaranty Trust Company of New York, *World Financial Markets.* New York: The Company, 1990, 2.

Diamond, D. W., and P. H. Dybvig. "Bank Runs, Deposit Insurance, and Liquidity." *Journal of Political Economy* 91:3, 1983, 401–19.

Djankov, Simeon, Rafael La Porta, Florencio Lopez-de-Silanes, and Andrei Shleifer. "The Regulation of Entry." *Quarterly Journal of Economics* 117:1, 2002, 1–37.

Dobbin, Frank, Beth Simmons, and Geoffrey Garrett. "The Global Diffusion of Public Policies: Social Construction, Coercion, Competition, or Learning?" *Annual Review of Sociology* 33, 2007, 449–72.

Dooley, Michael P., David Folkerts-Landau, and Peter Garber. "An Essay on the Revived Bretton Woods System." NBER Working Paper, 9971, September 2003.

Dosi, Giovanni, Keith Pavitt, and Luc Soete. *The Economics of Technical Change and International Trade.* London: Harvester Wheatsheaf, 1990.

Downs, Anthony. *An Economic Theory of Democracy.* New York: Harper and Row, 1957.

Drazen, Allen. *Political Economy in Macroeconomics.* Princeton, N.J.: Princeton University Press, 2002.

Duckenfield, Mark. *Business and the Euro.* London: Palgrave-Macmillan, 2006.

Dunning, John H. *Explaining International Production.* London: Unwin Hyman, 1988.

————. *Multinational Enterprises and the Global Economy.* Reading, Mass.: Addison-Wesley, 1993.

Duttagupta, Rupa, Gilda Fernandez, and Cem Karacadag. "From Fixed to Float: Operational Aspects of Moving towards Exchange Rate Flexibility." IMF Working Paper, 04/126, 2004.

Dyson, Kenneth, and Kevin Featherstone. *The Road to Maastricht: Negotiating Economic and Monetary Union.* New York: Oxford University Press, 1999.

Earle, Edward M. "Adam Smith, Alexander Hamilton, Friedrich List: The Economic Foundations of Military Power." In Peter Paret and Gordon A. Craig, eds., *Makers of Modern Strategy: From Machiavelli to the Nuclear Age.* Princeton, N.J.: Princeton University Press, 1986, 217–61.

Edwards, Sebastian. "How Effective Are Capital Controls?" *Journal of Economic Perspectives* 13:4, 1999, 65–84.

Ehrlich, Sean D. "Access to Protection: Domestic Institutions and Trade Policy in Democracies." *International Organization* 61:3, 2007, 571–605.

Eichengreen, Barry J. *Global Imbalances and the Lessons of Bretton Woods.* Cambridge: MIT Press, 2006.

————. *Golden Fetters: The Gold Standard and the Great Depression, 1919–1939.* New York: Oxford University Press, 1992.

————. "Hegemonic Stability Theories of the International Monetary System." In Richard N. Cooper, ed., *Can Nations Agree? Issues in International Economic Cooperation.* Washington, D.C.: Brookings Institution, 1989, 255–98.

————. "Is Europe an Optimal Currency Area?" CEPR Discussion Paper, 428, November 1990.

————. "The Political Economy of the Smoot-Hawley Tariff." *Research in Economic History* 1:2, 1989, 1–43.

Eichengreen, Barry J., Ricardo Hausmann, and Ugo Panizza. "Currency Mismatches, Debt Intolerance and Original Sin: Why They Are Not the Same and Why it Matters." NBER Working Paper, 10036, October 2003.

Eichengreen, Barry J., and Peter Temin. "The Gold Standard and the Great Depression." NBER Working Paper, 6060, 1997.

Eichengreen, Barry J., and Charles Wyplosz. "The Stability Pact: More Than a Minor Nuisance." *Economic Policy* 13:26, 1998, 67–113.

Esping-Andersen, Gøsta. *The Three Worlds of Welfare Capitalism.* Princeton, N.J.: Princeton University Press, 1990.

Ethier, Wilfred J., Elhanan Helpman, and J. Peter Neary, eds. *Theory, Policy, and Dynamics in International Trade: Essays in Honor of Ronald W. Jones*. Cambridge: Cambridge University Press, 1995.

European Commission. *Guide to the Case Law of the European Court of Justice on Articles 52 et seq. EC Treaty: Freedom of Establishment*. Brussels: European Commission, January 1, 1999.

Evans, Peter B. *Dependent Development: The Alliance of Multinational, State, and Local Capital in Brazil*. Princeton, N.J.: University Press, 1978.

Evans, Peter B., Harold K. Jacobsen, and Robert D. Putnam, eds. *Double-Edged Diplomacy: International Bargaining and Domestic Politics*. Berkeley and Los Angeles: University of California Press, 1993.

Fetter, Frank W. *Development of British Monetary Orthodoxy, 1797–1875*. Cambridge: Harvard University Press, 1965.

Findlay, Ronald, Rolf G. H. Henriksson, Håkan Lindgren, and Mats Lundahl, eds. *Eli Heckscher, International Trade, and Economic History*. Cambridge: MIT Press, 2007.

Finlay, Ronald, and Kevin H. O'Rourke. *Power and Plenty: Trade, War, and the World Economy in the Second Millennium*. Princeton, N.J.: Princeton University Press, 2008.

Finnemore, Martha, and Kathryn Sikkink. "Taking Stock: The Constructivist Research Program in International Relations and Comparative Politics." *Annual Review of Political Science* 4:1, 2001, 391–416.

Fischer, Stanley. "Exchange Rate Regimes: Is the Bipolar View Correct?" Distinguished Lecture on Economics in Government, Meeting of the American Economic Association, New Orleans, January 6, 2001.

———. "Modern Central Banking." In Forrest Capie et al, *The Future of Central Banking*. Cambridge: Cambridge University Press, 1994, 262–308.

Flandreau, Marc, Jacques Le Cacheux, and Frédéric Zumer. "Stability without a Pact? Lessons from the European Gold Standard, 1880–1914." *Economic Policy* 13:26, 1998, 117–62.

Fleming, J. Marcus. "Domestic Financial Policies under Fixed and Floating Exchange Rates." *IMF Staff Papers*, 9, November 1962.

Franzese, Robert J., Jr. "Institutional and Sectoral Interactions in Monetary Policy and Wage/Price-Bargaining." In Peter A. Hall and David Soskice, eds., *Varieties of Capitalism: The Institutional Foundations of Comparative Advantage*. Oxford: Oxford University Press, 2001, 104–44.

———. "Partially Independent Central Banks, Politically Responsive Governments, and Inflation." *American Journal of Political Science* 43:3, 1999, 681–706.

Frenkel, Jacob, and Assaf Razin. "The Mundell-Fleming Model a Quarter Century Later: A Unified Exposition." *IMF Staff Papers*, 34, December 1987.

Frey, Bruno S. *International Political Economics*. Oxford: Blackwell, 1984.

Frieden, Jeffry A. "The Dynamics of International Monetary Systems: International and Domestic Factors in the Rise, Reign, and Demise of the Classical Gold Standard."

In Barry J. Eichengreen and Marc Flandreau, eds., *The Gold Standard in Theory and History.* New York: Routledge, 1997, 206–27.

———. "Exchange Rate Politics." In Jeffry A. Frieden and David A. Lake, eds., *International Political Economy.* London: Routledge, 2000, 257–69.

———. "Invested Interests: The Politics of National Economic Policies in a World of Global Finance." *International Organization* 45:4, 1991, 425–51.

———. "Real Sources of European Currency Policy: Sectoral Interests and European Monetary Integration." *International Organization* 56:4, 2002, 831–60.

———. "Sectoral Conflict and US Foreign Economic Policy, 1914–1940." *International Organization* 42:1, 1988, 59–90.

———. "Third World Indebted Industrialization: International Finance and State Capitalism in Mexico, Brazil, Algeria, and South Korea." *International Organization* 35:3, 1981, 407–31.

Frieden, Jeffry A., and Barry Eichengreen, eds. *The Political Economy of European Monetary Integration.* Boulder, Colo.: Westview Press, 2000.

Frieden, Jeffry A., and Ronald Rogowski. "The Impact of the International Economy on National Policies: An Overview." In Robert O. Keohane and Helen V. Milner, eds., *Internationalization and Domestic Politics.* Cambridge: Cambridge University Press, 1996, 25–47.

Friedman, Milton. "The Case for Flexible Exchange Rates." In *Essays in Positive Economics.* Chicago: University of Chicago Press, 1953, 157–203.

———. "The Role of Monetary Policy." *American Economic Review* 58:1, 1968, 1–17.

Friedman, Milton, and Anna Schwartz. *A Monetary History of the United States, 1867–1960.* Princeton, N.J.: Princeton University Press, 1963.

Friedman, Thomas. *The World Is Flat: A Brief History of the Twenty-first Century.* New York: Farrar, Strauss and Giroux, 2005.

Gagné, Gilbert, and Jean-Frédéric Morin. "The Evolving American Policy on Investment Protection: Evidence from Recent FTAs and the 2004 Model BIT." *Journal of International Economic Law* 9:2, 2006, 357–82.

Galbraith, J. Kenneth. *The New Industrial State.* Boston: Houghton Mifflin, 3rd ed., 1978.

Gallarotti, Giulio M. *The Anatomy of an International Monetary Regime: The Classical Gold Standard, 1880–1914.* Oxford: Oxford University Press, 1995.

Gardner, Richard N. *Sterling-Dollar Diplomacy in Current Perspective.* New York: Columbia University Press, 1980.

Garrett, Geoffrey. "Globalization's Missing Middle." *Foreign Affairs* 83:6, 2004, 72–83.

———. *Partisan Politics in the Global Economy.* Cambridge: Cambridge University Press, 1998.

Garrett, Geoffrey, and Barry R. Weingast. "Ideas, Interests, and Institutions: Constructing the European Community's Internal Market." In Judith Goldstein and Robert O. Keohane, eds., *Ideas and Foreign Policy: Beliefs, Institutions, and Political Change.* Ithaca, N.Y.: Cornell University Press, 1993, 173–206.

Gereffi, Gary. "The Global Apparel Value Chain: What Prospects for Upgrading by Developing Countries?" Sectoral Studies Series, United Nations Industrial Development Organization, 2003.

Giavazzi, Francesco, and Marco Pagano. "The Advantage of Tying One's Hands: EMS Discipline and Central Bank Credibility." *European Economic Review* 32:5, 1989, 1055–75.

Gilbert, Milton. *Quest for World Monetary Order.* Ed. Peter Oppenheimer and Michael Dealtry. New York: Wiley, 1980.

Gill, Stephen, and David Law. *The Global Political Economy.* Hemel Hempstead: Harvester-Wheatsheaf, 1988.

Gilpin, Robert. *Global Political Economy: Understanding the International Economic Order.* Princeton, N.J.: Princeton University Press, 2001.

———. *The Political Economy of International Relations.* Princeton, N.J.: Princeton University Press, 1987.

———. "The Politics of Transnational Economic Relations." *International Organization* 25:3, 1971, 398–419.

———. *US Power and the Multinational Corporation.* New York: Basic Books, 1975.

———. *War and Change in World Politics.* Cambridge: Cambridge University Press, 1981.

Gittleman, Michelle, and John H. Dunning. "Japanese Multinationals in Europe and the United States: Some Comparisons and Contrasts." In Michael W. Klein and Paul J. J. Welfens, eds., *Multinationals in the New Europe and Global Trade.* Berlin: Springer-Verlag, 1992, 237–68.

Glyn, Andrew. "The Assessment: Economic Policy and Social Democracy." *Oxford Review of Economic Policy* 14:1, 1998, 1–18.

Goldstein, Judith L. *Ideas, Interests, and American Trade Policy.* Ithaca, N.Y.: Cornell University Press, 1993.

Goldstein, Morris, and Philip Turner. *Controlling Currency Mismatches in Emerging Markets.* Washington, D.C.: Institute for International Economics, 2004.

Gomory, Ralph E., and William J. Baumol. *Global Trade and Conflicting National Interests.* Cambridge: MIT Press, 2000.

Goodman, John B., and Louis W. Pauly. "The Obsolescence of Capital Controls? Economic Management in an Age of Global Markets." *World Politics* 46:1, 1993, 50–82.

Gorter, Joeri, and Ashok Parikh. "How Sensitive Is FDI to Differences in Corporate Income Taxation within the EU?" *De Economist* 151:2, 2003, 193–204.

Gourevitch, Peter. *Politics in Hard Times: Comparative Responses to International Economic Crises.* Ithaca, N.Y.: Cornell University Press, 1986.

Gourinchas, Pierre-Olivier, and Hélène Rey. "From World Banker to World Venture Capitalist: US External Adjustment and the Exorbitant Privilege." NBER Working Paper, 11563, 2005.

Gowa, Joanne S. *Allies, Adversaries, and International Trade.* Princeton, N.J.: Princeton University Press, 1995.

Gowa, Joanne S. *Closing the Gold Window: Domestic Politics and the End of Bretton Woods*. Ithaca, N.Y.: Cornell University Press, 1983.

———. "Public Goods and Political Institutions: Trade and Monetary Policy Processes in the United States." *International Organization* 42:1, 1988, 15–32.

Grabel, Ilene. "Ideology, Power, and the Rise of Independent Monetary Institutions in Emerging Economies." In Jonathan Kirshner, ed., *Monetary Orders: Ambiguous Economics, Ubiquitous Politics*. Ithaca, N.Y.: Cornell University Press, 2003, 25–54.

Graham, Edward M. *Fighting the Wrong Enemy: Antiglobal Activists and Multinational Enterprises*. Washington, D.C.: Institute for International Economics, 2000.

———. *Reforming Korea's Industrial Conglomerates*. Washington, D.C.: Institute for International Economics, 2003.

Gray, John. *False Dawn: The Delusions of Global Capitalism*. New York: Simon and Schuster, 1998.

Greider, William. *One World Ready or Not: The Manic Logic of Global Capitalism*. New York: Simon and Schuster, 1998.

Grieco, Joseph M. "Anarchy and the Limits of Cooperation: A Realist Critique of the Newest Liberal Institutionalism." *International Organization* 42:3, 1988, 485–507.

———. *Cooperation among Nations: Europe, America, and Non-tariff Barriers to Trade*. Ithaca, N.Y.: Cornell University Press, 1990.

Grimwade, Nigel. *International Trade: New Patterns of Trade, Production and Investment*. London: Routledge, 1989.

Groenewegen, Peter. "'Political Economy' and 'Economics.'" In John Eatwell, Murray Milgate, and Peter Newman, eds., *The New Palgrave: The World of Economics*. London: Macmillan, 1991, 556–62.

Grossman, Gene M. "Strategic Export Promotion: A Critique." In Paul R. Krugman, ed., *Strategic Trade Policy and the New International Economics*. Cambridge: MIT Press, 1986, 47–68.

Grossman, Gene M., and Elhanan Helpman. *Interest Groups and Trade Policy*. Princeton, N.J.: Princeton University Press, 2002.

———. "Outsourcing versus FDI in Industry Equilibrium." *Journal of the European Economic Association* 1:2–3, 2003, 317–27.

Grubel, Herbert J., and P. J. Lloyd. *Intra-industry Trade: The Theory and Measurement of International Trade in Differentiated Products*. London: Macmillan, 1975.

Guzzini, Stefano. *Realism in International Relations and International Political Economy*. London: Routledge, 1998.

Haggard, Stephan. *Pathways from the Periphery*. Ithaca, N.Y.: Cornell University Press, 1990.

Haggard, Stephan, and Sylvia Maxfield. "The Political Economy of Financial Internationalization in the Developing World." *International Organization* 50:1, 35–68, 1996.

Hall, Peter A., ed. *Governing the Economy: The Politics of State Intervention in Britain and France*. New York: Oxford University Press, 1986.

————, ed. *The Political Power of Economic Ideas: Keynesianism across Nations.* Princeton, N.J.: Princeton University Press, 1989.

Hays, Jude C. "Globalization and Capital Taxation in Consensus and Majoritarian Democracies." *World Politics* 56:1, 2003, 79–113.

Heimann, Fritz, and Gillian Dell. "Progress Report 07: Enforcement of the OECD Convention on Combating Bribery of Foreign Public Officials." Transparency International, July 18, 2007. Available at http://www.transparency.org/news_room/ in_focus/2007/oecd, accessed April 4, 2008.

Helleiner, Eric. *States and the Re-emergence of Global Finance.* Ithaca, N.Y.: Cornell University Press, 1994.

Helpman, Elhanan. "The Noncompetitive Theory of International Trade and Trade Policy." In World Bank, *Proceedings of the World Bank Annual Conference on Development Economics, 1989.* Washington, D.C.: World Bank, 1990, 193–230.

————. "Politics and Trade Policy." In Richard E. Baldwin et al., eds., *Market Integration, Regionalism, and the Global Economy.* Cambridge: Cambridge University Press, 1999, 86–116.

————. "The Structure of Foreign Trade." *Journal of Economic Perspectives* 13:2, 121–44.

Helpman, Elhanan, and Paul R. Krugman. *Trade Policy and Market Structure.* Cambridge: MIT Press, 1989.

Henderson, David. *The MAI Affair: A Story and Its Lessons.* London: Royal Institute of International Affairs, 2000.

Henisz, Witold, and Edward D. Mansfield. "Votes and Vetoes: The Political Determinants of Commercial Openness." *International Studies Quarterly* 50:1, 2006, 189–212.

Henning, C. Randall. *Currencies and Politics in the United States, Germany, and Japan.* Washington, D.C.: Institute for International Economics, 1994.

Hibbs, Douglas A. "Political Parties and Macroeconomic Policy." *American Political Science Review* 71:4, 1977, 1467–87.

Hirsch, Seev. "The US Electronics Industry in International Trade." *National Institute Economic Review* 34, 1965, 92–107.

Hirschman, Albert O. *Exit, Voice, and Loyalty: Responses to Decline in Firms, Organizations, and States.* Cambridge: Harvard University Press, 1970.

Hirst, Paul, and Grahame Thompson. *Globalization in Question: The International Economy and the Possibilities of Governance.* Cambridge: Polity, 2nd ed., 2000.

Hiscox, Michael J. "International Capital Mobility and Trade Politics: Capital Flows, Coalitions and Lobbying." *Economics and Politics* 16:3, 2004, 253–85.

————. *International Trade and Political Conflict: Commerce, Coalitions, and Mobility.* Princeton, N.J.: Princeton University Press, 2002.

Hoekman, Bernard M., and Michael M. Kostecki. *The Political Economy of the World Trading System: The WTO and Beyond.* Oxford: Oxford University Press, 2nd ed., 2001.

Hoekman, Bernard M., and Petros C. Mavroidis. *The World Trade Organization: Law, Economics, and Politics.* London: Routledge, 2007.

Hu, Yao-Su. "Global or Stateless Corporations Are National Firms with International Operations." *California Management Review* 34:2, 1992, 107–26.

Hufbauer, Gary Clyde. "The Impact of National Characteristics and Technology on the Commodity Composition of Trade in Manufactured Goods." In Raymond Vernon, ed., *The Technology Factor in International Trade.* New York: Columbia University Press, 1970, 175–231.

Hymer, Stephen H. *The International Operations of National Firms: A Study of Direct Foreign Investment.* Cambridge: MIT Press, 1976.

Ikenberry, G. John. "A World Economy Restored: Expert Consensus and the Anglo-American Postwar Settlement." *International Organization* 46:1, 1992, 289–321.

International Monetary Fund (IMF). *Argentina: 2002 Article IV Consultation.* IMF Country Report 03/226. Washington, D.C., July 2003.

———. *Balance of Payments Textbook.* Washington, D.C.: IMF, 1996. Available at http://www.imf.org/external/np/sta/bop/BOPtex.pdf, accessed April 4, 2008.

———. *Country Experiences with the Use and Liberalization of Capital Controls.* Washington, D.C.: IMF, 2000.

———. *World Economic Outlook, October 2001.* Washington, D.C.: IMF, 2001.

———. *World Economic Outlook, April 2007.* Washington, D.C.: IMF, 2007.

———. *World Economic Outlook, October 2007.* Washington, D.C.: IMF, 2007.

International Monetary Fund. Independent Evaluation Office. *Report on the Evaluation of the IMF's Approach to Capital Account Liberalization.* Washington, D.C.: Independent Evaluation Office, IMF, April 2005.

Irwin, Douglas A. *Against the Tide: An Intellectual History of Free Trade.* Princeton, N.J.: Princeton University Press, 1996.

Jackson, John H. *The World Trade Organization: Constitution and Jurisprudence.* London: Royal Institute of International Affairs, 1998.

———. *The World Trading System: Law and Politics of International Economic Relations.* Cambridge: MIT Press, 1997.

Jacobsen, John Kurt. "Much Ado about Ideas: The Cognitive Factor in Economic Policy." *World Politics* 47:2, 1995, 283–310.

James, Harold. *International Monetary Cooperation since Bretton Woods.* Washington, D.C.: IMF; New York: Oxford University Press, 1996.

Javorcik, Beata Smarzynska, and Shang-Jin Wei. "Pollution Havens and Foreign Direct Investment: Dirty Secret or Popular Myth?" *Contributions to Economic Analysis and Policy* 3:2, 2004, 1–32.

Jayasuriya, Kanishka. "Beyond Institutional Fetishism: From the Developmental to the Regulatory State." *New Political Economy* 10:3, 2005, 381–87.

Jones, Ronald W. "Factor Proportions and the Heckscher-Ohlin Theorem." *Review of Economic Studies* 24:1, 1956, 1–10.

Jones, Steven E. *Against Technology: From the Luddites to Neo-Luddism.* London: Routledge, 2006.

Kahler, Miles. "Economic Security in an Era of Globalization: Definition and Provision." *Pacific Review* 17:4, 2004, 485–502.

———. "Modeling Races to the Bottom." Graduate School of International Relations and Pacific Studies, University of California, San Diego.

———. "Rationality in International Relations." *International Organization* 52:4, 1998, 919–41.

Kalecki, Michael. "Political Aspects of Full Employment." *Political Quarterly* 14, October–December 1943, 322–31.

Kapstein, Ethan B. *Governing the Global Economy.* Cambridge: Harvard University Press, 1994.

Katzenstein, Peter J., ed. *Between Power and Plenty: Foreign Economic Policies of Advanced Industrial States.* Madison: University of Wisconsin Press, 1978.

Katzenstein, Peter J., Robert O. Keohane, and Stephen D. Krasner. *Exploration and Contestation in the Study of World Politics: An International Organization Reader.* Cambridge: MIT Press, 1999.

Keay, John. *The Honourable Company: A History of the English East India Company.* London: HarperCollins, 1991.

Keck, Margaret E., and Karen Sikkink. *Activists beyond Borders: Advocacy Networks in International Politics.* Ithaca, N.Y.: Cornell University Press, 1998.

Keefer, Philip, and David Stasavage. "The Limits of Delegation, Veto Players, Central Bank Independence, and the Credibility of Monetary Policy." *American Political Science Review* 47:3, 2003, 389–403.

Kenen, Peter B. "The Theory of Optimal Currency Areas." In Robert A. Mundell and Alexander K. Swoboda, eds., *Monetary Problems of the International Economy.* Chicago: University of Chicago Press, 1969, 41–60.

Kennedy, Paul. *The Rise of the Anglo-German Antagonism, 1860–1914.* New York: Humanity Books, 1988.

Keohane, Robert O. *After Hegemony.* Princeton, N.J.: Princeton University Press, 1984.

———. "The Theory of Hegemonic Stability and Changes in International Economic Regimes, 1967–77." In Ole R. Holsti, Randolph M. Siverson, and Alexander L. George, eds., *Change in the International System.* Boulder, Colo.: Westview Press, 1980, 131–62.

Keohane, Robert O., and Helen V. Milner, eds. *Internationalization and Domestic Politics.* Cambridge: Cambridge University Press, 1996.

Keohane, Robert O., and Joseph S. Nye. *Power and Interdependence: World Politics in Transition.* Boston: Little, Brown, 1977.

———, eds. *Transnational Relations and World Politics.* Cambridge: Harvard University Press, 1971.

Kindleberger, Charles P. *American Business Abroad.* New Haven: Yale University Press, 1969.

———. *A Financial History of Western Europe.* London: Allen and Unwin, 1984.

———. *The World in Depression, 1929–1939.* London: Allen and Unwin, 1973.

King, Gary, Robert O. Keohane, and Sidney Verba. *Designing Social Inquiry: Scientific Inference in Qualitative Research.* Princeton, N.J.: Princeton University Press, 1994.

King, Robert, and Mark Watson. "The Post-war U.S. Phillips Curve: A Revisionist Econometric History." *Carnegie-Rochester Conference Series on Public Policy* 41, 1994, 157–219.

Kirshner, Jonathan. *Appeasing Bankers: Financial Caution on the Road to War.* Princeton, N.J.: Princeton University Press, 2007.

———. "The Study of Money." *World Politics* 52:3, 2000, 407–36.

———, ed. *Monetary Orders: Ambiguous Economics, Ubiquitous Politics.* Ithaca, N.Y.: Cornell University Press, 2003.

Kobrin, Stephen J. "Testing the Bargaining Hypothesis in the Manufacturing Sector in Developing Countries." *International Organization* 41:4, 1987, 609–38.

Korten, David. *When Corporations Rule the World.* West Hartford, Conn.: Berrett-Koehler, 1995.

Krasner, Stephen D. *Defending the National Interest: Raw Materials Investments and US Foreign Policy.* Princeton, N.J.: Princeton University Press, 1978.

———. "State Power and the Structure of International Trade." *World Politics* 28:3, 1976, 317–47.

———. *Structural Conflict: The Third World against Global Liberalism.* Berkeley and Los Angeles: University of California Press, 1985.

Krueger, Anne O., ed. *The WTO as an International Organization.* Chicago: University of Chicago Press, 1998.

Krugman, Paul R. "Increasing Returns and Economic Geography." *Journal of Political Economy* 99:3, 1991, 483–99.

———. "Is Free Trade Passé?" *Journal of Economic Perspectives* 1:2, 1987, 131–44.

———. "A Model of Balance of Payments Crises." *Journal of Money, Credit and Banking* 11:3, 1979, 311–24.

———. *Re-thinking International Trade.* Cambridge: MIT Press, 1996.

———. "What Happened to Asia?" Unpublished paper, January 1998.

Krugman, Paul R., and Maurice Obstfeld. *International Economics: Theory and Policy.* Reading, Mass.: Addison-Wesley, 5th ed., 2000.

Kucera, David. "Core Labour Standards and Foreign Direct Investment." *International Labour Review* 141:1–2, 2002, 31–69.

Kurzer, Paulette. *Business and Banking: Political Change and Economic Integration in Western Europe.* Ithaca, N.Y.: Cornell University Press, 1993.

Kuttner, Robert. *The End of Laissez Faire.* New York: Knopf, 1991.

Kydland, Finn, and Edward S. Prescott. "Rules Rather Than Discretion: The Inconsistency of Optimal Plans." *Journal of Political Economy* 85:3, 1977, 473–92.

Kynge, James. *China Shakes the World: The Rise of a Hungry Nation.* London: Weidenfeld and Nicolson, 2006.

Lake, David A. "Leadership, Hegemony, and the International Economy: Naked Emperor or Tattered Monarch with Potential?" *International Studies Quarterly* 37:4, 1993, 459–89.

Lall, Sanjaya. "FDI and Development: Policy and Research Issues in the Emerging Context." Queen Elizabeth House Working Paper Series, 43, 2000.

———. "Imperfect Markets and Fallible Governments: The Role of the State in Industrial Development." In Deepak Nayyar, ed., *Trade and Industrialization*. New Delhi: Oxford University Press, 1997, 43–87.

Lane, Philip R., and Gian Maria Milesi-Ferretti. "International Financial Integration." IMF Working Paper, WP/03/86, April 2003.

La Porta, Rafael, Florencio Lopez-de-Silanes, and Andrei Shleifer. "Corporate Ownership around the World." *Journal of Finance* 54:2, 1999, 471–517.

Leamer, Edward. "A Flat World, a Level Playing Field, a Small World after All, or None of the Above? A Review of Thomas L. Friedman's *The World Is Flat*." *Journal of Economic Literature* 55:1, 2007, 83–126.

———. "The Heckscher-Ohlin Model in Theory and Practice." Graham Lecture. *Princeton Studies in International Finance*, No. 77, February 1995.

———. "The Leontief Paradox, Reconsidered." *Journal of Political Economy* 88:3, 1980, 495–503.

Lerner, Abba. "The Diagrammatical Representation of Cost Conditions in International Trade." Economica 12, August 1932, 346–56.

Levy, David L., and Aseem Prakash. "Bargains Old and New: Multinational Corporations in Global Governance." *Business and Politics* 5:2, 2003, 131–50.

Lijphart, Arendt, ed. *Parliamentary versus Presidential Government*. Oxford: Oxford University Press, 1992.

Lim, Ewe-Ghee. "Determinants of, and the Relation between, Foreign Direct Investment and Growth: A Summary of the Recent Literature." IMF Working Paper, WP/01/175, 2001.

Lindblom, Charles E. *Politics and Markets: The World's Political and Economic Systems*. New York: Basic Books, 1977.

Lindert, Peter H. "Key Currencies and Gold, 1900–1913." *Princeton Studies in International Finance*, No. 24, 1969.

Lipsey, Richard. "The Theory of Customs Unions: A General Survey." In Jagdish N. Bhagwati ed., *Selected Readings International Trade*. Cambridge: MIT Press, 1987, 357–76.

Lipson, Charles. *Standing Guard: Protecting Foreign Capital in the Nineteenth and Twentieth Centuries*. Berkeley and Los Angeles: University of California Press, 1985.

List, Friedrich. *The National System of Political Economy*. Trans. Sampson S. Lloyd. London: Longmans, Green, 1909.

Lohmann, Suzanne. "Federalism and Central Bank Independence: The Politics of German Monetary Policy, 1957–92." *World Politics* 50:3, 1998, 401–46.

Lohmann, Suzanne, and Sharon O'Halloran. "Divided Government and US Trade Policy: Theory and Evidence." *International Organization* 48:4, 1994, 595–632.

Loriaux, Michael. "The End of Credit Activism in Interventionist States." In Loriaux, ed., *Capital Ungoverned: Liberalizing Finance in Interventionist States*. Ithaca, N.Y.: Cornell University Press, 1997, 1–16.

Lucas, Robert E., Jr. "Some International Evidence on Output-Inflation Tradeoffs." *American Economic Review* 63:3, 1973, 326–34.

———. "Why Doesn't Capital Flow from Rich to Poor Countries?" *American Economic Review* 80:2, 1990, 92–96.

MacKenzie, Donald. *An Engine Not a Camera: How Financial Models Shape Markets.* Cambridge: MIT Press, 2006.

Maddison, Angus. *Phases of Capitalist Development.* Oxford: Oxford University Press, 1982.

Magee, Stephen P. "Endogenous Tariff Theory: A Survey." In David C. Colander, ed., *Neoclassical Political Economy, The Analysis of Rent-Seeking and DUP Activities.* Cambridge: Ballinger, 1984, 41–55.

Mahoney, James. "Nominal, Ordinal, and Narrative Appraisal in Macrocausal Analysis." *American Journal of Sociology* 104:4, 1999, 1154–96.

Mahoney, James, and Gary Goertz. "A Tale of Two Cultures: Contrasting Quantitative and Qualitative Research." *Political Analysis* 14:3, 2006, 227–49.

Manger, Mark. "Competition and Bilateralism in Trade Policy: The Case of Japan's Free Trade Agreements." *Review of International Political Economy* 12:5, 2005, 804–28.

Markusen, James R. "Foreign Investment and Trade." Centre of International Economic Studies, Policy Discussion Paper, 19, April 2000.

———. *Multinational Firms and the Theory of International Trade.* Cambridge: MIT Press, 2002.

Mattli, Walter, and Tim Büthe. "Setting International Standards: Technological Rationality or Primacy of Power?" *World Politics* 56:1, 2003, 1–42.

Mayer, Wolfgang. "Endogenous Tariff Formation." *American Economic Review* 74:5, 1984, 970–85.

McKeown, Timothy. "Hegemonic Stability Theory and 19th Century Tariff Levels in Europe." *International Organization* 37:1, 1983, 73–91.

McKinnon, Ronald I. *Money in International Exchange: The Convertible Currency System.* New York: Oxford University Press, 1979.

McKinsey Global Institute. *Mapping the Global Capital Market: Third Annual Report.* San Francisco: McKinsey & Co., January 2007.

———. *118 Trillion and Counting: Taking Stock of the World's Capital Markets.* San Francisco: McKinsey & Co., February 2005.

———. *New Horizons: Multinational Company Investment in Developing Economies.* San Francisco: McKinsey & Co., 2003.

McNamara, Kathleen R. *The Currency of Ideas: Monetary Politics in the European Union.* Ithaca, N.Y.: Cornell University Press, 1998.

Mehrling, Perry. *Fischer Black and the Revolutionary Idea of Finance.* Hoboken, N.J.: Wiley, 2005.

Midford, Paul. "International Trade and Domestic Politics: Improving on Rogowski's Model of Political Alignments." *International Organization* 47:4 1993, 535–64.

Milner, Helen V. *Interests, Institutions, and Information.* Princeton, N.J.: Princeton University Press, 1997.

———. "Rationalizing Politics: The Emerging Synthesis of International, American and Comparative Politics." *International Organization* 52:4, 1998, 759–86.

———. *Resisting Protectionism: Global Industries and the Politics of International Trade.* Princeton, N.J.: Princeton University Press, 1988.

Milner, Helen V., and Edward D. Mansfield. "The New Wave of Regionalism." *International Organization* 53:3, 1997, 589–627.

Moggridge, Dennis E. *The Return to Gold, 1925: The Formulation of Economic Policy and Its Critics.* New York: Cambridge University Press, 1969.

Moore, Michael. *A World without Walls: Freedom, Development, Free Trade, and Global Governance.* New York: Cambridge University Press, 2003.

Moran, Theodore H. *Harnessing Foreign Direct Investment for Development: Policies for Developed And Developing Countries.* Washington, D.C.: Center for Global Development, 2006.

———, ed. *Multinational Corporations: The Political Economy of Foreign Direct Investment.* Lexington, Mass.: D. C. Heath, 1985.

Morisset, Jacques, and Neda Pirnia. "How Tax Policy and Incentives Affect Foreign Direct Investment: A Review." World Bank Working Paper, 2509, 2000.

Morrow, James D. "When Do 'Relative Gains' Impede Trade?" *Journal of Conflict Resolution* 41:1, 1997, 12–37.

Mosley, Layna. *Global Capital and National Governments.* Cambridge: Cambridge University Press, 2003.

Mundell, Robert. "Capital Mobility and Stabilization Policy under Fixed and Flexible Exchange Rates." *Canadian Journal of Economics and Political Science* 29, 1963, 475–85.

———. "The Monetary Dynamics of International Adjustment under Fixed and Floating Exchange Rates." *Quarterly Journal of Economics* 74:2, 1960, 227–57.

Navaretti, Georgio Barba, and Anthony J. Venables. *Multinational Firms in the World Economy.* Princeton, N.J.: Princeton University Press, 2006.

Navarro, Vicente, John Schmitt, and Javier Astudillo. "Is Globalization Undermining the Welfare State?" *Cambridge Journal of Economics* 28:1, 2004, 133–52.

Neilson, Daniel L. "Supplying Trade Reform: Political Institutions and Liberalization in Middle-Income Presidential Democracies." *American Journal of Political Science* 47:3, 2003, 470–91.

Newfarmer, Richard, ed. *Profits, Poverty, and Progress: Case Studies of International Industries in Latin America.* South Bend, Ind.: Notre Dame University Press, 1985.

Nordhaus, William D. "The Political Business Cycle." *Review of Economic Studies* 42:2, 1975, 169–90.

North, Douglass C. "Institutions." *Journal of Economic Perspectives* 5:1, 1991, 97–112.

———. *Institutions, Institutional Change, and Economic Performance.* Cambridge: Cambridge University Press, 1990.

———. *Understanding the Process of Economic Change.* Princeton, N.J.: Princeton University Press, 2005.

Nye, John V. C. *War, Wine, and Taxes: The Political Economy of Anglo-French Trade, 1689–1900.* Princeton, N.J.: Princeton University Press, 2007.

Nye, Joseph S. *Bound to Lead: The Changing Nature of American Power.* New York: Basic Books, 1990.

Oatley, Thomas. "How Constraining Is Capital Mobility? The Partisan Hypothesis in an Open Economy." *American Journal of Political Science* 43:4, 1999, 1003–27.

Oatley, Thomas, and Robert Nabors. "Market Failure, Wealth Transfers, and the Basle Accord." *International Organization* 52:1, 1998, 35–54.

Obstfeld, Maurice, and Kenneth Rogoff. "The Unsustainable US Current Account Position Revisited." NBER Working Paper, 10869, November 2004.

Odell, John S. "Case Study Methods in International Political Economy." *International Studies Perspectives* 2:2, 2001, 161–76.

———. "Understanding International Trade Policies: An Emerging Synthesis." *World Politics* 43:1, 1990, 139–67.

Olson, Mancur. *The Logic of Collective Action: Public Goods and the Theory of Groups.* Cambridge: Harvard University Press, 1965.

———. *Power and Prosperity: Outgrowing Communist and Capitalist Dictatorships.* New York: Basic Books, 2000.

Oman, Charles P., Douglas H. Brooks, and Colm Foy, eds. *Investing in Asia.* Paris: OECD Development Centre, 1997.

Organization for Economic Cooperation and Development (OECD). *Corporate Tax Incentives for Foreign Direct Investment, No. 4.* Paris: OECD, 2001.

———. *Foreign Direct Investment and Economic Development: Lessons from Six Emerging Economies.* Paris: OECD, 1998.

Palan, Ronan. *The Offshore World: Sovereign Markets, Virtual Places, and Nomad Millionaires.* Ithaca, N.Y.: Cornell University Press, 2006.

Pauly, Louis B. *Who Elected the Bankers? Surveillance and Control in the World Economy.* Ithaca, N.Y.: Cornell University Press, 1997.

Persson, Torsten, and Guido Tabellini. *Political Economy: Explaining Economic Policy.* Cambridge: MIT Press, 2000.

Phelps, Edmund S. "Phillips Curves, Expectations of Inflation, and Optimal Unemployment over Time." *Economica* 34:3, 1967, 254–81.

Phillips, A. W. "The Relation between Unemployment and the Rate of Change of Money Wages in the United Kingdom, 1861–1957." *Economica* 25:4, 1958, 283–99.

Pierson, Paul. "The New Politics of the Welfare State." *World Politics* 48:2, 1996, 143–79.

Pinker, Steven. *How the Mind Works.* London: Penguin, 1997.

Pirie, Iain. "The New Korean State." *New Political Economy* 10:1, 2005, 25–42.

Polak, Jacques J. "The Changing Nature of IMF Conditionality." *Princeton Essays in International Finance,* No. 184, 1991.

Porter, Michael E. *The Competitive Advantage of Nations.* New York: Free Press, 1992.

Posen, Adam. "Central Bank Independence and Disinflationary Credibility: A Missing Link?" *Oxford Economic Papers* 50:3, 1998, 335–59.

Posner, M. V. "International Trade and Technical Change." *Oxford Economic Papers* 13:3, 1961, 323–41.

Prakash, Aseem, and Matthew Potoski. "Investing Up: FDI and the Cross-Country Diffusion of ISO 14001 Management Systems." *International Studies Quarterly* 51:3, 2007, 723–44.

Prestowitz, Clyde V. *Trading Places: How We Allowed Japan to Take the Lead.* New York: Basic Books, 1988.

Putnam, Robert D. "Diplomacy and Domestic Politics: The Logic of Two-Level-Games." *International Organization* 42:3, 1988, 427–60.

Quinn, Dennis P., and Carla Inclán. "The Origins of Financial Openness: A Study of Current and Capital Account Liberalization." *American Journal of Political Science* 41:3, 1997, 771–813.

Reich, Robert. "Who Is US?" *Harvard Business Review,* February 1990, 53–64.

Reinhart, Carmen M., Kenneth S. Rogoff, and Miguel A. Savastano. "Debt Intolerance." *Brookings Papers on Economic Activity* 1, 2003, 1–74.

Rhodes, Carolyn. *Reciprocity, U.S. Trade Policy, and the GATT Regime.* Ithaca, N.Y.: Cornell University Press, 1993.

Richards, John E. "Toward a Positive Theory of International Institutions: Regulating International Aviation Markets." *International Organization* 53:1, 1999, 1–37.

Rodrik, Dani. *Has Globalization Gone Too Far?* Washington, D.C.: Institute for International Economics, 1997.

Rogoff, Kenneth. "The Optimal Degree of Commitment to an Intermediate Monetary Target." *Quarterly Journal of Economics* 100:4, 1985, 1169–90.

Rogowski, Ronald W. *Commerce and Coalitions: How Trade Affects Domestic Political Alignments.* Princeton, N.J.: Princeton University Press, 1989.

———. "Trade and the Variety of Democratic Institutions." *International Organization* 41:2, 1987, 203–23.

Rosecrance, Richard N. *The Rise of the Trading State: Commerce and Conflict in the Modern World.* New York: Basic Books, 1986.

Rowe, David M. "World Economic Expansion and National Security in Pre–World War I Europe." *International Organization* 53:2, 1999, 195–231.

Rudra, Nita. "Globalization and the Decline of the Welfare State in Less-Developed Countries." *International Organization* 56:2, 2002, 411–45.

Rudra, Nita, and Stephan Haggard. "Globalization, Democracy, and Effective Welfare Spending in the Developed World." *Comparative Political Studies* 38:9, 2005, 1015–49.

Ruggie, John Gerard. "International Regimes, Transactions, and Change: Embedded Liberalism in the Postwar Economic Order." *International Organization* 36:2, 1982, 379–415.

Sachs, Jeffrey D., and Howard D. Shatz. "Trade and Jobs in US Manufacturing." *Brookings Papers on Economic Activity* 1, 1994, 1–84.

Sally, Razeen. *States and Firms: Multinational Enterprises in Institutional Competition.* London: Routledge, 1995.

Sandholtz, Wayne, Michael Borrus, John Zysman, Ken Conca, Jay Stowsky, Steven Vogel, and Steve Weber. *The Highest Stakes: The Economic Foundations of the Next Security System.* New York: Oxford University Press, 1993.

Sayers, Richard S. *Bank of England Operations, 1890–1914.* London: King, 1936.

———. *The Bank of England, 1891–1944.* Cambridge: Cambridge University Press, 1976.

Scharpf, Fritz. *Crisis and Choice in European Social Democracy.* Ithaca, N.Y.: Cornell University Press, 1991.

Schattschneider, E. E. *Politics, Pressures and the Tariff.* New York: Prentice Hall, 1935.

Schelling, Thomas. *The Strategy of Conflict.* Cambridge: Harvard University Press, 1960.

Scholte, Jan Art. "Global Capitalism and the State." *International Affairs* 73:3, 1997, 427–52.

Schonhardt-Bailey, Cheryl. *From the Corn Laws to Free Trade: Interests, Ideas, and Institutions in Historical Perspective.* Cambridge: MIT Press, 2006.

Seabright, Paul. *The Company of Strangers: A Natural History of Economic Life.* Princeton, N.J.: Princeton University Press, 2004.

Seabrooke, Leonard. *US Power in International Finance: The Victory of Dividends.* London: Palgrave Macmillan, 2001.

Seers, Dudley, ed. *Dependency Theory: A Critical Reassessment.* London: Pinter, 1981.

Sell, Susan K., and Aseem Prakash. "Using Ideas Strategically: Examining the Contest between Business and NGO Networks in Intellectual Property Rights." *International Studies Quarterly* 48:1, 2004, 143–75.

Sen, Amartya. *On Ethics and Economics.* Oxford, Blackwell, 1987.

Sen, Gautam. *The Military Origins of Industrialization and International Trade Rivalry.* London: Pinter, 1984.

Shatz, Howard J., and Anthony Venables. "The Geography of International Investment." World Bank Policy Research Working Paper, 2338, 2000.

Shiller, Robert J. *Irrational Exuberance.* Princeton, N.J.: Princeton University Press, 2nd ed., 2005.

Simmons, Beth A. "Central Bank Independence between the World Wars." *International Organization* 50:3, 1996, 407–44.

———. "The International Politics of Harmonization: The Case of Capital Market Regulation." *International Organization* 55:3, 2001, 589–620.

———. *Who Adjusts? Domestic Sources of Foreign Economic Policy during the Interwar Years.* Princeton, N.J.: Princeton University Press, 1994.

Simmons, Beth A., and Zachary Elkins. "The Globalization of Liberalization: Policy Diffusion in the International Political Economy." *American Political Science Review* 98:1, 2004, 171–89.

Sinclair, Timothy J. *The New Masters of Capital: American Bond Rating Agencies and the Politics of Creditworthiness.* Ithaca, N.Y.: Cornell University Press, 2005.

Singer, David Andrew. *Regulating Capital: Setting Standards for the International Financial System.* Ithaca, N.Y.: Cornell University Press, 2007.

Skidelsky, Robert. *John Maynard Keynes.* Vol. 3, *Fighting for Britain, 1937–1946.* London: Macmillan, 2000.

Sklair, Leslie. "Transnational Corporations as Political Actors." *New Political Economy* 3:2, 1998, 284–87.

Slaughter, Matthew J., and Phillip Swagel. "Does Globalization Lower Wages and Export Jobs?" *IMF Economic Issues,* 11, 1997.

Smarzynska, Beata K., and Shang-Jin Wei. "Pollution Havens and Foreign Direct Investment: Dirty Secret or Popular Myth?" World Bank Working Paper, 2673, 2001.

Snidal, Duncan. "The Limits of Hegemonic Stability Theory." *International Organization* 39:4, 1985, 579–614.

Soederberg, Susanne, Georg Menz, and Philip G. Cerny, eds. *Internalizing Globalization: The Rise of Neoliberalism and the Decline of National Varieties of Capitalism.* London: Palgrave Macmillan, 2005.

Spar, Deborah L., and David B. Yoffie. "Multinational Enterprises and the Prospects for Justice." *Journal of International Affairs* 52:2, 1999, 557–81.

Spencer, Barbara J., and James A. Brander. "Strategic Trade Policy." In Steven N. Durlauf and Lawrence E. Blume, eds., *The New Palgrave Dictionary of Economics.* Basingstoke: Palgrave Macmillan, 2008, DOI: 10. 1057/9740230226203.1632.

Steinmo, Sven. "The End of Redistributive Taxation: Tax Reform in a Global World Economy." *Challenge* 37:6, 1994, 9–17.

Stepan, Alfred C. *The State and Society: Peru in Comparative Perspective.* Princeton, N.J.: Princeton University Press, 1978.

Stewart, Kenneth G., and Michael C. Webb. "Capital Taxation, Globalization, and International Tax Competition." Econometrics Working Papers, 301, Department of Economics, University of Victoria, 2003.

Stiglitz, Joseph E. *Globalization and Its Discontents.* London: Allen Lane, 2002.

Stiglitz, Joseph E., and Andrew Weiss. "Credit Rationing in Markets with Imperfect Information." *American Economic Review* 71:3, 1981, 393–410.

Stolper, Wolfgang, and Paul A Samuelson. "Protection and Real Wages." *Review of Economic Studies* 9, 1941, 58–73.

Stopford, John M., Susan Strange, and John S. Henley. *Rival States, Rival Firms: Competition for World Market Shares.* Cambridge: Cambridge University Press, 1991.

Strange, Susan. "International Economics and International Relations: A Case of Mutual Neglect." *International Affairs* 46:2, 1971, 304–15.

———. *The Retreat of the State: The Diffusion of Power in the World Economy.* Cambridge: Cambridge University Press, 1996.

———. *States and Markets.* London: Pinter, 1988.

Swank, Duane C. *Global Capital, Political Institutions, and Policy Change in Developed Welfare States.* Cambridge: Cambridge University Press, 2002.

Swank, Duane C., and Sven Steinmo. "The New Political Economy of Taxation in Advanced Capitalist Democracies." *American Journal of Political Science* 46:3, 2002, 642–55.

Sweeney, Richard J. "The Information Costs of Capital Controls." In C. P. Rios and R. J. Sweeney, eds., *Capital Controls in Emerging Economies.* Boulder, Colo.: Westview Press, 1996.

Tax Justice Network. "Tax Us If You Can." Briefing Paper, September 2005.

Temin, Peter. *Did Monetary Forces Cause the Great Depression?* New York: W. W. Norton, 1976.

Thacker, Strom C. "The High Politics of IMF Lending." *World Politics* 52:1, 1999, 38–75.

———. *Big Business, the State, and Free Trade: Constructing Coalitions in Mexico.* Cambridge: Cambridge University Press, 2nd ed., 2006.

Trebilcock, Michael John, and Robert Howse. *The Regulation of International Trade.* London: Routledge, 3rd ed., 2005.

Triffin, Robert. *Gold and the Dollar Crisis: The Future of Convertibility.* New Haven: Yale University Press, 1961.

Turner, Barry. *Free Trade and Protection.* London: Longman, 1971.

Tyson, Laura D'Andrea. *Who's Bashing Whom? Trade Conflict in High-Technology Industries.* Washington, D.C.: Institute for International Economics, 1992.

Underhill, Geoffrey R. D. "Keeping Governments Out of Politics: Transnational Securities Markets, Regulatory Co-operation, and Political Legitimacy." *Review of International Studies* 21:3, 1995, 251–78.

United Nations Conference on Trade and Development (UNCTAD). *World Investment Report 1992: Transnational Corporations as Engines of Growth.* New York: UNCTAD, 1992.

———. *World Investment Report 2005: Transnational Corporations and the Internationalization of R&D.* New York: UNCTAD, 2005.

———. *World Investment Report 2006: FDI from Developing and Transition Economies, Implications for Development.* New York: UNCTAD, 2006.

Van Dormael, Armand. *Bretton Woods: Birth of a Monetary System.* London: Macmillan, 1978.

Vernon, Raymond. "International Investment and International Trade in the Product Cycle." *Quarterly Journal of Economics* 80:2, 1966, 190–207.

———. "Sovereignty at Bay: 10 Years After." *International Organization* 35:3, 1981, 517–39.

———, ed. *Big Business and the State.* London: Macmillan, 1974.

Viner, Jacob. *The Customs Union Issue.* London: Stephens and Sons, 1950.

———. "Power versus Plenty as Objectives of Foreign Policy in the Seventeenth and Eighteenth Centuries." *World Politics* 1:1, 1948, 1–29.

Vogel, David. *Trading Up: Consumer and Environmental Regulation in a Global Economy.* Cambridge: Harvard University Press, 1995.

Wade, Robert. "The Coming Fight over Capital Controls." *Foreign Policy* 113, Winter 1998–99, 41–54.

———. *Governing the Market: Economic Theory and the Role of Government in East Asian Industrialization.* Princeton, N.J.: Princeton University Press, 1990.

Wade, Robert, and Frank Veneroso. "The Asian Crisis: The High Debt Model versus the Wall Street–Treasury-IMF Complex." *New Left Review* 288, March–April, 1998, 3–23.

Waelde, Thomas, and Abba Kolo. "Environmental Regulation, Investment Protection, and 'Regulatory Taking' in International Law." *International and Comparative Law Quarterly* 50:4, 2001, 811–48.

Walter, Andrew. "Adam Smith on International Relations: Liberal Internationalist or Realist?" *Review of International Studies* 22:1, 1996, 5–29.

———. "Do Corporations Really Rule the World?" *New Political Economy* 3:2, 1998, 292–95.

———. "Globalization, Corporate Identity, and European Technology Policy." *Journal of European Public Policy* 2:3, 1995, 427–46.

———. "Globalization and Policy Convergence: The Case of Direct Investment Rules." In Richard A. Higgott, Geoffrey R. D. Underhill, and Andreas Beiler, eds., *Non-state Actors and Authority in the Global System*. London: Routledge, 2000, 51–74.

———. *Governing Finance: East Asia's Adoption of International Standards*. Ithaca, N.Y.: Cornell University Press, 2008.

———. "Leadership Begins at Home: Domestic Sources of International Monetary Power." In David M. Andrews, ed., *International Monetary Power*. Ithaca, N.Y.: Cornell University Press, 2006, 51–71.

———. "NGOs, Business, and International Investment Rules: MAI, Seattle and Beyond." *Global Governance* 7:1, 2001, 51–73.

———. *World Power and World Money*. New York: St. Martin's, 2nd ed., 1993.

Waltz, Kenneth N. *The Theory of International Politics*. Reading, Mass.: Addison-Wesley, 1979.

Warnecke, Steven J. *International Trade and Industrial Policies*. London: Macmillan, 1979.

Warren, Bill. *Imperialism, Pioneer of Capitalism*. London: Verso, 1980.

Webb, Michael C. *The Political Economy of Policy Coordination*. Ithaca, N.Y.: Cornell University Press, 1995.

Webb, Michael C., and Stephen D. Krasner. "Hegemonic Stability Theory: An Empirical Assessment." *Review of International Studies* 15:2, 1989, 183–98.

White, Lawrence H. *The Theory of Monetary Institutions*. Malden, Mass.: Blackwell, 1999.

Widmaier, Wesley. "The Social Construction of the 'Impossible Trinity': The Intersubjective Bases of Monetary Cooperation." *International Studies Quarterly* 48:2, 2004, 433–53.

Willett, Thomas D. "International Financial Markets as Sources of Crises or Discipline: The Too Much, Too Late Hypothesis." *Princeton Essays in International Finance*, No. 218, May 2000.

Williamson, Oliver E. "The New Institutional Economics: Taking Stock, Looking Ahead." *Journal of Economic Literature* 38:3, 2000, 595–613.

Wilson, Edward O. *Consilience: The Unity of Knowledge*. London: Little, Brown, 1998.

Womack, James P., Daniel T. Jones, and Daniel Roos. *The Machine That Changed the World: The Story of Lean Production*. New York: Harper Perennial, 1991.

Woo-Cumings, Meredith, ed. *The Developmental State*. Ithaca, N.Y.: Cornell University Press, 1999.

Wood, Adrian. "Globalization and the Rise in Labour Market Inequalities." *Economic Journal* 108:450, 1998, 1463–82.

Woods, Ngaire. *The Globalizers: The IMF, the World Bank, and Their Borrowers*. Ithaca, N.Y.: Cornell University Press, 2006.

World Bank. *The East Asia Miracle: Economic Growth and Public Policy*. Washington, D.C.: World Bank, 1993.

Wright, Richard. *The Moral Animal: Why We Are the Way We Are*. London: Abacus, 1994.

Wyplosz, Charles. "EMU: Why and How It Might Happen." *Journal of Economic Perspectives* 11:4, 1997, 3–22.

———. "International Financial Instability." In Inge Kaul, Isabelle Grunberg, and Marc A. Stern, eds., *Global Public Goods: International Cooperation in the 21st Century*. New York: Oxford University Press, 1999, 152–89.

Zoromé, Ahmed. "Concept of Offshore Financial Centers: In Search of an Operational Definition." IMF Working Paper, WP/07/87, April 2007.

Zysman, John. *Governments, Markets, and Growth: Financial Systems and Politics of Industrial Change*. Ithaca, N.Y.: Cornell University Press, 1983.

Index

adjustment: balance of payments (BoP) 86–91; and international interdependence, 96–99; theory and practice of, 91–96

adverse selection, 162

agenda setting, in democratic decision-making process, 79–81

agriculture, 1, 5, 138; and URA, 35n17

aid, 106. *See also* public international finance

Airbus, 53–54

aircraft industry, 53–54

Alesina, Alberto, 140

Alt, James E., 76

amendment, in democratic decision-making process, 79–81

Amity and Commerce treaty, 202

anthropology, 22

antidumping duties, 36n19

anti-Keynesian policy consensus, rise of, 129

Apple, 182

Argentina, 104, 153, 159

Asian financial crisis (1997), 159–61

associated enterprise, 173n8

balance of payments (BoP), financing and adjustment of, 86–99

balance-of-payments argument for trade protection, 50–51

balance of payments (BoP) deficit, 87

balance of payments (BoP) surplus, 87

bank loans, in private international finance, 102–3

Bank of England, 106, 108–10, 112n53. *See also* central banks

Basle Capital Adequacy Accord, 165

Basle Committee for Banking Supervision (BCBS), 164–65

Basle Concordat (1975), 164

Basle I and II, 164–65

Becker, Gary, 9, 15, 17

Bernstein, Peter L., 130

best-practice standards, 160–61. *See also* standard setting

bilateral investment treaties (BITs), 202–5

bilateralism, in international trade, 41–43

Boeing, 53–54

bonds, in private international finance, 103–4

borrowers: and default risk, 154; risks to, 101–4

borrowing: in convertible foreign currencies, 102–3; as means of funding deficits, 87–90; sustainable level of, 152–53. *See also* international financial institutions; private international finance; public international finance

boundary, of firm, 179, 181–83. *See also* multinational corporations (MNCs)

branded products, demand for, 185

Brander, James, 53–54

Bretton Woods Agreement, 114–18

Bretton Woods system, 97–98, 141; demise of, 118–21

Broz, J. Lawrence, 139

Bundesbank, 131

business cycles, 74

California effect, 223–24

Canada, and globalization, 235–36

deposit insurance schemes, 163

developed countries: defining, 153–54; and FDI, 177–79, 196–98

developing countries: defining, 153–54; and DSM, 38–41; and FDI, 177–79, 189–91, 194; and fear of floating, 139–40; and fiscal policy constraints, 152–54; and infant industry argument, 49–50; and nationalization of MNC assets, 189; and private international finance, 102–4; and product cycle theory, 51–53; and public international finance, 106–7; and URA, 35–36

developmental NGOs, and trade policy, 77

dispute settlement, relating to FDI, 206, 208, 209–10, 227; in WTO, 34

Doha Development Round, 36–38

dollar, US, as key currency, 100

dollarization, 139–40

dollar standard, 118–21, 134

domestic content requirements, 188n28

domestic employment, and trade protection, 51

domestic interests, in trade policy, 67–76

domestic politics, and international system, 14–15, 23–24

double taxation treaties (DTTs), 202n2, 202–5

Downs, Anthony, 14, 14n36

dual-use technologies, and trade protection, 63–65

Dunning, John, 180

East Asian developmental model, 159–61

East India Company, 171

econometrics, 18–19

economic crises: debt crises, 153, 158; and FDI, 190–93. *See also* financial crises

economic determinism, 20–21

economic development, and factor mobility, 73; and FDI, 194–95

economic nationalism, 196, 207

economics, role in IPE, xi–xiii, 2–7, 16–22, 228–32

economic theory: of exchange rates and adjustment, 91–95; and financial integration, 145, 147–48; FDI, 179–83; and international trade, 44–56, 58, 68–70, 83; of optimal currency areas, 137

economies: Rogowski's typology of, 71; of scale, 171, 171n4; of scope, 171, 171n4

EEC (European Economic Community), creation of, 41–42

efficiency hypothesis, 155n56, 155–58

Eichengreen, Barry J., 113

electoral districts, 81–82

electoral franchise, expansion of, 113, 128

electoral systems, and trade policy, 81–83

Elkins, Zachary, 125

eminent domain, 210

empiricism, in IPE, x

Endangered Species Act of 1973 (US), 39

endogeneity, of political institutions, 82–83

endogenous tariff theory, 68–70

environmental activists, opposition to WTO system, 44

environmental NGOs, 40, 77

environmental standards, and convergence hypothesis, 223–25

EU (European Union): and financial liberalization, 124; and multilateralism, 43–44; and RIAs, 206; and trade in agriculture, 1

eurodollar markets, 123

European Court of Justice, 206

European Economic Community. *See* EEC

European Monetary System (EMS), 95, 98, 136–39

European Monetary Union (EMU), 133, 136–39

European Union. *See* EU

evolutionary biology, 22

exchange rate: fixed/pegged, 91n4, 91–92, 94, 96–99, 107, 115–17, 134–36, 139–40, 145; flexible/floating, 91n4, 91–94, 99, 120, 133, 136, 139–40 (*See also* fear of floating); real, 92, 92n5

exchange rate commitments, 95–96, 135; credibility of, 138

exchange rate fixity, and monetary policy autonomy, 135

exchange rate policies, and financial integration, 139–40

expenditure-reducing policies, as adjustment measure, 93–94

expenditure-switching policies, as adjustment measure, 93–94

138n14, 138–39; exchange rate policy credibility, 96; and FDI, 177, 202; financial liberalization, 110, 124, 142, 153; protectionism in, 29; reserve holdings, 105, 120; resistance to currency revaluation, 98, 134; return to gold standard, 112
Gilpin, Robert, ix, 9–11
Global Compact, 210–11
globalization, 23, 23n61, 235–38; of labor markets, 237
gold: demonetization of, 120; reserve role of, 115
gold-dollar system, 116
gold exchange standard, 116, 118–21
Gold Pool, 117
gold revaluation proposal, 120
gold standard, 93, 96; and Bretton Woods Agreement, 115; international, 109–14
Government Procurement Agreement, 207–8
Gowa, Joanne S., 66
grants, 106
Great Britain: and European political integration, 139; and free trade, 28–29; and international gold standard, 110–12; and MNCs, 177; system of Imperial Preference, 30; and unilateral trade policy, 28–29
Great Depression, 115
greenfield investments, 174, 187, 190
Gresham's Law, 119n69
Grieco, Joseph M., 13, 65
Grossman, Gene M., 69
G10 reserve swap network, 141

Haggard, Stephan, 125
Hamilton, Alexander, 49
Hawley-Smoot tariff (US), 30, 73, 77–78, 82
Hays, Jude C., 157
Heckscher, Eli F., 46
Heckscher-Ohlin-Samuelson theory. See H-O-S theory
hegemonic coercion, and policy liberalization for FDI, 196–98
hegemonic stability theory (HST), 10–12, 14–16, 29–31, 115
hegemony, absence of, 114
hegemony, US, in construction of Bretton Woods system, 115. See also United States

Helleiner, Eric, 124
Helpman, Elhanan, 69
herding phenomena, 163
Hibbs, Douglas A., 146–47
hierarchy, in global monetary and financial markets, 85
highly concentrated sector, 69n21, 69–70
Hirschman, Albert O., 213
Hiscox, Michael, 73, 75–76, 229
home country, for MNCs, 164, 164n78, 173, 173n7
horizontal differentiation, 48n37
horizontal FDI, 179–81, 184–87
host country, for MNCs, 164, 164n78, 173, 173n7
H-O-S theory (Hecksher-Ohlin-Samuelson), 46–49, 48n40, 70–71, 190, 197, 220, 222, 229; factor proportions in, 46–49
HST. See hegemonic stability theory
human capital, as manufacturing input, 47
human rights activists, opposition to WTO system, 44
Hymer, Stephen, 186

ideational change, 21–22, 193–96
ideology: and CBI, 149; and constructivism, 22; in explaining financial liberalization, 129–30; and interest-based trade theories, 76–77
IFI conditionality, 101, 143–44
IFIs. See international financial institutions (IFIs)
IMF (International Monetary Fund), 106–7, 117–18, 142–43, 160, 234; establishment of, 115; and financial liberalization, 124–25, 129–30
immigration, 237
imperialism, 171
import substitution industrialization (ISI), 158–59
incentive policies (for FDI), and convergence hypothesis, 217–20
Inclán, Carla, 126
indebted industrialization, 158–59
India: distributional effects of inward FDI, 221; and emergence of a global labor

Prakash, Aseem, 77n35
preferential trade agreements (PTAs), 41–43
presidential systems, 79–81
President's Council of Economic Advisors (US), 65n8
primary (extractive) industries, FDI in, 177
Prince, Chuck, 162n72
private international finance, 100–104; reemergence of, 121–30
privatization of SOEs, 195
probabilistic laws, in social science, 17n43
procedural justice, and international trade, 57–58
product cycle theory, 51–53, 186–87
production, as core issue, xiii
proportional representation (PR) electoral systems, 78n39, 81–83
protectionism, 31, 36n19, 45, 56–57; in early modern era, 28–29; institutional theories, 78–83; interest-based theories, 60–78; justification for, 49–56
prudential regulation, 159, 163
public international finance, 100, 106–7; changes in, 141–44

Quinn, Dennis P., 126

ratification: in democratic decision-making process, 79–81; of international investment agreements, 211
rational actors, 6
rational expectations (RE) theory, 148
rationalism, 21–22, 25, 25n67
realism, 8–10, 12; and financial liberalization, 122–24; and trade policy, 61–67. See also neorealism
Reciprocal Trade Agreements Act (RTAA; US), 30–31
reciprocity: principle in trade liberalization, 31, 45; source of international cooperation, 12
referendums, in democratic decision-making process, 79–81
regional investment agreements, 205–6
regionalism, in trade policy, 41–43
Reichsbank, 112
relative gains, in international trade, 65–67
remittances from foreign residents, 101n25

research and development (R&D), in international trade specialization, 52
reversal risk, in international finance, 100–101, 107
Ricardo, David, 28, 45–46, 46n32, 109
Ricardo-Viner model, 72–74, 126–27, 229–30
risk, in international finance, 99–107; borrowers and, 101–4, 154; lenders and, 101–4
risk assessment/credit rating, 162n75
risk categories: currency risk, 100–105, 107; default risk, 154; in international finance, 100–101; legal risk, 101; liquidity risk, 99–107; market risk, 101; maturity risk, 100n24, 100–102; political risk, 101; reversal risk, 100–101, 107
risk insurance, 162n75
riskmetrics models, 165, 165n83
Rodrik, Dani, 57–58, 229
Rogowski, Ronald, 17–18, 70–71, 229
Ruggie, John Gerard, 128
rules of origin, 188n28
rules of the game, under gold standard, 110
Russia, financial crisis, 103

sale of assets to foreign residents, as means of funding deficits, 87
Samuelson, Paul, 46
Schattschneider, E. E., 73, 77–78
Schelling, Thomas, 11n26
Schmoller, Gustav, 49
Schumpeter, Joseph, 229
SDR allocations, 117
sectoral interests: in monetary and exchange rate policies, 146–47; in trade policy, 72–74
security externalities of trade: aggregate, 65–67; sectoral, 61–63; technological, 63–65
seigniorage, 109
self-fulfilling crises, 162
Sell, Susan, 77n35
Sen, Amartya, 6n13
service sector, and FDI, 177
Shrimp-Turtle case, 39–40
side payments, in democratic decision-making process, 79–81
Simmons, Beth A, 113, 125
simplification, in IPE, 17
simplifying assumptions, 25n67

Single European Act, 205–6
single market programme (European), 128.
    See Single European Act
Skidelsky, Robert, 22n58
Smith, Adam, 4, 28, 45, 62
Snidal, Duncan, 11n26
societal approaches, and FDI, 189–91; and
    trade policy, 67–76
South Korea: and Asian model, 159–61,
    195n40; BoP and financial crisis, 90–93,
    103, 103n30; FDI policy, 177, 190–91, 195;
    preference for bank finance, 104
sovereignty risk, in international finance,
    101, 104
specialization: and international trade, 45–49;
    and technology gaps, 51–53
specific factors (Ricardo-Viner) model, 72–74,
    126–27, 229–30
Spencer, Barbara, 53–54
stagflation, 147
standard setting, 55–56, 160–61; environmen-
    tal standards, 223–25; financial standards,
    55–56, 166–67; labor standards, 220–23,
    237; technical standards, 55–56
state interests approach: and exchange rate pol-
    icy, 137–38; and FDI policy, 191–93; and
    financial liberalization, 128; and trade pol-
    icy, 61–67
state-led development strategies, and financial
    integration, 158–61
state-owned enterprises (SOEs), and privatiza-
    tion, 195
"states *vs.* markets" dichotomy, 9
statistical techniques, use of, 18–19
Stolper-Samuelson theorem, 48, 70–71,
    126–27
Strange, Susan, xi–xii, 9
strategic industries, and trade protection,
    63–65
strategic trade theory, 53–56
subsidiary, of an MNC, 173n8
superpower détente, emergence of, 8
swap facilities, between central banks, 117
Sweden, 62
Switzerland, 124, 202

Taiwan, and Asian model, 159, 195; FDI
    exports, 177, 182
tariff "binding," 43
taxation: and efficiency hypothesis, 156–57;
    and MAI, 209
tax competition, and FDI, 218–20
tax policies, and convergence hypothesis,
    217–20
technical standards, and strategic trade policy,
    55–56
technological differentiation, 48n37
technology, and trade protection, 63–65
technology gaps, 51–53
Thailand, and Shrimp-Turtle case, 39–40
time inconsistency, in macroeconomic
    policymaking, 95–96
tobacco industry, 54
Toyota, 182
trade liberalization, 29n5, 30, 45–49
trade policy: institutional theories, 78–83; in-
    terest-based theories, 60–78; robust theory
    of, 83–84
trade protection, as adjustment measure, 93.
    See also protectionism
transnational corporations. *See* multinational
    corporations
transportation costs, 29, 180, 184
Treaty of Rome, 205
Triffin, Robert, 105, 119
TRIMS (Trade Related Investment Measures),
    34–35, 207
TRIPS (Trade Related Aspects of Intellectual
    Property Rights), 34–35, 39
turtle excluder devices (TEDs), 39–40
Two-Tier agreement, 120
Tyson, Laura D'Andrea, 64n8

UNCITRAL (UN Commission on Interna-
    tional Trade Law), 209n8
UN Convention against Corruption, 210–11
UNCTAD, 195, 202
unemployment, natural rate of, 147
UN General Assembly, Resolution 3171
    regarding Permanent Sovereignty over
    National Resources, 189
unholy trinity argument, 94, 145, 231